1957

THE COPLEY PRESS

The National Cyclopædia of American Biography

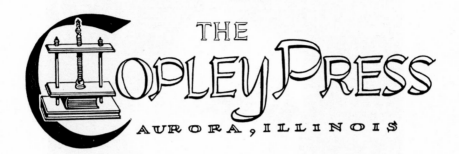

THE COPLEY PRESS

AURORA, ILLINOIS

FREEDOM

PRESS

THE COPLEY PRESS, INC.
428 Downer Place
Aurora, Illinois
1953

Printed in the United States of America by
The Arts & Crafts Press
San Diego, Calif.

To the Associates and Friends
of
The Copley Press

Preface

The 25th anniversary of incorporation of The Copley Press seems a fitting time to record the history of the newspapers which comprise the organization. This history tells of the men and women, past and present, who have taken or are taking leading parts in the operation of the Copley newspapers, and something of the cities in which they are published.

A biography of Col. Ira Clifton Copley, founder of The Copley Press, precedes the stories of the 15 dailies. In order to give a complete picture of the corporation, it is necessary to go back many years prior to 1928, when The Copley Press was created, for Col. Copley first engaged in the newspaper business in 1905, when he bought the Aurora Beacon.

This history is a chronicle of the growth of each Copley Press city and its surrounding area, as well as an account of the individual newspapers from their inception. The people of the 13 thriving cities, four typical of Illinois and nine of California, constitute civic units which reflect the strength, the vitality, courage, resourcefulness, culture, spirit and dignity of the United States of America.

With the press presenting the news in a factual and objective manner, Americans are the best informed of peoples. Thus Americans constantly are striving, with few exceptions, to maintain inviolate our great republic and our cherished system of free enterprise.

The initiative and growth of America also are evidenced in the many millions of lines of local and general advertising that are printed in the newspapers of the land. Through advertising, products of the nation are sold, in ever-increasing volume, to the consumers of the nation. The constant demand by the public for goods and services is the essence of a sound and expanding economy.

It would be impossible to relate the story of The Copley Press without the assistance of many persons. Thanks and appreciation particularly are due J. C. Safley, who offered to edit the material, assemble the photographs, write copy where required, and, above all, provide the guidance and continuity necessary to produce this book.

Thanks also are extended to the officers of the corporation and our many friends, who supplied data and photographs. All others who helped in research, in checking information, in providing pictures and in the preparation of copy, receive our special thanks, for we are indebted to them for valuable assistance.

JAMES S. COPLEY

Contents

THE COPLEY PRESS

The Copley Press, Inc.

The First Quarter Century

HEADQUARTERS OF THE COPLEY PRESS

AUDUS W. SHIPTON
President, The Copley Press

2

The Copley Press, Inc.

428 Downer Place   Aurora, Ill.

THE COPLEY PRESS was incorporated February 17, 1928, under the laws of the State of Illinois. The corporation operates five newspapers in Illinois and 10 in California. It also owns, with three exceptions, the real properties and buildings where the newspapers are published, and other real estate. General offices are maintained at 428 Downer Place, Aurora, Ill., with legal headquarters at the nearby town of Bristol, in Kendall County.

Col. Ira C. Copley, who owned the newspapers in Aurora, Elgin and Joliet, transferred them, together with his newspaper properties in San Diego, to the new corporation. The newspapers he purchased in Los Angeles County and in Springfield were transferred to The Copley Press, Inc., at later dates. When The Copley Press was incorporated, Col. Copley became president, B. P. Alschuler, vice president, and F. M. James, secretary and treasurer.

With establishment of The Copley Press, an organization was set up that co-ordinated operation of the various properties. The Colonel long had in mind the time when he no longer would direct the newspapers and he made arrangements insuring that they would continue to function on a high plane when he passed from the scene. For more than 19 years, he headed The Copley Press. Since his death, in 1947, the newspapers, pursuing, without variation, the wise policies of public service to which the Colonel dedicated them, have risen to even greater heights of achievement.

THE COPLEY PRESS

Sole owners of The Copley Press are the estate of Ira C. Copley (deceased), James S. Copley, of Aurora, and William N. Copley, of San Diego.

The Copley Press has passed its 25th anniversary and enters the second quarter century under auspicious conditions.

The Copley Press directly owns and operates four daily newspapers in Illinois. They are the Aurora Beacon-News, Elgin Daily Courier-News, Joliet Herald-News and the Illinois State Journal, in Springfield. It operates under lease the Illinois State Register, also in Springfield.

Two subsidiary corporations are owned by The Copley Press. They are (1) the Union-Tribune Publishing Co., which wholly owns and operates The San Diego Union and the Evening Tribune, and (2) Southern California Associated Newspapers, which wholly owns and operates seven daily newspapers in Los Angeles County, California. They are the Post-Advocate, in Alhambra; Burbank Daily Review; Evening Star-News, Culver City; Glendale News-Press; Daily News-Post, in Monrovia; South Bay Daily Breeze, in Redondo Beach, and Evening Vanguard, in Venice. In addition, Southern California Associated Newspapers owns 60 percent of the stock of the San Pedro Printing & Publishing Co., which owns and operates the San Pedro News-Pilot. Forty percent of the stock of the San Pedro Printing & Publishing Co. is owned by Clark F. Waite, Alden C. Waite, Chase Wanglin, J. A. Waite and Mrs. Lila Waite. Offices of Southern California Associated Newspapers are at 4044 Lafayette Place, Culver City.

The San Diego Union and the Illinois State Journal are seven-day morning newspapers. The Sunday edition of the Springfield newspaper bears the name, Illinois State Journal and Register. All the other Copley newspapers are six-day afternoon publications, except the Burbank Daily Review, which omits issuing on Saturday. In addition, the Aurora Beacon-News and the Joliet Herald-News print Sunday editions.

The Copley Press owns one-half of the San Diego Broadcasting Co., which owns and operates Radio Station KSDO in San Diego.

James S. Copley is chairman of the corporation of The Copley Press, and also is a member of the executive committee and a director. Audus W. Shipton, of Springfield, is president of the corporation, a member of the executive committee and a director. Other officers are William M. Hart, Aurora, vice president and director; C. Raymond Long, Elgin, vice president and director; John F. Lux, Joliet, vice president and director; J. Emil Smith, Springfield, vice president and director; Lester G. Bradley, San Diego, vice president and director; William Shea, San Diego, vice president and director; Richard N. Smith, North Hollywood, Calif., secretary, treasurer and director; Thomas H. Beacom, Winnetka, Ill., member of the executive committee and director; William N. Copley, San Diego, director; Clark F. Waite, Beverly Hills, Calif., director; Mrs. C. O. Goodwin, Aurora, assistant secretary and assistant treasurer; C. C. Weiland, Los Angeles, assistant secretary; D. F. Hartman, Culver City, assistant treasurer. Miss Eleanor C. Waegner, Los Angeles, is administrative secretary and confidential secretary to the financial officers, and H. Ambrose Erlanson, Sherman Oaks, Calif., is divisional audi-

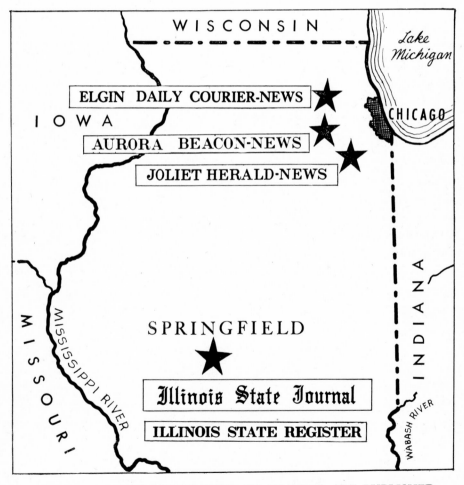

WHERE COPLEY NEWSPAPERS IN ILLINOIS ARE PUBLISHED

tor for Illinois and San Diego. Miss Ila M. Hunter is office manager in Aurora. Mrs. Agnes Coomes, Bristol, Ill., is registered agent.

Col. Copley, always partial to his old-time friends, with whom he spent many enjoyable days, named William W. Tracy, of Springfield, Ill., and Williamstown, Mass., counselor of the corporation. Following Tracy's death, Will H. McConnell, of Springfield, Ill., succeeded to the title, and continues with the organization in that capacity.

Because of Col. Copley's extensive financial relations in Chicago during his public utility years, he was close to those banking interests which eventually became the First National Bank of Chicago. The Colonel, always preparing for eventualities, arranged for the First National Bank of Chicago to be an executor of his estate.

When James S. Copley came out of the Navy, following World War II, the Colonel decided to bring all his business affairs up to date. The Chicago law firm of Hopkins, Sutter, Halls, DeWolfe & Owen was recommended to him for legal advice.

Col. Copley, in his will, designated the First National Bank of Chicago and James S. Copley as co-executors of his estate. In this capacity, the bank has been represented by Thomas H. Beacom, Edward F. Blettner, Jr., James Phinney Baxter, H. Richard Wilking, Forrest Williams and A. S. Thorwaldson. Blettner originally represented the bank on the board of directors of The Copley Press and on the executive committee, and was succeeded by Beacom, who is serving at present (June 1, 1953). The co-executors have relied for legal advice on Albert L. Hopkins, with help also being received from other members of the law firm, including T. Eugene Foster, Harry D. Orr, Jr., Donald J. DeWolfe and Thomas R. Mulroy.

Maynard J. Toll and other members of the firm of O'Melveny & Myers, Los Angeles, are attorneys for California interests of The Copley Press.

Officers of the Union-Tribune Publishing Co., are Lester G. Bradley, chairman of the board and director; James S. Copley, president and director; William Shea, vice president and director; A. W. Shipton, vice president and director; Richard N. Smith, secretary and director; Thomas H. Beacom, director; Walter J. Schneider, vice president, and Hugh R. Morick, assistant secretary.

Chairman of the board of Southern California Associated Newspapers is Clark F. Waite, who also is a director. Alden C. Waite, of Glendale, is

FRANCIS MARION JAMES
Vice President of The Copley Press, Who Died on May 7, 1953
Inset, When He Joined Copley Organization in 1902

7

RICHARD N. SMITH
Secretary and Treasurer, The Copley Press

8

president and a director. Vice presidents, who also are directors, are A. W. Shipton and Rear Adm. Robert Henderson, USN, ret. C. C. Weiland is assistant secretary and a director, as well as general auditor for all Copley newspapers. Other vice presidents are Barton Heiligers, Alhambra; Hugh B. Baumberger, Burbank; Robert L. Curry, Culver City; Carroll W. Parcher, Glendale; Charles F. Davis, Monrovia, and F. S. Haynes, Redondo Beach. Richard N. Smith is secretary of the corporation and C. V. Anderson is assistant treasurer and auditor.

Officers of the San Pedro Printing & Publishing Co. are J. A. Waite, president, treasurer and director; Clark F. Waite, vice president and director; James S. Copley, secretary and director; Richard N. Smith, assistant treasurer and director; Bynner Martin, vice president and publisher, and C. C. Weiland, assistant secretary.

Officers of the San Diego Broadcasting Co. are C. Arnholt Smith, of San Diego, president and treasurer; James S. Copley, vice president; Jack Heintz, San Diego, vice president and manager, and D. R. Giddings, secretary. Directors are Smith, Copley, Giddings and A. W. Shipton.

Audus W. Shipton, president of The Copley Press, began his newspaper career at the bottom rung of the journalistic ladder as a carrier boy in Woodstock, Ill. He attended the public schools in Woodstock and, in 1915, was graduated from Beloit College, Beloit, Wis., where he majored in journalism and commerce.

After graduation, he was assistant manager of the Woodstock Republican and, for a short time, was in the advertising department of Mandel Brothers Department Store, Chicago. From there he went to the Aurora Beacon-News, as advertising salesman.

At the outbreak of World War I, Shipton left the Beacon-News to enlist in the 129th Infantry Regiment, 33rd Division, and rose from private to captain.

After his discharge from the Army, he returned to the Beacon-News and, in June, 1921, was promoted to local advertising manager. When Col. Copley purchased the Illinois State Journal, on January 1, 1928, Shipton was transferred to Springfield as general manager. It was his responsibility to see that publication of the newspaper continued without interruption during erection, in 1929-30, of a new State Journal Building at the location of the old structure.

His appointment as publisher of the State Journal was made in 1933, and nine years later, with consolidation of the business of the State Journal and the Illinois State Register, Col. Copley announced Shipton's promotion to president of The Copley Press. At that time, the Colonel became chairman of the board and commented humorously that he had "kicked himself upstairs."

As president of COPRESS, Shipton each year makes numerous trips from his Springfield office in the State Journal Building to the home office in Aurora, to the northeastern Illinois newspapers and to California. He and James S. Copley preside at the annual conferences of The Copley Press. Miss Amelia J. Reich is secretary to Shipton. She started work with the Illinois State Journal in 1910.

Shipton has filled many civic positions over a long period of years, with emphasis on chamber of commerce work and the American Legion. He was post commander of the American Legion in Aurora and was three times president of Kiwanis, twice in Aurora and once in Springfield. His Masonic activities extend from the Blue Lodge through Scottish Rite and Shrinedom into the Jesters.

He was president of the University of Illinois Dads' Association in 1935. He was awarded an honorary Phi Beta Kappa key in 1951, for outstanding work for Beloit College and in the newspaper field, and in June, 1952, he was appointed to the Beloit College Board of Trustees.

Newspaper organizations with which he is affiliated include Sigma Delta Chi, national professional journalistic fraternity; the Illinois Daily Newspaper Markets, which he was influential in founding; Inland Daily Press Association, to which he gave valuable assistance in its political affairs problems, and the American Newspaper Publishers Association.

Francis Marion James, who was a vice president of The Copley Press, chairman of the finance committee and a director, died May 7, 1953, in Aurora, Ill. At the time of his death, James also was a vice president, treasurer and a director of the Union-Tribune Publishing Co., and first vice president, treasurer and a director of Southern California Associated Newspapers. In addition, he was a vice president, assistant treasurer and a director of the San Pedro Printing & Publishing Co.

James, who had been connected with the Copley organization since 1902, died in Copley Memorial Hospital. He was 79 years old. While en route from New York to California, he stopped in Aurora for a visit at his old home. He suddenly was taken ill and died a week later.

JAMES S. COPLEY
Chairman of the Corporation, The Copley Press

He was a close associate of Col. Copley, particularly in financial matters, during the Colonel's public utility years, and also in the various newspaper enterprises, beginning with the Colonel's purchase of the first daily news-paper, the Aurora Beacon, on December 1, 1905. Thus James, with the rapid expansion of Col. Copley's business interests, assumed increased duties and responsibilities, and became known as a financial expert in the manifold ramifications connected with operation of public utilities and newspapers.

James, who resided in Los Angeles, had held so many positions with Copley organizations that he said "it would take a long search through the minute books to pick up the exact dates."

Born at Hinckley, Ill., on November 30, 1873, James attended country school and then Hinckley High School, from which he was graduated. He held a bachelor of arts degree from Jennings Seminary, Aurora, and also a diploma in accounting and commercial law from the same institution. From July, 1894, to November, 1902, he was with the Sandwich Manufacturing Co., at Sandwich, Ill., as branch office cashier, in charge of credits and collections, traveling salesman and assistant to the chief accountant. He left the company to accept a position with Col. Copley. Thus began a long and distinguished career of financial management for the Colonel. It has been said,

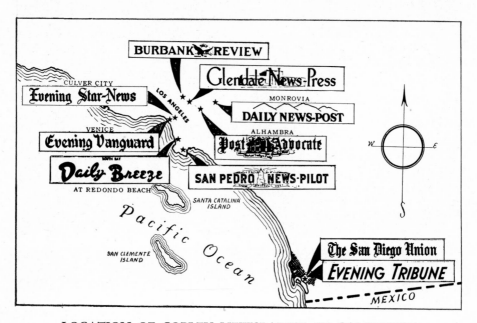

LOCATION OF COPLEY NEWSPAPERS IN CALIFORNIA

12

somewhat facetiously, yet aptly, that James "held the Colonel's purse strings."
In reviewing his career a few months prior to his death, he wrote:

"Starting November 20, 1902, I became chief accountant for three
public utilities then operated by Col. Copley—the Fox River Light, Heat &
Power Co., Joliet Gas Light Co., and La Grange Gas Co. Effective February
1, 1905, these companies, together with the Elgin American Gas Co., were
consolidated into the Western United Gas & Electric Co. About 1907, my
duties were expanded to include credits and collections. About 1911 or 1912,
those duties again were expanded to include what was called 'the new business department,' which covered the promotion and sale of the company's
products, principally gas and electricity, through the sale of appliances.
About 1913, my duties were further expanded by establishing and supervising
a public relations department.

"During World War I, in addition to the foregoing, I was delegated as
assistant to the president. This was done primarily to enable me to handle
before the Illinois Public Utilities Commission the company's applications
for authority to issue additional securities.

"On December 1, 1905, Col. Copley purchased his first newspaper, the
Aurora Beacon, and requested me to assume responsibilities there regarding
financial matters, including accounting and collections. In 1910, he acquired
the Elgin Courier and requested me to assume similar responsibilities for
that newspaper.

"Col. Copley acquired a majority of the stock of the Joliet News on
June 1, 1913, and the same day he became owner of a majority of the stock
of the Joliet Herald and requested me to assume similar responsibilities
with those publications. The newspapers were operated as separate publications until June 1, 1915, when they were merged as the Joliet Herald-News.
The Colonel acquired the majority of the Herald stock from John Lambert,
a resident of Joliet and a big steel mill owner, who helped organize the
U. S. Steel Corp. A. S. Leckie, publisher of the Herald under Lambert,
owned some stock in the Herald and continued as publisher until 1920.
Edward Corlett also held some of the Herald stock. When Leckie left the
organization, Col. Copley and Corlett acquired his stock on a pro-rata basis
and Corlett took over as publisher, continuing in that position until February 1, 1932, when he was succeeded by John F. Lux. Col. Copley acquired
Corlett's stock before completing organization of The Copley Press."

James, beginning in 1914, was connected with the Copley utility busi-

COPLEY PRESS GROUP PHOTOGRAPHED IN CULVER CITY

Left to right, H. Ambrose Erlanson, divisional auditor; Miss Rose M. Ladenburg, secretary to James S. Copley and A. W. Shipton; Miss Eleanor C. Waegner, administrative secretary and confidential secretary to the financial officers; Miss Jennie Leavitt, assistant to Miss Waegner; C. C. Weiland, assistant secretary of COPRESS; Donald F. Hartman, assistant treasurer of COPRESS.

ness in southern Illinois and also was associated with three West Virginia coal mining properties the Colonel purchased as adjuncts to his utility business.

Following Col. Copley's sale of his utility properties, effective February 1, 1926, James' work during the remainder of 1926 and all of 1927 was confined to the newspapers in Aurora, Elgin and Joliet and to the Colonel's personal affairs. When The Copley Press was organized, James became secretary and treasurer.

Richard N. Smith, secretary, treasurer and a director of The Copley Press, and who also holds official positions with COPRESS subsidiaries, joined the organization on June 1, 1944. He previously was trust officer of the Merchants National Bank in Aurora.

In order that he might have a title as a corporate officer, to enable him to sign official documents, Smith became an assistant treasurer on September 18, 1945, and received the added title of assistant secretary a year later. He was elected a director of COPRESS on February 12, 1952, and at the annual meeting on February 17, 1953, he was named secretary and treasurer. Smith was born in Chicago. His parents moved to Aurora shortly thereafter. His education was obtained in the West Aurora public schools and at Northwestern University (College of Commerce, 1926).

Mrs. C. O. Goodwin has spent many years in the service of Copley companies. A graduate of Palmer Secretarial School in Aurora in 1892, she was an instructor in that school in 1893. She was named treasurer of the Aurora Gas Light Co., a Copley concern, the same year. Mrs. Goodwin resigned at the time of her marriage and was succeeded by her sister, Miss Helen O'Meara. Mrs. Goodwin resumed employment with the organization in 1924 as assistant treasurer of Western United Gas & Electric Co., and was made acting treasurer in 1925. When the Colonel sold his utility properties in 1926, Mrs. Goodwin left his employment, but returned in 1928, when she became assistant secretary and assistant treasurer of COPRESS, which positions she continues to hold.

C. C. (Chris) Weiland, assistant secretary of COPRESS, is a native of Aurora, and first became connected with the Copley utility interests in March, 1903, in Aurora, after nearly three years with the Commercial Credit Co., of that city. Twenty years later, in March, 1923, Weiland moved to California and was associated with William May Garland, well-known real estate operator and property owner of Southern California, until May 15, 1929, when he again joined the Copley organization in the Los Angeles accounting department. He has been general auditor of all Copley Newspapers ever since. He also is assistant secretary and a director of SCAN and assistant secretary of the San Pedro Printing & Publishing Co.

D. F. Hartman, assistant treasurer of COPRESS, is in the Culver City offices. He joined the organization on June 1, 1949. Employed by the Los Angeles office of Ernst & Ernst, certified public accountants, he went "on loan" to SCAN headquarters to assist in preparation of financial reports. After working in that status for three months, he was invited to remain with

COPRESS. A native Californian, Hartman is a graduate of the University of Southern California.

Thirty-five years of work for Copley newspapers came to a close in

CHARLES D. CHAFFEE
Long in Circulation Work

San Diego, on April 12, 1942, with the death of Charles D. Chaffee. He started carrying a route for the Aurora Daily News at the age of 9, and, while attending high school, worked in that newspaper's mailing room. In 1907, he joined the Aurora Beacon, and thus began his association with Copley newspapers. Later he became circulation manager of the Beacon-News.

When Col. Copley consolidated the Joliet dailies in 1915, Chaffee was placed in charge of merging the circulation of the Daily News with that of the Joliet Herald. He did the same type of work for the Elgin Courier when it took over the Elgin Daily News.

He introduced the idea of taking tents with Aurora Beacon-News banners to plowing matches at Big Rock and Wheatland, Ill., and to the fair at Sandwich. There farmers were signed for subscriptions a year in advance.

In January, 1930, Chaffee was made director of circulation for Southern California Newspapers, Associated. He began part-time association with The San Diego Union and Evening Tribune in 1932, spending four days a week in San Diego, and in 1940 and 1941 assisted in the circulation department of the Illinois State Journal. Chaffee became circulation manager of the San Diego newspapers in 1941 and held that position until his death.

Col. Ira Clifton Copley

1864-1947

Founder of The Copley Press, Inc.

THE COPLEY HOME IN AURORA

17

COL. IRA C. COPLEY
Informal Photo Taken Not Long Before His Death

18

James S. Copley to Gain Control of Copley Press

7-30-57 *Herald*

Thru family settlement of a suit involving the estate of the late Col. Ira C. Copley, of Aurora, Ill., his newspaper properties held by The Copley Press, Inc., will come under the control of his son, James S. Copley.

The proposed family contract was submitted today to Judge Cornelius J. Harrington of the Circuit Court of Cook County, Illinois, for approval and will become effective when approved by the Court and the Treasury Department.

Copley, chairman of the corporation of The Copley Press, Inc., announced today the suit will be brought to a close by an agreement whereby The Copley Press, Inc., will purchase the stock of another son, William N. Copley, of Paris, France, and stock of other minority holders. The family agreement will give James S. Copley full control of the property.

Affected by the agreement are 16 California and Illinois newspapers and television station KCOP of Los Angeles. The purchase price and conditions of sale were not disclosed. In the suit filed in the Circuit Court of Cook County Illinois in 1955, against The First National Bank of Chicago and James S. Copley, as executors, William N. Copley had sought diversification of the estate of Col. Copley who died in 1947.

Copley newspapers in California include The San Diego Union, the San Diego Evening Tribune, Alhambra Post-Advocate, Burbank Daily Review, Culver City Star-News, Glen-News-Press, South Bay

JAMES S. COPLEY

Daily Breeze of Redondo Beach, San Pedro News Pilot, Monrovia News-Post, Venice Vanguard and Borrego Sun.

Illinois newspapers of The Copley Press include the Illinois State Journal and Illinois State Register of Springfield, the Aurora Beacon-News, the Elgin Courier-News and the Joliet Herald-News.

The sale of KCOP of Los Angeles, has been submitted to the Federal Communications Commission for approval.

'SHE'S O[...]

Save Trap In W[...]

ANDERS[...] oughta eve[...] cheer for [...] shouted som[...]

The crow[...] ment as a [...] out of the 4[...] rying 17-mo[...] ley in his [...] fallen into [...] well.

"She's ok[...] Roberts.

But for [...] Monday nigh[...] sure 17-mont[...] ley would co[...] 3-year-old br[...] David wept [...] begging for [...] out of the hol[...]

"That's all [...] whole time,"[...] said today.[...] ing and s[...] sister out o[...]

Richard [...] brown-haired,[...] were playing [...] day evening v[...] fixed supper.[...]

"Richard ca[...] house crying, [...] hole and got hu[...] old mother sai[...]

"I ran out[...] thought of [...]

Lack of Oil   Stol[...]

com-
bled.
elegram,"
otract and
n it."
ing most of
He has a
72.

E-DAY
aning
s'
ore

Cleaning

ARDNER ST

0¢ ea.
Bundle
itute
ry
ng
OR DAY

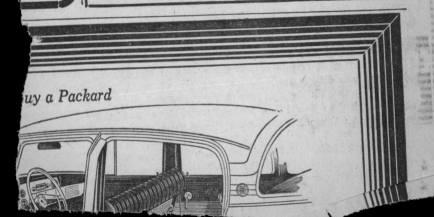

Col. Ira Clifton Copley

I

IRA CLIFTON COPLEY was a man of diverse interests. He was outstanding in many lines of activity, in any one of which he was considered an authority. First, he was a newspaper owner and operator and businessman. He was a philanthropist, a humanitarian, a member of Congress, a public utilities executive, a financier, an economist, a political scientist, a lawyer (although he never practiced the profession), a mathematician (he once was offered a position on the mathematics faculty of Yale University, but did not accept), a military man, an archaeologist, a world traveler, an ardent fisherman, a lodge- and clubman, and a most amiable host.

But more important than all of these attributes, he was a steadfast American citizen, fond of his home and family.

The title of Colonel came from two sources. First, he was a lieutenant colonel in the Illinois National Guard (1904-08) and later a colonel (1905-11) on the staff of Gov. Charles S. Deneen, of Illinois. Known to his intimate associates as Cliff, others addressed him as Colonel, while reference was made to him in the third person as the Colonel or Col. Copley.

The Colonel took a personal interest in the well-being of the army of employes in his far-flung enterprises. Hard work and loyalty were amply rewarded and words of commendation often were forthcoming. He had the ability to select for key positions in his organization men who were highly qualified in their particular fields and they were permitted wide latitude in operation of the business with which they were entrusted. The men who served him were strengthened by his guidance.

The Colonel's life span was seven days more than 83 years. He was born on a farm in Copley Township (named for his father, Ira Birdsall Copley), in Knox County, Illinois, on October 25, 1864, and died at 5:10 a.m., on Sunday, November 2, 1947, in Copley Hospital, Aurora, Ill. He had given to the city the hospital in which he died. The Colonel's illness was of brief duration. He entered the hospital on October 18 for treatment of a partial fracture of a bone in one of his legs. The injury occurred in Los Angeles a few days prior to his departure for his home in Aurora. His wife, Mrs. Chloe Copley, his sons, James S. and William N. Copley, and other members of the family were with him when death came.

He was thought to have been making excellent progress and was in good spirits until Wednesday, when suddenly his condition took an adverse turn. He rallied during the night and again gave doctors hope that he might recover. His son, William, who was in San Diego, left immediately with his wife for Aurora. James, then first vice president of The Copley Press, was in Aurora. Early Saturday, the Colonel lapsed into a coma, and it became apparent that his life was ebbing. His death wrote "30" to a brilliant newspaper publishing career that for him began midway in life.

Funeral services were conducted at 11 a.m., Tuesday, November 4, in Trinity Episcopal Church, Aurora. The Rt. Rev. William W. Horstick, bishop of the Eau Claire (Wis.) Diocese of the Episcopal Church, officiated. Bishop Horstick, former pastor of Trinity Episcopal Church, long had been a friend of Col. Copley and his family. The Colonel was a Universalist, but contributed to Trinity Church.

The Psalms read by the bishop were the 26th, 27th and 121st, while the lesson was from the 8th chapter of St. Paul's Epistle to the Romans, beginning with the 14th verse. In keeping with the simplicity of the services, the only music was that by the church organist.

Editors and publishers of Col. Copley's Illinois newspapers carried the casket to the place of burial in Spring Lake Cemetery. Pallbearers were A. W. Shipton, J. Emil Smith and V. Y. Dallman, of Springfield; C. Raymond Long, Elgin; John F. Lux, Joliet, and Charles W. Hoefer, Aurora. Many long-time friends and associates, headed by Gov. Dwight H. Green, of Illinois, attended the services.

COL. COPLEY AND GOV. DWIGHT H. GREEN, OF ILLINOIS

In memory of the Colonel, operations on all his newspapers in Illinois and California were suspended during the funeral hour.

From all parts of the world expressions of sympathy to the family of the Colonel were received. The president of the United States, noted legislators, prominent financiers, journalists, people from all walks of life, paid respect to the memory of Ira Clifton Copley, the man who lived by the code, "Be on the square."

The Colonel's old-time friend, House Speaker Joseph W. Martin, Jr., characterized him as "a builder in the best sense of the word. He loved his country and devoted his great talents to making it a better land."

Congressman (now Vice President) Richard M. Nixon, of California, said: "Col. Copley exemplified the American story," while Ohio's Senator

Robert A. Taft commented that Col. Copley "held the respect of leaders in Washington for his clear thinking and sound judgment on domestic and world affairs." Senator William F. Knowland, of California, said the Colonel was "a man who placed the public interest above all else."

The Colonel must have had a premonition that death was near because, only four days before the end came, he visited the publishers of his newspapers in each of the three northeastern Illinois cities—Aurora, Elgin and Joliet—and said: " I just wanted to come over and visit with you."

Prophetic was a remark he made to one of his editors in San Diego not long before he left California for Illinois, but before his injury occurred. At a social gathering, comment was made to the Colonel on how well he appeared to be.

"Yes," he replied laconically, "but I don't want to live longer than I am able to take care of myself."

His passing marked the end of a chapter, but the memories of his directing genius have inspired all who were associated with him to carry on. He led a good, full life, and he left a regiment of men and women the better for having known him.

His humanity reflected in his philanthropies was well known to those associated with him. He espoused the cause of justice with an unflinching will.

The Congress of the United States, on November 18, paid tribute to Col. Copley. Congressman Chauncey W. Reed, of West Chicago, representing the Eleventh Illinois Congressional District, which Col. Copley had served for 12 years, eulogized him as an "inspiration to the youth of a friendly nation," and added: "America is the richer because he lived."

Col. Copley's rise in business resulted from hard work, coupled with unusual ability. He was an ardent adherent of the American philosophy of toil and thrift as the keys to success, and of equal opportunity for all. He was impatient with those who were indolent and who felt the public owed them a living.

While extraordinarily successful himself, the Colonel often remarked in his later years that no individual in the future could acquire in a lifetime what he had accumulated, because of the existing governmental policy of almost confiscatory taxes on high earnings. This he deplored because of the stifling effect it had on ambition and initiative.

The Colonel was not immune from making errors in business judgment and occasionally they were extremely costly to him, but he took them in stride as inevitable in the course of extensive operations.

Col. Copley was a man of medium stature. He usually wore a mustache which was closely cropped. Occasionally he was smooth-shaven. His clothing, made by New York tailors, was of the best fabric, but always conservative in pattern and design. He took excellent care of himself physically and ever was watchful lest he become overweight. He insisted that those of his executives who became ill have the best of medical attention.

He was handicapped during his entire lifetime by weak eyes, yet he refused to wear glasses. In infancy, he contracted scarlet fever, which affected his eyes, and a film formed over the pupils. He also was snow-blinded when young. It was said that his parents left Knox County and settled in Aurora, so the son could have the benefit of treatment by an eye specialist there. He could see well enough when the light was good, but encountered ocular difficulties at night. Despite the inconvenience, he was an avid reader of newspapers and books.

The Colonel was one of the founders of and contributed heavily to the Wilmer Ophthalmological Institute, in Baltimore, Md. The institute was directed by the noted eye specialist, Dr. William Holland Wilmer, whose patient the Colonel had been, and was designed to develop the science of ophthalmology and provide improved methods of eye relief.

Col. Copley was a wizard at figures. While his newspapers always were operated on a high plane editorially and from a business point of view, and he insisted that no expense be spared in upholding these aims, he at the same time took a keen interest in the balance sheet. His mind was a vast storehouse of mathematical data and he could draw from it, with uncanny accuracy, figures pertaining to every phase of this business or that. Estimates and guesswork in dollars and cents he disdained. What he wanted and demanded was exactitude.

His son, James S. Copley, tells about his father's devotion to the facts.

"One day, when I was just a youngster," he recalled, "I went in to Dad and said: 'They say'—I didn't get any further. He demanded: 'Who are they?' And when I began to temporize, Dad said: 'Jim, always remember that what they say isn't as important as who said it.'"

A young publisher, in telling Col. Copley of the improvement he had planned for the newspaper building, once remarked that new window sills were to be installed because "we are heating the outside." The Colonel quickly asked: "How much of the outside are you heating?" And when the publisher became confused, Col. Copley said: "That is a lesson—that you never need to exaggerate with me."

"We have no friends to favor and no enemies to punish," was Col. Copley's admonition to A. W. Shipton, when Shipton went from Aurora to Springfield to assume management of the just-purchased Illinois State Journal, early in 1928.

"If you make a success of this job," he continued, "it will be because you select capable men to head the paper's departments and charge each of them with the responsibility of developing good seconds in command."

Another warning was to be fair to all, never to play favorites. The Colonel's idea was that the latter would destroy the objectivity of the publisher or manager in meeting day-to-day problems. "You must have friends, of course, but never so intimate that you become the servant of their desires," he said.

Col. Copley held that publication of newspapers was a privilege rather than a prerogative and it was the duty of newspapers to publish all news in an unbiased manner, irrespective of the politics of the owner. His philosophy was that news was news regardless of whom it affected, even if it included a member of his family or one of his newspaper employes.

An example of the operation of this principle was an occurrence at the Coronado ferry one afternoon when Col. Copley was returning from Los Angeles. One of his San Diego newspapers, following his policy, carried headlines stating that I. C. Copley had been called before a board in Washington and the newsboy was shouting: "Read all about Col. Copley." The Colonel called the newsboy to his side, and, after inquiring about the item, bought five papers.

The next day he was telling his circulation manager about the incident and the manager said: "The dumb fellow, I will fire him immediately." In reply, the Colonel remarked: "What do you want to do that for, he sold five papers, didn't he?"

It was another Copley preachment "never to make the same mistake twice." This was a credo he often repeated during the early annual conferences of the organization (The Copley Press) he loved so well and was ambitious to build in strength. The results he attained bespeak the soundness of his business philosophy.

His door always was open to receive anyone with a particular problem,

COL. COPLEY IN YOSEMITE NATIONAL PARK

for which he invariably would provide a prompt solution. As a result, his
advice often was sought.

Col. Copley built a great group of newspapers by giving each publisher complete autonomy. Of course, the publisher was responsible to the

25

Colonel, but he did not interfere so long as the publisher held to the creed that what was best for the community was best for the newspaper.

"Every community in which we publish a newspaper," he said, "has a complete identity of its own. Therefore, each newspaper should have its own identity, reflecting the views and life of the community in which it is published.

"You cannot do mass thinking for a group of newspapers or for a group of communities. Each is different, each needs to have the close personal touch with community life that only the home-town newspaper can give.

"A newspaper must have personality—a definite personality just like an individual. It must have integrity, it must have responsibility and it must have its finger on the pulse of its community and perform the service which is best for the area in which it is published."

The orders for "must" editorials, which often come from owners of newspaper groups, were notably absent in the Copley newspapers. Col. Copley always insisted that his newspapers print all the local news of consequence and take editorial stands favoring the public welfare.

He selected as publishers men who knew and loved their home towns. Some of the men now publishing Copley newspapers—in fact, the majority —came up from the ranks, knowing expertly their home towns and their newspapers. His instructions to them were: "Treat everyone fairly."

Col. Copley never permitted anyone to criticize one of his publishers without requesting that the publisher be present. In the event he received a letter of complaint, he would acknowledge the complaint with the statement that the matter would be discussed with the man in charge. The policy helped management and, in most cases, clarified situations which, had they been handled differently, might have developed into unpleasant misunderstandings.

An illustration of the policy's operation is reflected in connection with an advertisement that had been submitted to one of his newspapers. The advertisement was political in character and as such carried the political rate, which was higher than the commercial rate. The advertiser, dissatisfied with the decision, called on Col. Copley, who in turn summoned his publisher and, after the matter had been considered further, the Colonel sustained the publisher's decision and advised the advertiser that any subsequent discussion would be with the publisher and not with him. The man

COL. COPLEY, ROBERT W. RICHARDS AND A. W. SHIPTON
Farewell Said as Richards Left to Cover War in Pacific

became highly indignant and said that, if it were necessary to discuss the subject with the publisher, he never would return to the office. Col. Copley replied: "That's a matter that is entirely in your hands, but, I reiterate, any further discussion will be with the executive and not with me."

Col. Copley was intensely human in his relationships, not only with the publishers of his newspapers, but with all the employes of the company, regardless of the rank they had in the organization. When he visited his newspaper plants, he stopped to chat with clerks, reporters, printers, pressmen—in fact all who produced the newspaper.

He knew and often remarked about the number of employes in the organization, the number of carriers, in whom he held a special interest, and the successes which his papers were accomplishing individually over the years. He watched operations daily with painstaking and fatherly care through a system of reports, devised by his long-time friend and able confidant, Francis Marion James.

"How does Col. Copley get such intense loyalty from the people who produce the Copley newspapers?" someone once asked. The answer was simple. He was loyal to them, intensely so, sometimes even to the point of giving an erring person chance after chance to make good.

He had a policy of never "dropping in" on any of the publishers of his newspapers without advance warning, a policy which endeared him to the man who had taken the afternoon off to play golf and wasn't expecting the boss. He always called by telephone the day before and politely asked: "Will you be in tomorrow? I'd like to come over and visit."

He trusted his people implicitly and all he asked of them was that they produce a newspaper that would be a credit to the Copley organization and to the community it served.

His hospitality was legendary and a party at the Colonel's house not only included the "high brass," but many of the rank and file. And he found real enjoyment in their company.

Those of The Copley Press who spent many years in its service often remarked on his memory. "He had a memory like an elephant," a publisher said. "And that not only was for the things that he had heard and seen, but also for any promise that he might make. That promise always was kept."

His punctuality was legendary. When going on a journey, he was at the railroad station long before train time. If the Colonel said he would meet a person at 4:30 o'clock, he would arrive at 4:29.

His achievements and those of The Copley Press were founded on actual warm-hearted interest in the people of the organization because he considered them as members of his family. And this was not from a paternalistic attitude, but because he genuinely loved them.

II

Ira Clifton Copley was born of a pioneer family in the simple surroundings that characterized farm life in Illinois at the time of the Civil War. He traced his ancestry in America to Thomas Copley, an Englishman, who settled in Massachusetts about 1625. The Colonel's father, Ira Birdsall Copley, was a native of Harpersfield, Delaware County, New York. He was born in 1825 and went west to Knox County, Illinois, in 1849. There he met and married Ellen Madeline Whiting, of Galesburg, on November 10, 1853. Her family had moved to Illinois from Connecticut. She was born in 1837 at West Hartford, Conn.

ORIGINAL AURORA GAS WORKS, BUILT IN 1868

Ira Clifton Copley, whose birthdate was October 25, 1864, was the sixth of 12 children. The family comprised six sons and six daughters. Four sons died in infancy. They were Richard W. (1858-1861), Willie A. (1866-68), Freddie J. (1869) and Bertie T. (1870). Three daughters died in early childhood. They were Cora A. (1856), Luella I. (1857-61) and Ida W. (1871-72). A son, Clarence A., born in 1860, died in 1882.

A daughter, Elvira (Mrs. Rae Copley Raum), died in San Diego in 1934, at the age of 72. Another daughter, Ella M. (Mrs Charles Collier), died in San Diego in 1921, aged 55. Edyth (Mrs. F. Karl Lamb), born in 1875, died in Los Angeles in 1948. The father died in San Diego, November 24, 1893, and the mother's death also occurred in San Diego, in 1914.

In 1867, when Ira C. Copley was 3 years old, his father and his mother's brother, R. H. Whiting, of Galesburg, assumed ownership of the Aurora Gas Light Co. This was the original company organized in 1861 by Aurora men and later it was developed into the Western United Gas & Electric Co. The Aurora Gas Light Co. was chartered by an act of the state legislature, which gave the company a perpetual franchise for Aurora.

His father owned 30 percent of the capital stock of the Aurora Gas Light Co., and became manager of the property. His uncle owned 70 percent. His mother made out the bills and did other clerical work. Copley and Whiting began building on the west bank of the Fox River in Aurora and, by December, 1868, a gas works was completed at a cost of $60,000. The first sale of gas took place on December 22 of that year and Aurora stores and buildings were lighted by gas for the first time on Christmas Eve.

Gas was sold at $4.50 for 100 cubic feet. Coke, a by-product in the manufacture of gas, was of no use in those days, so it was wheeled to the adjacent river bank and dumped into the water to create filled-in land to add to the gas plant property.

It was in Aurora that the formal education of Ira C. Copley began. Upon graduation from West Aurora High School in 1881, he enrolled in Jennings Seminary, in preparation for Yale University. He received his bachelor of arts degree from Yale in 1887.

Following graduation, he began the study of law at Chicago's Union College. Classes were conducted at night and, to help defray his expenses, he tutored in mathematics. His first pupil was Burton Holmes, later noted as a travel lecturer.

Copley then was known as a "night owl," who enjoyed staying up late and chatting on many subjects, including politics and world events.

Two months before time to receive his degree in law, he withdrew from school and returned to Aurora to manage the Aurora Gas Light Co. Shortly thereafter, he took the Illinois Bar examination and was admitted to practice of law, but never followed the legal profession. Many years later, on May 9, 1923, in impressive ceremonies at Lincoln Memorial University at Harrogate, Tenn., near Cumberland Gap, Col. Copley received the honorary degree of doctor of laws.

Ira C. Copley assumed charge of the Aurora Gas Light Co. on February 2, 1889, succeeding his father. The company had languished almost to the point of being snuffed out like a flame on a gas jet. Considerable dissatisfaction had developed because of the poor quality of gas and, on February 1, 1889, a competitor, operating under the name of the Excelsior Gas Co., had received a franchise to construct a gas plant and mains.

Electricity also had been developed as an illuminating medium in competition with gas by the L. O. Hill Co., which had built a generating plant and, under contract with the city, had begun lighting Aurora streets with electricity in 1882. Aurora, one of the first two cities in America to have its streets so illuminated, often was called the "City of Lights." Another company had been chartered in 1887 as the Aurora Electric Light & Power Co.

Then Ira C. Copley stepped into the picture. In addition to being manager, he was elected a director and president of the Aurora Gas Light Co. While others concentrated their efforts in developing gas for illuminating purposes, the 25-year-old former law student saw a real future in gas for

ELECTRICITY FROM THIS PLANT LIGHTED AURORA IN 1882

use as fuel. With this impelling obsession, he inflamed the imaginations of many businessmen in Illinois to the point where they were willing to lend him money to enlarge the original plant and, on October 25, 1890, his 26th birthday, his company purchased the property and franchise of the competing gas company. He then bought his uncle's interest in the Aurora Gas Light Co., his father retired, and Ira C. Copley was in sole charge. In January, 1891, the property of the L. O. Hill Co. was bought by the stockholders of the Aurora Gas Light Co.

In 1894, he and W. W. Tracy, an investment banker in Chicago, together with Col. Fred Bennett, of Joliet, acquired all the stock of the Joliet Gas Light Co. In 1900, Copley, with associates, organized another company, the La Grange Gas Co., with offices in La Grange, Ill., to sell service along the Burlington, North Western and Milwaukee Railroads. The Aurora Gas

31

Light Co. took over the property of the Aurora Electric Light & Power Co. in 1902, and, in anticipation of further extension of gas and electric power properties, the name of the combined companies was changed to the Fox River Light, Heat & Power Co. Thus the foundation was laid for a great network of utility enterprises in the Midwest. Illinois was growing fast and, as its population increased, the Copley companies prospered.

By that time, Copley, who had become proficient as a gas engineer, conceived the idea of transmitting gas under pressure for long distances and he carried out experimental work which satisfied him that artificial gas could be transmitted under pressure as a practical proposition, so a gas main was laid to Batavia in 1902. Copley was the pioneer in the transmission of artificial gas for long distances and Batavia became the first town in the world to be supplied with gas in that manner. In this connection he met and entertained gas engineers from America and Europe, who visited Aurora to study the new method of gas transmission. By 1903, gas mains had been extended to St. Charles and Geneva, Ill., in addition to Batavia.

A consolidation of the various enterprises under the name of Western United Gas & Electric Co. took place on February 1, 1905. This merger involved the Fox River Light, Heat & Power Co., the Joliet Gas Light Co., the La Grange Gas Co. and the Elgin American Gas Co., a subsidiary of the American Gas Co., of Philadelphia. The population served by these companies was 240,000.

In 1905, Western United Gas & Electric Co. acquired the property and franchise of the Aurora Steam Heating Co., and, in 1910 and 1911, purchased the electric plants in Wheaton and Glen Ellyn, Ill.

With a vastly expanded territory to be served and with the proof of the success of transmitting artificial gas under pressure, Col. Copley determined that it would be advisable to construct one large central gas manufacturing plant. He accordingly made an exhaustive personal investigation of the largest and most efficient gas plants in operation in England, Germany and Austria, which included two trips to those nations. In 1911, Col. Copley organized the Coal Products Manufacturing Co., a corporation for the manufacture of gas, coke and other by-products. This corporation entered into a contract with the Koppers Co. to construct, near Lockport, Ill., a by-products coke oven plant. It was the first company in the United States to build an establishment for supplying gas as a principal product and coke as a by-product.

COL. IRA CLIFTON COPLEY

The Illinois Commercial & Mining Co. was incorporated under Col. Copley's direction in 1914. The company was organized to market coke, coal tar and ammonium sulfate, the by-products of the Coal Products Manufacturing Co.

In 1914, a farmer living near Ava, Ill., about 16 miles from Murphysboro, reported existence of natural gas on his property. He had drilled a small gas well, which was producing gas that was used to heat and light his home. Col. Copley consulted geologists of Northwestern University, who recommended exploratory drillings. In order to carry on these operations, the Mid-Egypt Gas & Oil Co. was organized as a subsidiary of the Illinois Commercial & Mining Co., and many acres were leased and wells were drilled, which produced natural gas and oil. A pipeline eventually was laid connecting Murphysboro with 16 natural gas wells and enough gas was produced to supply the southern territory for a few years. For transmission of the oil, a separate company, known as the Mid-Egypt Pipeline Co., was organized as a "common carrier."

Coal, an essential raw material necessary to the manufacture of gas, became increasingly scarce as World War I progressed. In order to obtain a source of supply that would assure continuous production by the Coal Products Manufacturing Co., Col. Copley and the company's engineers decided it was imperative for the Illinois Commercial & Mining Co. to lease or purchase coal-producing mines. In 1917, coal lands containing a well-equipped mine were leased at Ethel, Logan County, West Virginia. A second mine was opened on this property soon after it was leased. These mines supplied the Coal Products Manufacturing Co. with about 250,000 tons of coal a year and it thus was able to maintain uninterrupted production of gas throughout the war and during the strenuous years following.

In addition to operation of the mines, it was necessary for Col. Copley's company to maintain housing for the miners and to assume management and general supervision of the commissaries. On the property in Ethel, W. Va., there was an attractive and clean village, with 111 miners' houses, two general stores and an excellent schoolhouse.

In 1920, two more mines were purchased in West Virginia. They supplied the Coal Products Manufacturing Co. with approximately 150,000 tons of Pocahontas coal annually. In the same year, the Illinois Commercial & Mining Co. bought all the stock of the Gus Blair Big Muddy Coal Co., which operated a mine on the outskirts of Murphysboro, Ill. The name was changed to Western United Gas Coal Co. and the entire output, amounting to about 115,000 tons annually, was used by the Southern Illinois Gas Co. and the Coal Products Manufacturing Co., excepting a small amount sold locally. West Virginia coal previously had been employed universally in coke ovens, but, at Col. Copley's request, a system was developed which permitted the use of Illinois coal.

Owing to the large number of companies owned by, and affiliated with the Illinois Commercial & Mining Co., it was decided that legal steps should be taken to make it a holding company. At a special meeting of the stockholders, on May 9, 1921, the charter was amended and the name was changed from Illinois Commercial & Mining Co. to Western United Corp. The capital stock was increased from $360,000 to $16,000,000, consisting of 60,000 shares of common capital stock of a par value of $100 a share, aggregating $6,000,000, and 100,000 shares of preferred stock, par value $100 a share, aggregating $10,000,000. President of the corporation was Col. Copley. The Western United Corp. served gas to 65 communities, electric current to 12, and steam heat to one.

When the so-called Samuel G. Insull interests began to cast envious eyes on the properties of Western United, a war developed between the two companies for territory to be served with electricity. Lines were constructed by both companies and much litigation ensued before the Illinois Commerce Commission. Difficulties were settled by an order of the commission defining the territories to be served by each company and an agreement was reached between the companies, under which certain disputed territories were served by a new company, with each contestant owning one-half.

Col. Copley organized, in 1921, the Aurora, Elgin & Fox River Electric Co., which purchased at receiver's sale the street railways in Aurora and Elgin and the interurban railway connecting the two cities.

In December, 1924, Col. Copley was elected vice president and general manager of the Western Public Service Co., organized to effect a working agreement between the Western United Gas & Electric Co. and the Public Service Company of Northern Illinois, both of which had been supplying electric current in the districts. The following month, contracts were made providing for management by Stone & Webster, Inc., of Boston, Mass., of the gas, electric power and light, street and interurban railways, water and steam business of the Copley companies.

Col. Copley disposed of all his utility holdings on February 1, 1926, to

E. H. Rollins & Sons and A. E. Fitkin & Co., and resigned as president of the Western United Corp. Rollins & Sons subsequently bought the Fitkin interests in the holding company and some time later Rollins & Sons sold to the Insull interests.

In 1893, Miss Celia O'Meara (now Mrs. C. O. Goodwin), long to remain with Col. Copley as his aide, confidante and business associate, made his acquaintance and entered his business world. It was in the late 1890's that a long-time association with B. P. Alschuler, brother of the renowned Judge Samuel Alschuler, began. Alschuler, John C. Murphy and John K. Newhall were names of Copley's intimates, and when his business enterprises increased to a point where legal advisers became a part of the operation, it was Alschuler and Murphy who assumed the responsibility.

During the years of his great expansion of public utilities, Col. Copley conducted almost parallel courses in his two other great interests—politics and newspaper publishing. (Detailed accounts of Col. Copley's newspaper activities appear in other chapters in this book.)

III

Almost from the year he left college, he plunged with ardor into local and state politics. He became an important figure in the Republican Party in Illinois, the party and the state which sent Lincoln to the presidency.

ILLINOIS PENITENTIARY AT STATEVILLE

From 1894 to 1898, he was a member of the Illinois State Republican Central Committee, and at the same time was president of the Illinois League of Republican Clubs.

For several years, Col. Copley was a state park commissioner and, in 1909, he was appointed a member of the commission to build the new Illinois penitentiary at Stateville. The penitentiary was unusual in construction, in that it was circular in shape, permitting inspection of all cells from a central point. Col. Copley was deeply interested in the construction and devoted much time to it. He served on the penitentiary commission for a period of 17 years.

In 1910, Col. Copley was elected to Congress from the Eleventh Illinois District, by the second largest majority ever given any Illinois congressman to that date. The district comprised Kane, McHenry, DuPage and Will Counties. His popularity in his district was attested by the fact that he was repeatedly re-elected, serving six consecutive terms, from 1911 to 1923.

In the 62nd Congress, he was a member of the Building and Grounds Committee; the 63rd, Post Office and Post Roads and Industrial Arts and Expositions Committees; the 64th, Post Office Committee. He had no committee assignment during the 65th Congress, but in the 66th he was named a member of the tax-writing House Ways and Means Committee, on which he also served in the 67th Congress, and which gave him great political prestige.

He conducted the most personal of congressional campaigns. No hamlet in his district was too small to be overlooked. He spent hours—not only during the campaign but after election—chatting with the men and women of these small communities. His political appointments always were in the interest of the community, and not from political expediency.

During his service in Congress he sponsored much forward legislation. He was given credit for having virtually written the income tax provisions that were based on the ability of persons to pay their share of the tax burden according to their incomes, figured on a graduating scale. He promoted mothers' pensions and fought excess profits tax measures. He introduced the first legislation to prohibit the exploitation of child labor; however, he was ahead of the thinking of his colleagues in this industrial field, and the bill was defeated.

For promoting such legislation, a decade after he had left the halls of Congress, Col. Copley gave credit to President Franklin D. Roosevelt,

W. W. TRACY AND COL. COPLEY
They Were Close Friends for Many Years
Picture Taken in 1945 in Front of Aurora Beacon-News Building

37

with whom he often did not agree on matters of public policy. He also indorsed Roosevelt's swift action during the bank crisis of 1933 and supported him without stint in World War II as commander-in-chief of the Army and Navy. The Colonel always put his country foremost.

While a member of Congress, Col. Copley was quite liberal in his views, considering the thought of the times. In fact, when Theodore Roosevelt founded the Bull Moose movement in 1912, Col. Copley ran for re-election on the Progressive ticket and was elected. During one of his congressional campaigns, he made a speech in Woodstock, Ill., in which he said that he favored President Wilson's progressive policies and he voted for the Federal Reserve Act, passed during the Wilson administration.

Following is the vote received by Col. Copley and his opponents in the general elections in the Eleventh Illinois Congressional District from 1910 to 1920, and the vote cast in the Republican primary in the same district in 1922:

1910

Ira C. Copley, Republican	17,899
Frank O. Hawley, Democrat	11,276
Jonas G. Brook, Progressive	1,106
James H. Brower, Socialist	1,047

1912

Ira C. Copley, Republican	25,750
Thomas H. Riley, Democrat	14,330
William P. Lea, Progressive	876
P. H. Murphy, Socialist	1,167

1914

Ira C. Copley, Progressive	18,371
Frank W. Shepherd, Republican	17,197
John A. Logan, Democrat	9,098
H. H. Nicodemus, Socialist	662

1916

Ira C. Copley, Republican	38,418
William C. Mooney, Democrat	15,715
William C. Langhorst, Socialist	1,309
R. C. Copley, Progressive	212

1918

Ira C. Copley, Republican	25,744
Carl F. Schutz, Socialist	1,954

1920

Ira C. Copley, Republican	68,691
Anton Nemanich, Jr., Democrat	14,885
Frank L. Raymond, Socialist	1,825

1922 PRIMARY

Frank R. Reid, Republican	38,934
Ira C. Copley, Republican	32,729

In the 1916 election, the name, *R. C. Copley,* listed as a Progressive, appeared on the ballot in addition to that of Ira C. Copley, Republican. Explanation of the virtual duplication was given in a story in the Aurora Beacon-News on November 1, 1916, which read:

CONG. COPLEY OPPOSED
BY MYTHICAL OPPONENT

MAN VOTING FOR CONGRESSMAN GAVE HIM WRONG INITIAL.

R. C. Copley, a mythical person, is the candidate for congress on the progressive ticket.

There is no such person as R. C. Copley in the Eleventh congressional district, but the name is on the ballot. The only name on the progressive ticket.

A Will county voter, who refused to leave the progressive party ranks, wanted to write in Congressman Copley's name and his "I" was taken for an "R."

Congressman I. C. Copley couldn't file a petition withdrawing as he is not R. C. Copley. As things stand he is opposed by himself.

IV

His business success assured by the time he was 27, Ira C. Copley wooed and won the attractive Miss Edith Strohn. She was born in Sheboygan, Mich. Her father was W. W. Strohn and her mother, Mary Nelson Strohn. Her father was a successful lumberman, and also was interested in shipping on the Great Lakes. The family moved to Oconomowoc, Wis., where Edith Strohn and her brothers and sister were reared. She attended St. Mary's Seminary at Knoxville, Ill., and was graduated with high honors. While visiting schoolmates at Aurora, she met Col. Copley, and, after a short courtship, they were married on March 3, 1892, in Los Angeles, to which city her parents had moved from Wisconsin. They enjoyed a happy wedded life lasting 37 years.

A woman of culture and refinement, tactful and considerate, Mrs. Copley had the faculty of quickly making friends and tying them to her in bonds of deep affection. There was no circumference to her circle of friendships. Statesmen, politicians, bankers, professional- and businessmen, the well to do and the needy men and women all found in her society the attentive ear of a sympathetic listener, a giver of sound advice when sought, and an eager and practical provider of aid where required. Before and during World War I, when her husband served in Congress, she aided him with grace and dignity in the discharge of his important duties. Her home in Washington was a welcome meeting place for members of the cabinet and their wives, the diplomatic corps, and members of the Senate and House of Representatives.

She accompanied Col. Copley on frequent trips to Europe, and won the high regard of those with whom she came in contact, as she had done in her native country.

A finished musician, an art connoisseur, and possessing the genius of transforming a house into a home, she exemplified the highest type of American womanhood. She was a director of the Juvenile Protective Association of Aurora, and kept in constant touch with and aided juvenile protective societies throughout the nation. She displayed special interest in hospital improvement and devoted much of her attention to the maintenance of a high standard of treatment at the Aurora Hospital. Her forebears having fought in the Revolutionary War, she became an honored member of the Daughters of the American Revolution.

Early in their married life, Col. and Mrs. Copley lived in the Copley family home at 251 South Lake Street, Aurora, later renumbered 327 South Lake, except for a short period during the World's Columbian Exposition in Chicago, when they resided on Lincoln Place. They lived in Washington, D. C., after Col. Copley's election to Congress in 1910, but also retained their Lake Street home.

The Copley residence at 434 Downer Place, Aurora, where they lived for many years, was planned by Jarvis Hunt, noted architect, in 1906. The land was purchased a considerable time before construction of the house

EDITH STROHN COPLEY
She and Col. Copley Were Wed March 3, 1892, in Los Angeles
Mrs. Copley Exemplified the Highest Type of American Womanhood

41

was started and several years elapsed between laying the foundation and completion of the dwelling. Col. Copley and Mrs. Copley moved into the house in 1917.

Col. Copley enjoyed social life. He was an extensive entertainer and gave and attended many social affairs. It was a tradition of his to entertain his friends at his home in Aurora whenever he was in the city, and he tried to be there to act as host every October 25, his birthday. In fact, after he had entered Copley Hospital, he insisted upon having a party at his home on October 25, 1947, and he was taken there from the hospital in a wheel chair.

Another tradition was to have parties in his home on presidential election nights. The Downer Place house always was open for club, church, political and charity affairs and for friends.

He loved the good things of life and had for his family and served to his guests on innumerable occasions the best in food and drink. At one time, he purchased the entire stock of *un cave* in France and imported it to the United States. He had wine cellars in his Aurora home and in California.

Col. Copley's preoccupation with the well-being of children perhaps stemmed from the fact that in their early married life he and his wife suffered tragedies visited on few couples. Three children, all boys, died in infancy, but their love of children led them to adopt two boys, James Strohn Copley, in 1920, at the age of $3\frac{1}{2}$ years, and William Nelson Copley, in 1921, at the age of $2\frac{1}{2}$. The boys' middle names were taken from Mrs. Copley's family names—Strohn from her maiden name and Nelson from her mother's maiden name.

Col. and Mrs. Copley's concern for the welfare of youngsters, especially those likely to be underprivileged, was manifested in 1926 by their donation to the City of Aurora, at Christmas time, of two playgrounds, fully equipped. Until then, Aurora had no public playground. In addition, Col. Copley set aside other property that might later be converted into playgrounds according to the needs of the community.

Another example of his interest in children was his contributions to the Galena Street Home for Children. At the time the home was built through the efforts of the Kiwanis Club of Aurora, Col. Copley, when approached for a donation, wrote a check for the balance owed.

He also was a staunch supporter of the Community Chest. The first meeting to plan and activate the Community Chest of Aurora was held in the Colonel's Downer Place home.

He underwrote much of the expense of the Juvenile Protective Association in Aurora and made it possible for numerous young men to obtain higher education through loans of generous proportion.

The Colonel was an early owner of automobiles. His first cars were bought in 1906. One was a U.S.-made Mercedes, a four-cylinder, chain-drive car that cranked in front. The same year he purchased the chassis of a Darracq, of French manufacture. The engine was of six cylinders. The Colonel had two bodies built in Chicago for the chassis. One was a touring body, with no top, the other a landaulet. They were interchangeable. The landaulet was a closed body for use in winter and in rainy weather. It was the first enclosed automobile in Aurora and

JOHN T. BENNETT
The Colonel's Chauffeur

subjected its owner to much criticism in the opposition newspaper, the politically-owned Aurora Daily News. The newspaper dubbed the car "the limousine." It was one of six cars of the French make in the United States at that time.

John T. (Jack) Bennett, who resides in Coronado, Calif., and who became Col. Copley's chauffeur in 1906, recalls many interesting experiences in his service with the Colonel. He drove for the Colonel until the Colonel's death and remained with the Copley family until 1949, when he retired, after 43 years of employment. Bennett left the Rambler automobile factory in Kenosha, Wis., to work for the Colonel.

When they started on a motor trip, reaching their destination was an uncertainty. Mechanical breakdowns and flat tires were frequent, roads were bad everywhere except in the cities, which were the only places to have paved streets. Spades were a part of the equipment, for use in digging out wheels mired in mud. When a sudden shower occurred, the Colonel would order Bennett to drive under a tree for shelter, because the car was topless. That was a dangerous spot, Bennett observed, because lightning might strike a tree.

Col. Copley took the landaulet to Washington, when he was a member of Congress, and Bennett went along as chauffeur. In 1912, the Colonel owned a Packard. Painted Yale blue, it was known as "the Ringling car," because the color was that of circus equipment. The Colonel also owned Cadillacs, but the names of his other cars have become obscure with the passing of the years. Among them were Stoddard-Dayton, Stutz, Knox, Rickenbacker and Cole.

Col. Copley was an excellent card player. Before the days of auction and bridge whist, he was a member of the City Club of Aurora and played with great skill the old-fashioned game of whist. Throughout his life, he played auction when it was in favor, and contract. He never could quite conform to the rules of bidding, inasmuch as he was an individualist, but, if his partner understood his system of bidding, the game was played by them with considerable success. He sometimes amused himself by playing solitaire.

The Colonel was an enthusiastic yachtsman and his Diesel seagoing yacht, the *Happy Days*, was his pride and joy. Designed on his order by Cox & Stevens, ship architects, of New York, the 235-ton *Happy Days* was built by Krupp Works at Kiel, Germany, and was delivered to the Colonel at Kiel on April 1, 1927. The contract was awarded to the German firm because, during the post-war, pre-Hitler depression in Germany, a ship could be built there for one-third the cost prevailing in the United States. Its overall length was 196 feet, 7 inches; length at waterline, 165 feet, 3 inches; beam, 27 feet, 1 inch, and draft 13 feet, 11 inches. The Colonel and his family went to Germany to take possession of the *Happy Days*.

MOORED IN FRONT YARD
'Happy Days' at Coronado

COL. COPLEY ENJOYED MANY CRUISES ON HIS YACHT *HAPPY DAYS*

Construction was of substantial character. Decks and exposed wood-work were of teak. The various deck fittings and gear used in operation were heavy. The craft comprised three decks. The interior was attractive and the finish in good taste, in keeping with the Colonel's desire to provide for himself and his guests the most pleasing and livable quarters possible. Furniture, floor coverings and draperies were carefully selected. Wall spaces and overheads in the rooms for the owner and guests were paneled and the trim and molding produced a pleasing effect. The dining room was finished in a green tint, the living room and library were fitted with fireplaces and the rooms were finished in sanded teak. There were seven large rooms for the owner and guests and each room had a separate bath directly adjoining.

The *Happy Days* carried a full crew of 31. Maximum speed was 13½ knots an hour and on extended voyages a speed in excess of 12 knots could be maintained indefinitely. The *Happy Days* was able to cruise 8000 miles without refueling.

The name of the yacht, as the Colonel's friends knew, was taken from his salute in offering a toast to those dear to him, for he always saluted them with the words, "Happy Days!"

The *Happy Days* afforded Col. Copley and his family many happy days at sea and gave him ideal opportunities to extend the gracious and generous hospitality for which he was widely known. Winston Churchill once was his guest, along with 30 of the Colonel's friends from the California Club, Los Angeles. Col. Copley's cruises on the *Happy Days* were extensive. On it he visited many European ports, including Constantinople and the North Cape of Norway. He cruised the eastern and western coasts of the United States.

Early in 1942, following outbreak of World War II, the yacht was sold to the U. S. Navy and was used as a training ship and later as a weather ship. After the war, the Navy sold the yacht and the *Happy Days* was converted into a refrigerator ship in the fishing industry.

The Colonel was much interested in the arts and during his travels in the United States and abroad bought numerous paintings for his home in Aurora.

He was the owner of a valuable painting of John Hancock, done by John Singleton Copley. Col. Copley felt that this portrait was of particular significance to him, not only by reason of its art qualities and due to the fact that it was the work of America's top-ranking pre-Revolutionary portrait

PORTRAIT IN OFFICES OF COPLEY PRESS
Painted in London by Raymond Woog

47

PICTURE IN COPLEY MEMORIAL HOSPITAL
Portrait Painted in New York by S. Dickinson

painter, but also because John Hancock was an illustrious American patriot whose signature was the first to be appended to the Declaration of Independence. John Hancock subscribed to the Declaration in extraordinarily large handwriting and is reported to have said at the time that he did not want King George III to need to put on his spectacles in order to see his signature. Col. Copley, in his true-hearted Americanism, was a great admirer of the Founding Fathers of the United States and ever ardently revered the imperishable document they promulgated.

One painting that he bought was not what it was purported to be. On a trip abroad, he met in Italy a friend, John Esmond. They were looking at paintings and were told that they could procure a valuable Corot. They looked at the painting and the Colonel purchased it, but, when it arrived in America, customs officers imposed an import tax on the ground that it was not genuine. Whatever became of the picture is not known, but it was not one of the Colonel's prized possessions.

Although he appreciated art, the Colonel had only two portraits painted

COPLEY CORONADO HOUSE AT RIGHT, HOTEL IN CENTER

of himself. The portrait in offices of The Copley Press, at 428 Downer Place, Aurora, was painted in London in 1936. It is marked "W" in a circle, and is the work of Raymond Woog. Visitors to COPRESS headquarters see this portrait when they enter. The portrait in the Copley Memorial Hospital was done in New York in 1944, signed by S. Dickinson. The Colonel sat twice for the painting.

Following acquisition of The San Diego Union and Evening Tribune, Col. Copley, in 1928, bought the 20-room Coronado residence of the late John D. Spreckels. The house, situated on a five-acre estate across the street from Hotel del Coronado, faces Glorietta Bay. Built by Spreckels in 1906, it was a showplace in Coronado. After remodeling the house extensively, the Copleys occupied it when they were in the San Diego area. Many distinguished guests were entertained there. It was one of the Colonel's jokes that the *Happy Days* was moored in his front yard. After his death, the property was sold, in 1949, to a syndicate, which converted the residence into an apartment hotel.

Some time after they acquired the Coronado property, Col. and Mrs. Copley decided to take a trip east, particularly to attend the dedication of

COPLEY MEMORIAL HOSPITAL IN AURORA

THE COLONEL EMPHASIZES HIS REMARKS
Speaking Before Aurora Rotary Club

the Wilmer Ophthalmological Institute, toward the founding of which both had contributed. While in Baltimore, personal tragedy struck on the Colonel's birthday, October 25, 1929, when Mrs. Edith Strohn Copley died in St. Agnes Hospital. Mrs. Copley had suffered from sinus trouble. A minor operation was performed and fatal complications developed.

The Colonel and Mrs. Copley often had discussed the matter of providing an endowment for the Aurora Hospital and, when in Aurora, while en route to Baltimore, the subject again was considered.

On September 4, 1930, Col. Copley gave to the Aurora Hospital Association 2¾ acres adjoining the hospital. The land was valued at $150,000. He also provided for an endowment of $250,000 to be paid in five annual installments beginning January 1, 1932, the income to be used for maintenance and upkeep of the hospital, or in any other manner deemed appropriate. Col. Copley agreed at this time to bequeath the hospital an endowment of $1,000,000 in his will.

In gratitude for these gifts, the name of the institution was changed from Aurora Hospital to Copley Hospital, and a stipulation was made that, after Col. Copley's death, the name would be changed to Copley Memorial Hospital.

The Aurora Hospital Association was organized and chartered in 1888. The first patient was received in a rented building. Construction of a hospital was begun in 1890 on the site of the present nurses' home. An addition was built five years later. In 1913, a hospital was erected on the land now occupied by the Copley Memorial Hospital. This was made possible by contributions from public-spirited citizens. An important role was played by Col. Copley, who suggested that plans for a three-story structure be abandoned in favor of a four-story building. At that early date, he envisioned the future growth of the institution.

At the present time, the 200-bed Copley Memorial Hospital has eight operating rooms, two delivery rooms, an X-ray department with a full-time roentgenologist and a laboratory with a full-time pathologist. Col. Copley's contributions have helped to hold down hospital charges and provide modern equipment and facilities. The Copley Memorial Hospital stands as a glorious monument to his benevolent generosity.

Col. Copley married Mrs. Chloe Davidson Worley on April 27, 1931, in Paris, France. She was a daughter of Charles Lybrand Davidson, Chicago banker. She had resided in Pasadena and Aurora. After their wedding, Col. and Mrs. Copley toured France and England and made a Mediterranean cruise on the *Happy Days*. Guests on the voyage were M. and Mme. Michel Clemenceau, of Paris; W. W. Tracy, then of Williamstown, Mass., and Philip Pitt Campbell, of Washington, D. C. The Copleys returned to the United States in August, 1931.

On their Los Angeles visits they stayed at the Biltmore Hotel, but fi-

THE COLONEL AND MRS. CHLOE COPLEY
They Were Married in Paris, April 27, 1931
Photo Was Taken at Sun Valley, Ida.

53

nally, in 1937, bought property on Muirfield Road, which they used on future occasions when they were in Los Angeles.

The Colonel and Mrs. Chloe Copley were remarried in Aurora on June 19, 1944. The ceremony was performed by the Rt. Rev. William W. Horstick, the clergyman who later preached the Colonel's funeral sermon. The Colonel decided on the remarriage in order to render invulnerable his holdings and commitments and to avoid legal complications that might arise in the event the Paris records of their marriage were destroyed in World War II.

Following the death of Col. Copley, Mrs. Chloe Copley traveled extensively, but always retained a keen interest in the Colonel's business affairs. She was generous with her time and money in various charitable enterprises. Mrs. Copley died in Los Angeles on August 1, 1949. She had been spending the summer in Los Angeles and died unexpectedly of a heart ailment.

ARDENT FISHERMAN
The Colonel in High Sierra

The Chloe D. Copley Memorial Library at the hospital in Aurora was endowed by Mrs. Eleanor Worley Blenman, her daughter; Comdr. William Blenman, USN, the daughter's husband, and William W. Wilbourne III, the daughter's son. Each year they make a contribution of books.

Col. Copley's fraternal and club affiliations were extensive. Masonic organizations and lodges in which he held membership were Aurora Lodge, No. 254, Ancient Free and Accepted Masons; Aurora Chapter, No. 22, Royal Arch Masons; Aurora Council, No. 45, Royal and Select Masters; Aurora Commandery, No. 22, Knights Templar; Ancient Accepted Scottish Rite, Chicago; Medinah Temple, Ancient Arabic Order, Nobles of the Mystic Shrine, Chicago; Aurora Lodge, No. 705, B. P. O. Elks, and Ben Hur Lodge, No. 870, Independent Order of Odd Fellows, Aurora.

COL. IRA CLIFTON COPLEY

He was a member of the Aurora Union League Club and Aurora Country Club. In Springfield, he belonged to the Sangamo Club and the Abraham Lincoln Association. His Chicago Clubs were the Union League, the Chicago, the Arts and the Tavern. He was a life member of the Art Institute of Chicago. In New York City, Col. Copley belonged to the Metropolitan Club and in Washington, D. C., to the Chevy Chase Club and the National Press Club. As a graduate of Yale University, he held membership in the Graduate Club Association, New Haven, Conn., and the Yale Club, New York City. He was a member of the Bath and Tennis Club as well as the Everglades Club, in Palm Beach, Fla. While in Paris, Col. Copley joined the Inter-Alliance Club.

When Col. Copley's interests necessitated his spending a considerable part of his time in California, he became a member of a number of clubs on the West Coast. In San Francisco, he belonged to the Bohemian Club and the Pacific Union Club. In Los Angeles, he held membership in the California Club, the Bolsa Chica Gun Club, the Los Angeles Country Club and the Bel Air Bay Club of Pacific Palisades. He also belonged to the Cuyamaca Club in San Diego, the San Diego Club, the Coronado Beach & Tennis Club, La Jolla Beach & Tennis Club, and the Club Internationale of Ensenada, Mexico. He was a life member of the San Diego Historical Society.

Col. Copley's epitaph might well be the tribute paid him in the dedication to a volume published in 1921 by the Western United Corp., the public utilities parent company of which he was the architect, builder and president:

"He possesses the engineer's knowledge of chemistry and mechanics; the financier's knowledge of money and accounting, and an exceptional fund of business sense, patience and foresight."

Mrs. C. O. Goodwin, of Aurora, long-time business associate of Col. Copley in his far-flung enterprises, and who did extensive research for his biography, commented:

"Col. Copley was never a man of today. He always was a man of tomorrow. In going over all of this material, I am aghast at his vision and his achievements. Over the years, as they came along, we grew along with them, took them casually and for granted. Now I am astounded at the magnitude of his accomplishments."

55

The Illinois State Journal, in an editorial on November 3, 1947, the day following the Colonel's death, said:

"Above and beyond his intrepid business record, Col. Copley will be longest remembered for the Aurora Hospital he endowed, the public parks he donated, the college needs he underwrote and the deep affection he held for the young people who are the future strength of the United States he loved so well. Thus has a champion of free enterprise lived compassionately and established a priceless heritage."

Col. Copley once told a group of associates with whom he counseled:

"Wealth, position, power are not the measure of a man. It is the disposition he had to do the right thing, his dependability, the conscience that is his and the desire he has to serve."

James Strohn Copley

JAMES S. COPLEY AND PRESIDENT EISENHOWER

57

JAMES STROHN COPLEY
Chairman of the Corporation, The Copley Press
President and Publisher, The San Diego Union and Evening Tribune

58

James Strohn Copley

JAMES STROHN COPLEY, chairman of the corporation of The Copley Press, was born August 12, 1916, in St. Johnsville, N. Y. He was adopted by Col. and Mrs. Ira C. Copley at the age of 3½. He received his early education in various elementary schools in Washington, D. C., Aurora, Ill., and Pasadena, Calif., always under the watchful eyes of the Colonel and Mrs. Copley.

At the age of 14, he entered Phillips Academy, in Andover, Mass. There he embarked upon his own newspaper career by becoming business and advertising manager of the school's semi-weekly, the Phillipian. By 1934-35, Jim not only had brought the Phillipian to a point where it showed a profit, but had added many features to increase its reader interest and improve its service. He introduced comic strips and speeded circulation to the point where it was delivering stories of big games to the crowds leaving the stadium, in the manner of metropolitan newspapers.

Journalism followed at Yale in much the pattern set at Andover. Jim spent his four undergraduate years in the advertising department of the Yale Record, and upon graduation was ready to embark on the professional newspaper education outlined by his father.

The first step was at Culver City, where he became assistant to Publisher William Shea, on the Star-News. Once more he found himself assigned to the circulation department. There he not only supervised carriers, but often was called upon to deliver papers himself when the "routes were down," which he did with the assistance of a recently-purchased jalopy.

After a year at Culver City, Jim moved on to the Alhambra Post-Advocate and then to the Glendale News-Press, where his broadened experience qualified him to supervise an extensive remodeling program occasioned by the rapid growth of the News-Press.

The next journalistic step took Jim to San Diego. There he became assistant to Lester G. Bradley, then publisher of The Union and Tribune-Sun, largest of all the Copley newspapers. This time Jim's desk was in the advertising department and before long some of the troublesome assignments began to find their way to him. One particularly tough account was that of a store proprietor who was in the habit of tearing the proof of each ad to pieces and remaking it to suit himself. So vexing was this individual that at the start Jim was inclined to think the account not worth the trouble required to service it. Before giving up, however, he decided to investigate the case from every angle. After long and detailed study, he was convinced the account was worth saving and he determined to save it. He called upon the advertiser at his store. What the two said to each other remains a secret, but the incident marked the end of the advertiser's attempts to rewrite his own advertising copy.

The attack on Pearl Harbor interrupted Jim's newspaper career. When he announced his intention of joining the Navy, his father at first deplored the move. Jim's eyes were sub-standard and Col. Copley had come to depend more and more upon him in the management and conduct of the newspapers. But the Colonel was extremely proud when his son was accepted by the Navy and commissioned an ensign (USNR) in March, 1942.

Jim had made application for Naval Intelligence, but was assigned to duty with the Incentive Section of the Office of Public Relations in Washington, D. C. During his four years' service, he received two promotions and was named secretary of the Navy Board for Production Awards. In this capacity he had full responsibility for presenting to the board recommendations for the coveted "E" award. On February 1, 1946, Jim was placed on the Navy's inactive list.

In 1946, he married Jean Maclachlan Boyd, whom he had met in Washington. They have three children, William Boyd, a stepson attending Stanford University, and Janice and Michael Clifton, both 4 years old as this is written (1953).

Following his marriage, he spent his time in Illinois and California, in order to be near his father and also to assume the responsibilities of first vice president of The Copley Press. Col. Copley died November 2, 1947. With his passing, a tremendous burden fell upon Jim's shoulders.

Jim was named co-executor with the First National Bank of Chicago, of Col. Copley's estate, and shortly thereafter was made a member of The Copley Press executive committee. In these new and top-level capacities he faced the responsibility of making important and far-reaching decisions. In his hands and those of the executive committee lay the destinies of The Copley Press and the careers and jobs of hundreds of persons on the staffs of its newspapers. Not the least important task was that of solving the difficult financial problems created by the heavy tax structure on his father's estate. The immediate years following Col. Copley's death were filled with almost endless day and night conferences, while Jim and his associates wrestled with and finally bested the seeming insurmountable problems of those exhausting days. By 1950, the organizational structure of The Copley Press had been brought to a point where Jim felt he could return to active newspaper work, something which always had been close to his heart. This he did by becoming publisher of The San Diego Union and the Tribune-Sun, as well as president of the Union-Tribune Publishing Co.

The Copleys reside in Aurora, Ill. By working on a tight schedule, Jim is able to spend several months of the year in his San Diego office. When he took over The San Diego Union and Tribune-Sun, he immediately plunged into the civic and social life of the community as well as the active operation of the newspapers. His personal stewardship of the San Diego properties has carried them into their period of greatest growth.

Rapid increases in circulation and advertising and consequent growth of the newspapers themselves brought a requirement for greater facilities. As an answer, Jim launched in San Diego an expansion and development program, the largest any Copley executive ever had undertaken. Plant facilities were expanded from approximately 27,000 square feet to more than 75,000 square feet. Installation of eight new Goss Headliner press units, auxiliary press and stereotype equipment, other machinery and modernization called for the heaviest investment ever made in one property by The Copley Press.

Along with the business and plant development in San Diego, Jim applied himself to bringing about consummation of many civic projects. In 1952, he threw himself whole-heartedly into the support of the Eisenhower-Nixon ticket. Early in the campaign, he went to Denver for a long personal conference with Gen. Eisenhower and came away with comprehensive and first-hand knowledge of all the campaign factors. He personally directed the campaign waged by the Copley newspapers in support of the Republican ticket. San Diego County gave Gen. Eisenhower a plurality of 73,400 votes and Republican leaders generally credited The San Diego Union with having performed a major part in winning the local victory. Other Copley newspapers received similar credit for having won substantial victories in their communities.

During The Copley Press meeting in 1952, Jim Copley was elected chairman of the corporation of The Copley Press. A. W. Shipton, president, made the motion. Said Shipton: "I have known Jim from early boyhood. I have been intimately associated with him. I have watched his development with happy pride. His capacity was well demonstrated when his father died and he had to assume the burden along with the First National Bank of Chicago of settling the estate. This has required his application to many perplexing problems and he has demonstrated a maturity of mind considerably in advance of his years. Under his direction, I prophesy The Copley Press will continue to grow and prosper, a just reward for a young man with a fine mind and the ability to use it. My hat is off to him."

Shipton's praise of Jim Copley is typical of the comments of his associates in publishing as well as in the fields of politics, finance and civic endeavor. His plans for Copley Press newspapers, as he has outlined them to his fellow workers, provide for a group of the very best newspapers it is possible to publish. Jim has stated over and over that he will be satisfied with nothing but superiority in newspaper operations and in newspaper personnel. It is his fixed determination that all Copley newspapers shall become more and more important factors in American life, not to be excelled in their contributions to the well-being of these United States of America, and to the people who dwell within them.

William Nelson Copley

COPLEY, FOND OF TRAVEL, SPENDS MUCH TIME IN EUROPE

WILLIAM NELSON COPLEY
Director, The Copley Press

William Nelson Copley

WILLIAM NELSON COPLEY'S active career with The Copley Press began when his letters to his father appeared in Copley newspapers during World War II. At present he is a member of the board of directors of The Copley Press. Bill, as he is known by his associates, was a private in the U. S. Army, and saw action in the North African campaign and on the Sicilian and Italian fronts. His letters, in which he described Army life, sometimes grimly, often humorously, but always vividly, were outstanding. They were run anonymously in the Copley newspapers. Each carried an explanatory note that it was "an American soldier's letter to his father." Some of the letters were written from Fort Eustis, Va., and Fort Totten, N. Y., where he underwent training. Others were from North Africa and Italy.

In recent years, Bill has spent much time in France, Spain and Switzerland and has written for The Copley Press many articles on his experiences and observations in those nations.

Upon his discharge from the Army, Bill Copley became a reporter for the Tribune in San Diego, where he did feature writing. Being of an artistic turn of mind, he later devoted his time to painting, and, with a partner, opened a studio in Beverly Hills, Calif., where several showings by noted artists were held. Later he rented an abandoned firehouse in Los Angeles, with a view to providing a place for his own painting, and where young artists without means also could work and exhibit their pictures.

Ambitious to further his own ability in art, Bill went to Paris in 1951 for study. He found, however, that living in Paris is difficult for an American. Writing from Paris for COPRESS in April, 1952, he said:

"Learning to live in France doesn't come easily. I've been at it a year and it seems that I'm just beginning to learn things. You wonder how the French, who've been here all the time, have figured things out as well as they have. It was a big day in my life when I finally found a studio, and I accomplished the feat in a little less than a year, which is almost a record. Anybody who comes to Paris seriously starts looking for a studio, ever since La Boheme. It's the thing to do. And you don't necessarily have to be a painter. A couple of stamp collectors I know feel that a studio is indispensable to their profession. It's part of the myth of living in Paris. It's mad.

"According to our standards of real estate, a studio in Paris should be the cheapest thing on the market. There are a lot of them and they never could have been expensive to build. You're lucky if you find one with electricity and most of them don't have either gas or water. But they're still the most desirable things to have in Paris.

"It was only after I got my studio that I began to realize how slowly one learns things here. My studio was a nice empty cube. So I said I'll put a stove here, run in some electricity and water, and go to the bathroom at the corner cafe.

"A friend of mine introduced me to an entrepreneur called Ivo Rublic, who promised me to have the job done in three days. I started sending out postcards inviting people to the housewarming. That was six weeks ago.

"An entrepreneur is a sort of free-lance contractor who is bound by tradition to promise to have everything done in three days. They also give reasonable estimates. More than that, they are completely charming people and, like dentists here, are really artists in disguise.

"To engage an entrepreneur is like being adopted by a cat. You become attached to him immediately and you can be pretty sure that he'll never leave you, though he may wander enough to make you worry about him.

"When I found out that Ivo wasn't going to get the job done in the three days, and it didn't look as though he'd make it by three weeks, I decided to take a trip and settle my nerves. Only to make the gesture effective, I had to find Ivo and let him know that I was taking a trip to settle my nerves.

"I spent the day looking for him at all his favorite cafes and finally left what I thought was a nasty note on his door. I came back to the studio for a last wistful look and there he was. I told him that I was taking a trip to settle my nerves and that I'd left a nasty note on his door.

"I left that night from Saint Germaine, but not before seeing Ivo again. He'd gone home and read the note. I was getting into the car when he saw me. He ran up to me and hugged me like a bear. There were tears in his eyes and he kept repeating, 'That wasn't a nasty note.'

"Ivo is an artist from Czechoslovakia. Everybody in his home town said he was a good painter and advised him to go to Paris to become famous. Then he won a prize for painting which turned out to be more money than he was allowed to take into France. So he had a party for his friends and distributed the money among them like one deals a hand at bridge. Then he went to Paris and discovered that it was full of artists and that most of them were broke.

"He married a pretty little Hungarian girl, and they built an apartment for themselves. The place was the size of a broom closet.

"She was a dancer and when she injured her back he cared for her for two years there when she couldn't move from her bed. It was then that he put his painting away and became an entrepreneur. When she was better he sent her to America with what he had earned.

"But they're not happy without each other. Sometimes he says he is so unhappy he can't work. So she's coming back. And when he's paid his debts, he says, he'll paint again. He even set the date. But knowing Ivo, I'm sure it will happen just that way, though he may be a little late, like he was with my studio.

"Ivo looks like Skeezix and is the happiest person I've ever known, except when he's sad, which is a little less than half the time. We've become such good friends by now that I can't even write him any more nasty notes. As for the studio, it will be finished some day, and I'm no longer nervous about it. Actually, I rather dread the day when it will be all done, because, like the cat who adopts you, I would miss his irregular visits.

"And I've learned a little bit more about life here: That if things aren't done when you want them done, because you may think you can afford to have things done when you want them done, all is far from lost; that time can get stretched like a big rubber band, and instead of getting older, you get younger in the process."

In another article from Paris, published in December, 1952, Bill Copley told graphically of life in Czechoslovakia, behind the Iron Curtain, as related to him by a refugee doctor friend.

"It is no fun to anticipate a winter in Paris without any money, but my friend, the doctor, still thinks he's better off than he was in Prague," Copley wrote. "I had asked him if things were really as bad in Czechoslovakia as we were made to believe. He said I couldn't imagine how bad things were.

"Prague, he told me, hadn't been hurt too badly by the war. When the Communists took over, they brought with them another third of the town's population as administrators. They took over most of the downtown area for their offices and made a big bite into the nicer kind of housing. Adjustments were made to offset this. Now no one can live in an apartment where there is more than one room for each person. Barracks have been built outside the city. Often a whole family will inhabit a room.

"The doctor said that anybody with a business of his own, no matter how small, suddenly found himself an employe where he had been the proprietor. All stocks of food and clothing were taken over by the state and rationed.

"Life, he said, became completely Sovietized. Library books were burned and replaced by the Soviet choice. All newspapers fell under the control of the party. The Paris Communist publication Humanite was the only western paper allowed on newsstands. The state took over the theaters. Shakespeare was banned. Nothing but Soviet plays and movies could be shown.

"According to the doctor, any position of responsibility in the community required six months of political training. Directors of any enterprise had to be party members.

"My friend, the doctor, said that things were particularly hard on him. He lost his office and instead had to work in a medical center a minimum of eight hours a day for a salary corresponding to $100 a month. This did not include house visits and night calls which had to be taken care of after his eight hours and for which he could ask no pay.

"The worst thing about it, he said, was that, in order for everyone to get in his eight hours, the doctors constantly were rotated so that a patient never got to see the same doctor twice. Also, since life was notoriously healthy under the régime, the doctors were fined if they found that more than 4 percent of their patients had anything the matter with them.

WILLIAM NELSON COPLEY

"He said that, when the strain began to show on him, it was suggested that he rest by taking his turn at the recreation center. This particular recreation center was a reconverted hotel in the country, which could accommodate 40 men, women and children recreationers.

"Recreation began at 7:30 in the morning by a meeting in the dining room with a 30-minute political speech before a 15-minute breakfast. After breakfast, they were led out for a walk in the country. There were frequent rests, during which they could listen to more instruction.

"There was another speech in the dining room before lunch, and after lunch they were given an hour of complete liberty to do whatever they wanted. Most of them seemed to want to sleep during this time. Then another hike, with speeches and an hour-long, before-dinner speech. After dinner there were two hours of discussion before they were put to

WILLIAM NELSON COPLEY
Pictured When a Student

bed. My friend said that most of the recreationers found their vacations rather dull and got into the habit of marking off the days on the calendar.

"Another unique institution in contemporary Czechoslovakia, according to my friend's description, is the volunteer brigade. A truck arrived at his door around 7 o'clock in the morning and he volunteered to go to the fields and help with the potato crop, knowing, he said, that he would be arrested if he refused. The particular fields were about 80 miles out of town, but they were directed in the singing of party songs all the way out. The volunteers worked until nightfall, when they were given supper, a speech, and some straw to lie on. After 12 days of this, they were returned to Prague and were paid for their efforts. At the same time, however, he said they were asked to donate the pay toward construction of a Socialist library.

"What upset my friend, the doctor, most of all was the fear of prison. He said one had to figure on one out of every 10 persons being a spy and some people didn't feel safe in their own families. There were 300 new prisons in the country and he said that remarks against the state brought stiffer sentences than felonies.

"The doctor said that he'd been thinking of leaving for a long time and had spent six weeks in jail because somebody had overheard him talking about it. After he got out of jail, his mind was made up.

"I asked him if people ever went back after they escaped.

" 'Oh yes,' he said, 'I have several friends who went back. They're serving sentences from 20 to 30 years.' "

In North Africa, Bill served for a time as interpreter for a U. S. colonel, for he spoke French fluently. Writing in midsummer of 1943, he said in one of his dispatches:

"I mean to tell you of the action that we had, limited though it was. The facts, as I may tell them, are simply that we have been in action and have destroyed enemy aircraft. The best representation that I can give of what the sensations were is to suggest it to be almost identical with those accompanying an athletic contest of importance. There can be no moral evaluation on courage of this kind. Reactions are universal and natural.

"First, when one senses an unsympathetic presence approaching, he finds himself almost wishing to have it go away. One shivers, though being far from cold. Then it becomes noisy and there is work to do and one feels the intoxicating thrill banishing other sensations. Here is proof that warfare belongs indisputably to the male nature. Yet it is no different than what we know is a fast-moving athletic contest. The desire to be superior is dominant.

"Thus it was with us. For others who have more to face, it may well be another matter, though I would guess it to be the same thing, more intense and more possessing. Simply it seems another part of life to be responded to and a part of human nature. The vanity associated with such thing is not noble, but it is a fact, and one reflects with pride though nowhere is there justification. I am grateful for having known even a little of the climaxing moments in the military way. Many useless illusions are thus destroyed. Perhaps I have tried to glean too much from very little, but always I have been curious of life. All soldiers carry with them a ridiculous fear of being afraid, which passes with the realization that all are equally timid. In telling of this, I make no claim, for there is none to make, but from a fleeting glimpse I feel I have come to be a little better brother of man.

"Always I am happy in my adventures, and always I dream of the day when I can return to you a better man."

Writing to his father from Italy, in November, 1944, after he had been on the front line, Bill said in a letter that appeared in the Copley newspapers:

"At present I am enjoying my first relief since I went on the line. Never before have I appreciated anything as much as this, as I am enjoying a nice feeling of having deserved it. Here there is a wealth of those little things which go so far to restore a sense of well-being. There are fires to keep us warm, mail, beer, coca cola. A couple of radios are installed and working. If the comfort is not completely solid, it is certainly enough of a contrast to previous conditions to seem luxurious.

"As far as my month on the line, looking back it doesn't seem so very bad at that. There was a mixture always of the suddenly pleasant with the rough and uncomfortable. I have been most impressed by the ability of the body and spirit to adapt itself to any extreme condition.

"I think the reason that most war literature, or even reporting, fails to be finally convincing is because it does not account for the initial adjustments men make to war conditions. Thus I have always read of wars and battles, never quite believing that men can so casually endure. But 'casually endure' is just what they do, and it actually seems rather effortless. And that they endure, and how they endure, is what should be remembered only of a war. These boys are all heroes, and this greatest aspect of war heroism should surpass the tales of accidental feats of spectacular bravery.

"For me, I feel that my experiences have marked the end of my search for reality. There is no need to seek further. I have been in the upper air of few illusions. It is the end of one education and the beginning of another, much greater. It is a rare privilege to live and feel emotion, confident that what you live and feel is real and true, beyond even your power of self-deception. An education should start from here.

"Mentioned in my last how I came to capture a German. It was without a doubt the silliest experience of my life, a sheer accident born from the confusion of a war situation. Picture your son quivering safely behind a rock when from nowhere comes a thunder of human steps and this madly frightened German comes racing by within a foot of our crouched hero.

"Indeed if it had not been such a whole-hearted retreat, it might have made a very convincing charge, but he passed me without even taking the trouble to notice me. Feeling something was expected, I called after him in a tone of rather hurt offense. At this he wheeled around and we found ourselves facing each other with our rifles, both too surprised to make immediate sense of the situation.

"Just how long we contemplated each other I will not, of course, ever know. I'd say now it was a minute, though I don't suppose it could have been more than 10 or 15 seconds. Then from nowhere I heard my own voice in a tone of strictest Hollywood tradition, 'Drop that gun!'

"The greatest surprise came immediately when he actually did drop his gun. After looking at myself in the mirror a little later, it made better sense. I had not washed or shaved in over 10 days and rather scared myself. As soon as things focused themselves back to reality, I sat right down and laughed my head off.

"During the whole scene, neither of us had thought to unlock our rifles. My victim, I'm now sure, was fully convinced that I intended to kill him, and I feel that it's rather unfortunate that he didn't know how void my mind was of any such idea. Yet if he had known how surprised I was, he might be writing home about it instead of me. Only he was such an unwarlike-looking individual.

"As a catch he probably represents the poorest in the German army. He is probably a nice little fellow with a dominating wife and a perplexed daughter. I imagine him to have been a fussy little watchmaker in a remote provincial town. Surely if he hadn't had the silly fortune to run into me, some harm would have come to him.

"We do not know how much longer things will go on here. There may be another round or two. But I still have my record of many months overseas and will petition it as soon as it becomes convenient.

"Your loving son,

"BILL."

Pfc. William N. Copley spent four years in the Army. He was overseas 27 months. He was inducted in July, 1941, at Fort Sheridan, Ill., at the end of his junior year at Yale University, and, after training in the United States, he went to England a year later with the 62nd Coast Artillery. In November, 1942, he participated in the invasion at Oran, in North Africa, and was awarded a campaign star. After three months near the Tunisian border, his organization was transferred to Algiers.

There assigned to the plotting and range section of anti-aircraft, he handled a battery of telephones, making calculations and forwarding computations to gunner crews. "This section of Algiers was considered suicide for the luftwaffe," he said, "after we knocked down 20 out of 20 one afternoon."

From Algiers to Bizerte and on to Palermo, the invasion was of a different kind. The enemy was a huge carnivorous red ant that attacked weary, footsore soldiers as they lay on their bunks at night. Copley invented what appeared to be a sleeping accommodation that would prove a boon to his companions. Rigging up an improvised hammock from burlap and tent rope, Copley swung his experiment between two trees and sprayed the butts with poisonous oil.

"I might have been awarded the Legion of Merit, for efficiency," he confided, "except that my innovation backfired; just before I fell asleep, it flipped over and I was tossed to the ground and broke my arm."

After two months in the hospital at Rabat, Copley spent eight months with one of the toughest military police contingents in the war zone, at Oran.

"Spoiling for the kind of action I joined the Army for," Copley volunteered for combat duty and was readily accepted by the fighting men of the 85th Infantry Division. In 60 days of action near Bologna, he received another campaign star, won the Combat Infantry Badge, had captured a German prisoner and was on his way home.

He was honorably discharged from the Army at Fort Sheridan, August 30, 1945.

He was born January 24, 1919, and at the age of 2½ years was adopted in 1921 by Col. Ira C. Copley and Mrs. Edith Strohn Copley. He was married, September 15, 1945, to Doris Weed, of Los Angeles. They are the parents of two children, William Bryant Copley, born November 19, 1946, and Claire Strohn Copley, born August 14, 1948. The couple later was divorced.

Bill is on assignment by executives of The Copley Press to write a series of articles from abroad describing conditions in Europe. He presently (June 1, 1953) is in Paris. He has been requested particularly to write of the mental attitude of the people and of the economic and social conditions he observes, not only in France, but in other countries in which he travels. The numerous special articles have been appearing in Copley newspapers. They have elicited many favorable comments by readers and have provided interesting sidelights on current news from Europe.

Bill is a member of the board of directors of The Copley Press and when he is home he attends all corporate and business meetings.

AURORA BEACON-NEWS

"Devoted to Community Service"

PICTURESQUE FOX RIVER BISECTS CITY OF AURORA

WILLIAM M. HART
Editor and Publisher, Aurora Beacon-News
Vice President, The Copley Press

Aurora Beacon-News

4-6 Main Street
101 South River Street

Aurora, Ill.

THE AURORA BEACON-NEWS traces its history back to 1846, when on December 18, the Aurora Beacon was founded. Cordwood, vegetables, poultry, and no doubt an occasional ham or side of farm-cured bacon were accepted by the struggling young publishers in payment of the yearly subscription, which was $2, if paid in advance. Otherwise the charge was $2.50. The Beacon was a six-column, four-page newspaper.

Several attempts had been made previously to establish newspapers in the little Illinois town of a few hundred people. All were failures until two brothers, M. V. Hall and B. F. Hall, bought the printing equipment of the defunct Aurora Democrat and established the Beacon as a weekly, 106 years ago.

At first the Beacon did not know on which side of the political fence it belonged, for M. V. Hall was an ardent Whig, while B. F. was an equally strong Democrat. The Democrat finally sold his interest to the Whig. The Beacon was one of the first newspapers to espouse the Republican cause and has been staunchly Republican ever since.

It is doubtful that the profits from the newspaper enabled them to do so, but, in 1848, the two brothers joined a third brother in selling exchange and, in 1856, established the Bank of Aurora, which, however, was put out of business by the approach of the Civil War. B. F. Hall was elected the first mayor of Aurora in March, 1857.

In the winter of 1853-54, the Beacon was sold to James N. and Dudley Randall, and later changed hands several times in the early struggle to become established. Then, on Saturday, September 6, 1856, the Aurora Daily Beacon appeared, with A. C. Gibson as editor. It was a five-column, four-

77

page paper. On April 30, 1857, August Harmon became editor. The first number of the daily is preserved at the Aurora Historical Museum.

The villages of Aurora and West Aurora, with a combined population of about 7000, just had united to form the City of Aurora. The little city was not large enough to support a daily paper and, in July, 1857, the Beacon was consolidated with the Aurora Guardian and publication was continued as a weekly called the Aurora Republican-Union. James N. Randall and Simeon Whitely had established the Guardian in 1852. One month after publication, Whitely established a separate office and began publication of the Aurora Republican, an eight-column folio.

Publication of the Beacon was revived in September, 1857, by Oscar B. Knickerbocker & Co. The Republican was sold to George S. Bangs, December 6, 1858, and consolidated with the Beacon under the latter name. The first issue by Bangs & Knickerbocker was on December 30, 1858.

Both men afterward became postmasters at Aurora. Bangs was a shrewd politician and an able executive. He was appointed postmaster by President Lincoln in 1861 and was slated to become marshal of the District of Columbia, but the death of Lincoln interfered. Bangs and George Buchanan were the originators of the present system of railway post offices, of which Bangs was appointed superintendent in 1869.

No history of the Aurora Beacon would be complete without further reference to Oscar B. Knickerbocker and John Henry Hodder, who were proprietors of the paper many years and under whose management the Beacon became a political power in the county and throughout the state. Both were strong men and important factors in the development of their city.

Knickerbocker was born in New York state, where he learned the printer's trade and later worked as a reporter on the Albany Evening Journal under Thurlow Weed. He came to Aurora in 1857 and worked at his trade for James N. Randall, who became associated with August Harmon in the publication of the Beacon.

When the Beacon and Republican were consolidated a year later, the firm became Bangs & Knickerbocker. In 1866, Bangs sold his interest to Hodder. The firm of Knickerbocker & Hodder continued to mold public opinion during the next 19 years.

Knickerbocker was a devout Christian gentleman and a forcible writer. Under his editorial leadership and the business direction of Hodder, the

LAST DAILY BEACON
Dated December 30, 1911

FIRST BEACON-NEWS
Issued January 2, 1912

Beacon flourished and continued to grow until the former's death in 1885, after which Hodder operated the newspaper alone until his death.

Hodder was a native of England, where he learned the trade of printer and bookbinder. He came to Aurora in 1854 and entered the employ of D. and J. Randall as a printer about the time of their purchase of the Beacon from the Hall brothers. In 1856, he started the first bookbindery in Kane County. The bindery afterward became a part of the Beacon plant.

For a time Hodder became associated with Knickerbocker in the firm of Knickerbocker & Co., publishers of the Beacon. He later went into business for himself, then in 1863 became printshop foreman of the Beacon and in 1866 purchased the interest of George Bangs.

The weekly Beacon became a semi-weekly in August, 1869, and a daily once more on March 30, 1891. There were four other struggling little daily newspapers in the small city at the time—the News, Post, Express and a German-language paper.

Competitive conditions were impossible; something had to be done. The News had been established on Washington's birthday in 1874 by Charles M. Faye, editor, and Jacob Siegmund, publisher. In September, 1875, Faye sold to his partner. Faye afterward had a distinguished career as editor of the Chicago Daily News. He had been a compositor in the printing department

79

of the Beacon. It is said that once during the early days of the News, when a circus was in town and he was left alone, he wrote the entire issue of the News, set the type, kicked off the edition on a small Gordon press, and then delivered it to the waiting subscribers.

On February 1, 1876, Willis B. Hawkins bought a half interest in the News for $800. He was a brilliant young man, a good deal of a humorist and wit and afterward became more or less a national figure in the journalistic field, having served as editor of the Washington Star and later as owner and editor of a New York publication called Brains.

In 1891, the News was sold to W. S. Frazier, a manufacturer of road carts and a local politician. He was elected mayor of Aurora in the spring of the same year. Ownership of the News afterward passed to his son, Lincoln B. Frazier, with A. M. Snook as editor.

The Aurora Evening Post was started in 1878 by L. A. Constantine. Its chief bid for fame was in the fact that Frank A. Vanderlip started his upward climb as a Post reporter. Vanderlip became successively financial editor of the Chicago Tribune, assistant secretary of the United States Treasury in the cabinet of President Theodore Roosevelt, and president of the then largest bank in America, the National City Bank of New York.

Pierce Burton, who had the nerve to publish a Republican paper in Demopolis, Ala., the Southern Republican, immediately after the close of the Civil War, bought the Aurora Weekly Herald in 1871. The Herald had been established in 1866 by Thomas E. Hill, one-time mayor of Aurora. In 1882, Burton established a daily edition called the Express.

Into this crowded field, the Beacon entered as a daily in 1891. Consolidation or elimination was inevitable.

In 1902, Charles Pierce Burton, son of Pierce Burton, then publishing the Express, tried to sell to Charles H. Smith, a local manufacturer with wealth and political aspirations. In a super-feat of salesmanship, he sold Smith on the idea that he needed a newspaper, but Smith bought the Beacon instead of the Express, which subsequently was sold to Frazier of the News. The News also had absorbed the Post in the meantime.

The Beacon was purchased by Col. Ira C. Copley on December 1, 1905, from Charles H. Smith and A. J. Hopkins. There were three competing newspapers in Aurora at that time—the News, the Post and the Express. Three years later, Snook left the editorship of the News and joined Col. Copley's staff as general manager of the Beacon.

Beacon--Extra.

AURORA, ILL., MONDAY, OCTOBER 9th, 1871.

Tremendous Fire in Chicago.

All the Business Part of Chicago Destroyed.

THE GREATEST FIRE OF MODERN TIMES.

Scores of People Burned.

3,000 ACRES BURNED OVER.

Our citizens were startled this morning to hear that Chicago was burning, we therefore took the first train into the city, and he found that every wagon on the streets was burdened with goods, almost vainly seeking a place of safety. Men lay in the streets lifeless, and exhausted. Rumor says in one building thirty-six persons were burned.

Last night on the corner of Dekoven and Jefferson streets, on the west side about five blocks from the freight depot, a woman was milking a cow and the animal kicked over a kerosene lamp which exploded and set fire to a little wooden shed. This soon spread into some small buildings which communicated with a large manufacturing establishment near by, on the river, and took all between this point up to Randolph street, sweeping all before it. It then leaped the river in one broad sheet of flame, and branched off in every direction, lapping from roof to roof like a prairie fire. From the West street depot to Lake Michigan, it is all one fearful scene of blackened and desolated waste, and the flames are still rushing northward furiously, eating up all before it. Not a vestige left of the once fair proportions of that grand business centre of the North-West. That part of the city as far as Lincoln Park, is one flat place, with nothing left upon it but ruins. The ruins extend from Eldridge Court and Harrison street, south.

It was impossible to get over on the north side. The extent of the fire is a track of land over one mile wide and five miles long.

All the original town of Chicago is burned— Court House, Sherman House, Opera House, Post Office, McVicker's, Tremont, Board of Trade building. Not a printing office or hotel of note of note left.

Not a passenger depot but is burned, except the Pittsburg & Fort Wayne.

Colleges, churches, the new Methodist, Presbyterian and Robert Collier's churches on the North Side are burned.

The telegraphs are all down.

At nine o'clock the water works burned, and all supply of water ceased, except from the river.

At ten o'clock we made our way to the court house square, with much difficulty. It was a scene of terrific devastation. Here we saw T. B. Bryan, watching his two-story safe, which was about the only thing standing, except the court house walls. While there, the west end of the court house fell. All the prisoners were liberated, except three murderers, who were secured.

Steam Engines are in the city from Detroit, St. Louis, Milwaukie;—also from Elgin and Aurora;—but can do little to restrain the flames.

O. H. Placy, of this city, escaped barely with his clothes, from his office—warned only by the crackling of the flames.

The books and papers were saved from the C. B & Q general offices.

No tongue can tell the horror of the scene, no pen can depict or imagination portray the misery and desolation caused by this great calamity. As we looked over the now flat and burning prairie, which, yesterday, was Chicago, we felt that no estimate of the great loss of property and life could definitely be made, suffice it to say, Chicago is in ashes. The Northwest is ruined and the wildest excitement is raging from Omaha to St. Paul and from Detroit to St. Louis. Our country is fire stricken.

There will be a mass meeting at the City Hall, at 7 o'clock, this evening, to take action for the relief of the sufferers by the CHICAGO FIRE.

A train has started from Galesburg with box cars picking up provisions for the Chicago sufferers. All who can afford to bring provisions to the depot are requested to do so, and they will be forwarded free of charge by the Co. The train will come along about three o'clock to-morrow morning. Anything left to-morrow will be sent in. All should be cooked. Rally now, and aid the unfortunate!

Kane County Circuit Court adjourned for two weeks, on account of the Chicago fire, this morning.

APPROXIMATE SIZE OF EXTRA ON HISTORIC DISASTER

81

Late in December, 1911, the Beacon took over the News, which previously had absorbed the other competing dailies, and continued publication as The Aurora Daily Beacon-News. The first combined issue was dated January 2, 1912. The News was bought from Charles H. Smith, who had acquired it following the sale of the Beacon to Col. Copley.

The guiding genius in the entire great enterprise known as The Copley Press was, of course, Col. Copley himself. He was a resident of Aurora all of his life, except during early childhood. He was only 3 years old when his parents moved to the city from Knox County, Illinois. His father, Ira B. Copley, became manager of the Aurora Gas Light Co.

Young Copley was given a thorough education. He was graduated from the West Aurora High School in 1881; later from Jennings Seminary in Aurora. In 1887, he was graduated from Yale University, where he became an expert gas engineer. He then took a course at the Union College of Law in Chicago.

Thus equipped, he became manager of the Aurora Gas Light Co. He at once began to develop the property with far-seeing vision and through the years succeeded in building up the mighty Western United Gas & Electric Co., which serves the rapidly-growing district west of Chicago, and became its president.

The key to his business success is shown in a remark he made to a friend who had commented on the wonderful opportunity offered by the territory he was developing.

"Yes," said the Colonel with a smile, "the opportunity was there and we saw it."

Col. Copley served six terms in Congress. After that he gave full time to his growing business interests. Although he spent much of his time in California, he retained his legal residence in Aurora, where various Copley playgrounds and the Copley Memorial Hospital, gifts from him to the city, attest to his public spirit and love for the old home town.

Col. Copley's earliest philanthropic efforts were directed toward establishing a college in Aurora. He led a small group of influential citizens, who engineered the transfer of a college from Mendota, Ill., to Aurora, a project made possible by his promise that the institution never would lack support. Since its founding in 1912, Aurora College benefited from Col. Copley's contributions, which amounted to approximately one-ninth of the

A. M. SNOOK
President and Publisher, 1908-30

A. M. HIRSH
President and Publisher, 1930-41

total subscription each year. In 1944, he deeded to the college a large amount of property for post-war expansion.

George E. Stephens came to the Beacon in 1905 from the Galesburg (Ill.) Register, as the paper's first editor under the ownership of Col. Copley. He was a keen newspaperman and pungent writer. The influence of the paper gained markedly while he was with it. He resigned in 1916 to become editor of the Illinois Manufacturers News and is now with the National Credit Men's Association and its publication.

Stephens had a pleasing personality and made many friends in Aurora. His ability to make friends and his interest in politics led Gov. Morrow, of Kentucky, to engage him as his first secretary. In that role he had an important part in promoting the interests of the Republican Party in that normally Democratic state. Later he became contributing editor to a number of important trade papers in Chicago, his present home.

A. M. Snook, who had come to the Beacon from the Daily News, and his successor, A. M. Hirsh, guided the Beacon-News to greater achievement. Both for many years were outstanding men in the community. They were active on the paper up to the time of their deaths.

Snook was born in Oswego, Ill., but was a resident of Aurora most of his life. During his childhood, the family was poor and the boy may be said to have matriculated in the "school of hard knocks." Young Snook finally obtained a job as a reporter for the Aurora Daily News. He had found his calling.

Combining business capacity with energy and a "nose for news," he soon rose to the position of managing editor. Under his guidance, the News prospered, absorbing its various competitors as it progressed. In 1908, Col. Copley, who had bought the struggling Beacon, persuaded the successful young journalist to join that newspaper and made him president and publisher.

Snook served in that dual capacity until his death in October, 1930, first with the Daily Beacon and, after its consolidation with the Daily News in 1912, with the Beacon-News. He guided the paper through its most critical years until, at the time of his death, it had become Aurora's one great newspaper.

The Beacon-News had become so well established when Snook died that a business brain rather than a newspaperman could take over. Hirsh, his successor, had had no journalistic experience. He was a clothing merchant and one of the best businessmen in the city. He also was an expert politician and for years it was said of him that "Hirsh runs Aurora." He was one of those rare men, an exceedingly able politician who sought no office for himself. Though he never held a political job, he became a veritable "Warwick" in municipal and state affairs. Col. Copley attributed much of his own political success to the acumen of his friend, Al Hirsh, and Hirsh was a strong factor in the election of Gov. Green, of Illinois.

His most conspicuous work, however, was that of city builder. When Col. Copley purchased the Daily News, the entire north half of Aurora's famous island was a swampy tract which had been bought in 1837 for $12.72. Hirsh headed a syndicate that transformed the morass into Aurora's shopping center, with handsome stores, the two leading hotels, one of them the tallest building in Illinois outside Chicago, one of the most beautiful theaters in Kane County, six fine bridges, a state armory, the handsome Beacon-News Building, and an enormous amount of taxable property that contributes to the beauty and prosperity and convenience of the largest city in Kane County.

"The most useful man Aurora has produced in 50 years," Col. Copley said of him. It was inevitable that Hirsh should have been selected as Snook's successor. He served as president and publisher of the Beacon-News until his death on March 12, 1941.

Three days later, a successor to Hirsh was appointed by Col. Copley in the person of Charles W. Hoefer, who had been advertising director of the Beacon-News.

CHARLES W. HOEFER
Publisher, 1941-1951

Like many other strong men, Hoefer began his business career as a newspaper carrier boy, working for the Joliet News. He afterward became office boy, and, by diligence, ability and faithfulness, worked his way toward the top. He developed a special genius in the advertising field and when, in 1915, Col. Copley consolidated the Joliet News with the Joliet Herald, Hoefer came to Aurora as promotion manager of the Beacon-News. Within a few months he was made advertising director. His grasp of the business made him the logical successor of Hirsh.

Hoefer retired December 31, 1951, for reasons of health. There was reluctance to see him go. The paper under his direction had 10 of the most prosperous years in its history and gained almost 8000 in circulation. He was liked by everyone. He was with the paper 36 years. Twenty-six of these years he was advertising director. He was a major factor in the growth and importance of the paper.

It was upon his urging that Publisher Snook added a Sunday morning issue. The idea was that this would please people of the area by giving them a wealth of personal and community news on a day when they ordinarily would be without it. This and a full presentation of consequential items of the day would give the home folk a paper they would prefer over all others, including the metropolitan press from nearby Chicago.

The thought was sound. The Sunday Beacon-News, with many columns of the printed word, and comics and pictures and personal items, outdistanced in the Aurora field the Chicago papers in circulation from the start and widened the gap with the years. The paper gave complete coverage of an area with a 30-mile radius.

This made for a much larger reading community than Aurora and environs and brought an appreciable increase in patronage to Aurora stores. In turn they expanded advertising, which worked for the good of all.

Hoefer was a born salesman and had a belief in advertising that made him a persuasive evangelist. He presented his views in such fashion that many who never before had used newspaper advertising were convinced of its value. Some started in a small way at stated intervals in each week. Others took bigger displays. Copy was improved by increased attention and the aid of skilled copy writers the Hoefer program provided.

This improvement in the paper was as much a factor in its growth as was the emphasis upon daily reporting in detail the news of three nearby and important cities, Batavia, Geneva and St. Charles. Thousands of people in these towns now are subscribers to the Beacon-News. They read every day of what goes on in their home towns. Their sports events are well covered. Their promotions are forwarded in word and picture. They are good patrons of Aurora business houses.

Devoted as he was to his paper, Hoefer found time to give personal attention to almost every phase of Aurora life. He was a leader in the movement for the comprehensive Fox River Valley Pleasure Driveway and Park District and served as its first president after the agency for the beautification of the valley and the creation of numerous play and recreation places was voted by the people.

He was one of the founders of the Aurora Foundation, which receives gifts and administers them for community benefit. He was active in the Chamber of Commerce and served on innumerable committees for advancement and betterment of the community. He belongs to the Elks and Aurora Country Club.

William M. Hart, for 16 years director of advertising for the Joliet Herald-News, became publisher of the Aurora Beacon-News, January 1, 1952. Prior to entering the advertising field, he gained national renown as a news writer with articles and stories having to do with a riot in the Joliet State Prison. Ways and means to effect prison reforms which he suggested later were put into effect in Illinois and also in other states.

He is a man of creative and stimulating ideas. He has boundless energy. He likes people and they like him. As publisher of a newspaper devoted to the public welfare and the forwarding of the business of a community, he is a natural. In a matter of weeks after his arrival in Aurora his presence for

AURORA BEACON-NEWS SERVES TYPICAL ILLINOIS CITY

good was felt. He had met the mayor and business and labor leaders and people in the forefront of all phases of the city's life. They took to him just as did employes of the newspaper on first get-together meetings. They had a feeling that here is one who knows what he is doing. Not a few of them felt that they had an acquaintance of a sort with him from having heard national broadcasts of one of his riot writings on "The Big Story" hour. It all made for a happy beginning.

Insofar as direction and building of the Beacon-News was concerned, Hart came well equipped. He is familiar with the mechanics of newspaper production, organization and administration. He knows about printing and deadlines for news and advertising and the steps that must be followed to enable the newsboy to have the paper at the door of the householder early.

"Get it to them," is a watchword of his.

Like his predecessor at the Beacon-News, he is keen about the home town. In Joliet, he long was active in public affairs. At the time he came to Aurora, he was a member of the Joliet Planning Commission. He was past chairman of the Will County Community Chest and past vice president of the Joliet Association of Commerce. He served as secretary of the Joliet Police and Fire Commission under three administrations and was secretary and member of the Joliet Water and Sewer Board, which put in a $4,000,000 improvement. He is a charter member of the American Legion, a Rotarian, and was chairman of the program committee of that group. He is a member of the Aurora Country Club, the Elks, Loyal Order of Moose and the National Press Club.

Hart also has served on various committees of the National Advertising Executives Association, of which he has been a member for many years. As a young man, he was lieutenant of an infantry company in World War I. The training he received in the service added to his ruggedness and gave him valued experience in command and responsibility. It was after he returned from the war that he began reporting for the Herald-News. His experiences and understanding gained in the Army served him in good stead in getting news, sizing up its values and hastening it to print.

The Army life also heightened his appreciation of people and motives. It made a naturally friendly person keener about his fellows. It won him the highest esteem in the old home town and brought quick recognition of his stature in his new field, Aurora.

In 1917, a young advertising man, Audus W. Shipton, came to the

Beacon-News from the Woodstock (Ill.) Sentinel. Twenty-five years later, he became president of The Copley Press. In Aurora, young Shipton proved to be a brilliant writer of copy and an extraordinary salesman. He made friends everywhere he went and, because he liked people, awakened a responsive liking in them. World War I came along, however, and on July 21, 1917, he joined the 129th Illinois Infantry and with that famed outfit went to France. From the war he returned to the Beacon-News in June, 1919, and began a steady rise in his profession.

Fred C. Flanders, the present managing editor, joined the Aurora Beacon as a reporter in 1906 and has been continuously employed by the Beacon-News and its predecessor newspaper for 47 years. Previously he was employed by the old Aurora News, while he attended Northwestern University Law School in Chicago. He was employed on the old News for about a year before joining the Beacon. In 1907, he became sports editor, later city editor, and in 1912 was named managing editor. When the Beacon took over the News in 1912, he put out the final issue of that paper and then returned to his duties with the Beacon, which now had become the Beacon-News.

Flanders has been writing editorial page copy, in addition to his other activities, for 20 years. The Beacon-News prides itself in having a live local editorial page, and the contributions by Flanders in the way of home editorials have made this part of the Beacon-News one of the most popular features. It is his thought that a newspaper, in order to have appeal and influence, must have as a foundation a strong and electrifying editorial page, a sparkling society page, and a sports page replete with news and gossip. He has seen the Beacon-News grow from a newspaper of 3800 circulation to one with more than 28,000 subscribers.

John A. Corkery, city and news editor of the Beacon-News, began his newspaper career in 1902 as a reporter for the Beacon, while still a high school boy. He left in 1903 to join the staff of the old Aurora News, returning to the Beacon in 1907. He has served as police reporter, sports editor, city editor (since 1923), and over-all news editor. He is an indefatigable worker with a keen understanding of what it is that people want in a newspaper. Corkery has an amazing capacity for organization. He has thousands of friends in the Fox River Valley, and, as a consequence, probably receives more news tips than any other person connected with the Beacon-News. His newspaper associates have a deep liking for him. He

PUBLISHER AND AIDES CHECK DAY'S EDITION

Publisher William M. Hart, center, and Beacon-News executive staff. Seated at left, Fred C. Flanders, managing editor, and at right, John A. Corkery, city and news editor. Standing, left to right, Frank L. Lee, classified advertising manager; Roy W. DuSell, pressroom foreman; William B. Chawgo, auditor; H. J. Sommerer, composing room foreman; Robert R. MacDonald, credit manager; William C. Buckberg, circulation manager, and Albert W. Gerbin, advertising manager.

inspires loyalty and effort, and in the community his friends are legion. It was under his direction that the Aurora Centennial edition of 1937 was issued. This was one of the largest and most comprehensive and interesting papers of its kind ever published in the United States. It contained 288 pages and covered every phase of Aurora life from the community's earliest days to the date of issue. Corkery recently was given a Pall Mall award for an outstanding story in connection with his assistance to Aurora police in solving the Jesek murder case.

Corkery was honored by his newspaper associates and Aurora civic leaders at a testimonial dinner in the Sky Club of the Leland Hotel the night of February 3, 1953. The occasion was in the nature of a birthday celebration. Corkery, who reached the age of 67 years three days later, was acclaimed by his fellow workers as "hale and hearty and capable of a day's work that would exhaust men many years his junior."

Frank L. Lee, director of classified advertising, has been continuously employed by the Beacon-News for 47 years. He started as a reporter and was named classified advertising director in 1908. Beacon-News classified advertising has been an important part of the newspaper. Lee's department recently established a record when a Sunday issue carried more than

800 classified ads. In addition to heading the classified department, Lee writes a Sunday column, "The Lighter Side of Life," which is widely read.

William C. Buckberg, circulation manager, began his career at the Beacon-News in 1921. He has developed approximately 200 carrier routes, and the able direction of his department has made it possible for the Beacon-News to have 115 percent coverage of the City of Aurora. Buckberg is widely known among Illinois circulation managers, who often seek his advice on carrier problems and other matters pertaining to circulation.

Robert R. MacDonald, credit manager, has been employed by the Beacon-News since 1925. His active interest in watching credits has built up an excellent record of collections.

H. J. Sommerer, composing room foreman, dean of the third floor, has been employed by the Beacon-News continuously for 46 years. He is so active in his work that his production of lines set on news copy often exceeds the record of the younger operators. In addition to setting news, he finds time to direct the composing room, an organization of 35 employes.

Roy W. DuSell, pressroom foreman, who has been employed by the Beacon-News for 47 years, is acknowledged as one of the best pressmen in Illinois. The Beacon-News often has been complimented for the attractive appearance of the newspaper, great credit for which must be given DuSell.

Albert W. Gerbin, advertising manager, recently appointed to that position, has been employed at the Beacon-News for 12 years. Active, young and energetic, Gerbin is bringing enthusiasm and energy to the display department. He is well acquainted with all the local retail accounts in Aurora.

William B. Chawgo, auditor, has been employed by the Beacon-News for 10 years. Prior to that time, he was with the U. S. government in the Internal Revenue Department. He has a wide knowledge of business matters and tax problems, and ably directs the business office. He was of great assistance to the publisher during the erection of the new press, mail room and circulation unit.

In the personnel of the old Beacon, before it was taken over by Col. Copley, and in that of the merged papers, were some outstanding figures. Mention has been made of B. F. Hall, George Bangs, Willis Hawkins, Charles M. Faye and Frank A. Vanderlip.

Fred Irving Anderson, who went to the New York World from the Aurora Daily News, has become a successful author. Frank M. Tenney, a

THREE-STORY BUILDING HOUSES AURORA BEACON-NEWS

former reporter, became an editor on the Great Falls (Mont.) Leader.

Truman A. DeWeese was editor of the Aurora Beacon in the early 1890's. He was a brilliant writer and one of the first columnists in the country. His column, a weekly feature of the Beacon, was called "Snap Shots by A Snapper." He became an editorial writer for the Chicago Times-Herald and later achieved notable success in the advertising field, practically establishing in the nation one of the better known breakfast foods. He also was well known as a public speaker. One of his humorous addresses was delivered at a Gridiron Club dinner in Washington. He died in the 1930's. His daughter, Dorothy, a well-known newspaper woman, once worked her way on a trip around the world on a feature writing assignment and spent a number of years in China.

Miss Mae Barclay, society editor of the Beacon-News for more than 32 years, had an important part in building the paper. She was an excellent reporter and a brilliant writer, startling at times in her handling of news and so observant and informed that her page was read by a great part of the male population. She came to the Beacon from the Aurora News in 1908. She was a private secretary to Col. Copley before she went to the News as a reporter shortly after the turn of the century. She retired in 1940 and died in 1951.

The late Charles Pierce Burton, who sold the Express to the News, was the author of a popular and successful group of boys' books, known as the Bob's Hill Stories, and wrote for Harper's Monthly and other magazines.

The present Beacon-News Building is a three-story structure of reinforced concrete with basement and mezzanine floor. Floor space is 24,000 square feet. The business office, classified and circulation departments are on the first floor, advertising, editorial and engraving departments on the second floor, and the composing room and stereotype flat casting on the third floor. The stereotype department is in the basement, where the pressroom also formerly was located.

In the autumn of 1952, the first unit of a new building was constructed at River and Holbrook Streets. It comprises the pressroom, mail room, garage and paper storage facilities. Plans have been developed for a second unit to house the business office, classified, circulation, editorial and engraving departments on the first floor, with composing room, display advertising and stereotype departments on the second floor.

A new Goss 96-page, six-unit press was installed in the new building,

FIRST UNIT OF NEW BUILDING, FINISHED IN 1952

and printing started there in February, 1953. The press enables the Beacon-News to print in two colors and black on almost any combination of newspaper sizes. It can maintain an average of 32,000 papers an hour and, with reconstruction of the folder, it will be possible to put 80 pages through the folder in a single issue.

Trackage facilities at the rear of the plant permit direct transfer of newsprint rolls from railroad cars to the paper storage room.

Other equipment includes six Linotypes, which are used for news; six Intertypes, three for ads, two for news and one for ads and news; a Ludlow, for casting ad lines; a Ludlow stripcaster and a Monotype stripcaster.

Aurora, with a population of 50,508 by the 1950 census, is a typical Illinois city located 39 miles west of Chicago. It has diversified interests, but principally it is a manufacturing city. Also, it is an important railroad point and a distribution center for many nearby towns and for a large agricultural area. Within a radius of 12 miles are the towns of Batavia, Bristol, Geneva, Montgomery, Mooseheart, Naperville, North Aurora, Oswego, Sugar Grove and St. Charles.

The population of Aurora is primarily of English, German and Swedish extraction and is representative of the European stock which is typical of Midwestern industrial centers. Nearly 90 percent of the population is native-born and many are descendants of settlers who migrated to Aurora from the eastern states more than a century ago. More than 64 percent of the residences are owned by the occupants.

Almost 200 manufacturing industries are located in Aurora and they make a wide range of products, all the way from small brushes to railroad cars and road-building equipment. Among the products are transmission machinery, conveyors, pneumatic tools, street sweepers, pumps, hardware, electronic equipment, storage batteries, machine parts, wallpaper, store fixtures, steel furniture, metal castings, clothing, typewriter ribbons, carbon paper, boxes and fasteners. More than half of the city's workers are engaged in manufacturing. Coal from nearby mines provides fuel at substantial freight savings, while oil and natural gas are transported into the area by an expanding network of pipelines.

ELGIN DAILY COURIER-NEWS

"A Good Neighbor and Friendly Servant Since 1874"

ELGIN'S BUSINESS DISTRICT BORDERS THE FOX RIVER

C. RAYMOND LONG
Editor and Publisher, Elgin Daily Courier-News
Vice President, The Copley Press

96

Elgin Daily Courier-News

164 DuPage Street   Elgin, Ill.

FOR ALMOST FOURSCORE years the Elgin Daily Courier-News and its Fourth Estate forebears have been virile forces in the development of the Elgin region business-wise, industrial-wise, agriculturally and culturally. And spanning the more purposeful years of this association with the community, from 1910 to the present, the Courier-News has been under the ownership and guidance of the Copley organization.

When the pioneer forerunner publication of the Elgin Daily Courier-News was founded in 1874, Elgin was in the age of the horse and buggy, the kerosene lamp and the board sidewalk. It was a town of 7000 population. Its residents were yet to talk over the first telephone wire, switch on the first incandescent light, drive over the first paved street.

Today Elgin is a growing city of 45,000. It is a center of precision manufacture and has a rich agricultural hinterland. Elgin proudly claims 44 churches and emphasizes the fact that 92 percent of its residents own their homes. Ninety-four percent of the streets are paved.

The Courier-News meantime has helped write the story of the city's development, has helped establish the tempo of Elgin's progress, with the result that the newspaper today serves an expanding trading area of more than 150,000 population in one of the more important marketing, industrial and agricultural centers of northeastern Illinois.

Elgin has been an important business, industrial and residential center for more than a century. The first settlement was established in 1835, and in 1846 Elgin was incorporated as a village. The Chicago & Galena Union Railroad reached Elgin in 1849 and growth of the community assumed the proportions of a boom. Elgin was incorporated as a city in 1854.

Elgin is located in the heart of the Fox River Valley, 38 miles west of Chicago. It is surrounded by prosperous farmlands and recreational areas. Economically and industrially, it is largely a self-contained community, with well-established institutions. Elgin was the first city in Illinois to establish a public school system.

The population of Elgin increased 13.6 percent between 1940 and 1950—from 38,333 to 43,534. This more than doubled the rate of increase recorded during the preceding decade and reflects the accelerated growth of industry in Elgin during recent years.

Manufacturing has been an important factor in Elgin since Civil War days and growth and development of the city largely have paralleled the expansion of its industry. Today the city has a well-diversified group of industries, the majority of which manufacture consumer goods for the national market.

The advantages of the city as a location for industry attracted men who have established Elgin's reputation as a manufacturing center for quality products. Among the items manufactured in the city are watches, precision instruments, electric toasters, plastic products, fasteners, watch cases, tools, automotive parts, compacts, motorized street sweepers, metal containers, paper cartons, container-filling machinery, architectural woodwork, ferrous and nonferrous castings, furniture, flexible metal hose, leather products and pressure cylinders.

Eighty-four industrial firms are located in and immediately adjacent to Elgin, and 127 companies are situated in the Elgin area labor district.

When Col. Ira C. Copley added the Elgin Daily Courier to his newspaper holdings in 1910, Elgin was a city of 25,876. In the years intervening, with the community virtually double in size, the impact of the newspaper upon Elgin and its environs has scored even more impressive gains.

This was not a happenstance. It was the result of the newspaper's dedication to its first responsibility to serve the common welfare by contributing its continuing best efforts to building the community.

Today the Courier-News is delivered to more than 21,000 homes in Elgin and in 41 communities in the Elgin trade area, which encompasses northern Kane County and generous portions of McHenry, Lake, Cook, DuPage and DeKalb Counties. Circulation coverage of the newspaper in the City of Elgin, incidentally, is so complete that it actually exceeds the

CITY CIRCULATION EXCEEDS NUMBER OF FAMILY UNITS

number of family units, totaling 12,069, compared with 11,165 family units, by recent count.

Over the years, residents of the Elgin region have witnessed the rise and decline of many newspapers. In 1845, the Western Christian, the city's first news publication, was established. It was a Baptist denominational organ which editorially advocated the abolition of slavery. It made Elgin its home for four years, moving to New York state in 1849.

All of this occurred just a decade after the Gifford and Kimball families migrated from New York state to found a village in the Fox River Valley and name it after an old Scottish hymn, "Elgin." In the century since that time, there has been a passing parade of daily and weekly publications, each serving a time and purpose, each leaving its imprint, lasting or transitory, upon the developing community.

There was a time, too, shortly before the turn of the century, when the press of Elgin included three daily and six weekly newspapers, each struggling from deadline to deadline to herald the community's story while avoiding the economic shoals of the day.

But the old has given way to the new. Today finds the Elgin Daily Courier-News the only survivor of all the publications that have gone before, and solely charged with community responsibility for telling the news story, providing editorial opinion, presenting the mercantile message, and carrying on in the best traditions of a free press in the promotion of all that is best for Elgin and the Elgin countryside.

That the newspaper has met this challenge is evidenced by the fact that the Courier-News today enjoys a wider readership acceptance than was accorded any other newspaper in the more than a century of Elgin's transition from a cluster of cabins and a gristmill to a progressive city with a shoulder to the wheel and an eye to the future. Further evidence may be seen in the volume of circulation, the use of the advertising columns, and in the manifold services rendered to the community.

The Elgin Courier-News came into being on January 2, 1926. On that date, two of the city's oldest and best known daily newspapers—the Elgin Daily News, established in 1876, and which later was to absorb a paper founded in 1874, and the Elgin Daily Courier, Vol. I, No. 1 of which was issued on March 18, 1884—were merged to give Elgin one bigger and better newspaper. At the time of the consolidation, the Elgin Daily News was the oldest daily newspaper, in point of continuous publication, in Kane County.

From 1910, when Col. Copley acquired the Elgin Daily Courier, until 1926, when the merger with the Elgin Daily News was effected, it had been the Colonel's wise and constant goal to combine the publications into one newspaper in order better to serve all of Elgin and its rapidly growing market region. The acquisition of the News late in 1925 achieved this purpose and opened the door to development of Elgin's one greater newspaper of the modern day, the Elgin Daily Courier-News.

Delving into Fox Valley newspaper lore, it is recorded that Dudley Randall, who previously had been in the newspaper business in Aurora, founded Elgin's first regularly-published daily newspaper in 1874. Randall called it the Daily Bluff City. Illinois journalism was 60 years old at the time, the state's first newspaper, the Illinois Herald, having been established in the early capital city of Kaskaskia, in 1814. Meanwhile, Randall's hand-set Daily Bluff City was boasting of "a growing Elgin with its 6000 souls," and was telling of a new watch works which was spreading Elgin's reputation over the nation.

On June 17, 1876, the first issue of the Elgin Daily News was published and over the span of the next half century, until its consolidation with the Elgin Daily Courier, the News absorbed several publications. Some of these flourished for a period of years, such as the Daily Bluff City, while others blossomed and withered in a matter of months with the passing of a single political campaign. Several of the early-day newspapers represented combinations of other publications which dated back to the Elgin Gazette of 1847.

Following the News on the Elgin newspaper stage was the Elgin Daily Courier, founded by Harry D. Hemmens and W. S. Doherty in 1884. In an announcement published on founding day, March 18, the co-owners of the new journalistic enterprise observed:

"It is the intent and it will be the endeavor of the publishers to make a bright and readable paper, elevated in tone and clean in every particular. The constant study of the publishers will be to do justice by all and to fairly reflect the manifold interests of this city and section.

"First of all, the new journal will aim to be a newspaper. Politically, it will support the principles of the Republican Party, earnestly yet fairly, and without prejudice . . .

"We do as well as we can today and we will do better as the days come and go . . ."

Written by the editorial pioneers of yesteryear, this statement of principle is similar in many respects to the present-day basic policy as published each day on the editorial page of the Courier-News. This statement pledges:

D. A. MacKENZIE
Publisher, 1920-29

FRANK P. HANAFIN
Former Elgin Publisher

"A square deal for all with no enemies to punish or entangling friendships to reward."

Doherty died in 1886, leaving Hemmens to direct the affairs of the Courier. This he did alone until 1903, when the Courier Publishing Co. was organized to manage and expand the property. Writing a few years ago of that period and of the subsequent sale of the newspaper to Col. Copley in 1910, Hemmens observed:

"In 1903, Albert L. Hall proposed that, if I would sell approximately a half interest in the Courier for a song, he would organize a stock company among his and my friends and raise capital to modernly equip the plant. The plan was carried out, the Courier Publishing Co. incorporated, and Mr. Hall took charge as manager and editor. I was, and remained, president of the corporation.

"The first two years were unprofitable, so more stock was sold, most of it to Mr. Hall's relatives and myself. I then ceased to hold a majority interest. Business, however, picked up and prospered from then on.

"We became nervous, some years later, over constant reports that the News was about to be sold to Col. Copley, fearing that, if so, the competition might be such that we could not keep up, with our vastly smaller resources.

Hence, when I started on a trip to Alaska, I left a power of attorney with a trusted friend. At Seattle, the evening before the morning I was to sail, I received a telegram from Elgin stating that all the stock but mine had been sold to the Colonel, who very fairly and even generously was willing to take my shares at the same figure, or that I should ride along with him if I preferred.

"I had no previous intimation that negotiations were pending, hence it was a bit of a jolt, but, after very brief consideration, I concluded that the Colonel's ideas as to changes and improvements very likely would be over my head, and sold. Then I went north and counted glaciers. I was out of business."

In addition to Albert L. Hall, who was manager and editor of the Courier at the time Col. Copley purchased the property, and who in the late years of his life served as editor of Chicago area community newspapers, other editors and publishers of the Courier and the Elgin Daily Courier-News have included Frank P. Hanafin, more recently engaged in the newspaper business in Litchfield, Ill.; the late D. A. MacKenzie, the late C. B. Strohn, the late R. Eaton Fedou, and C. Raymond Long.

R. EATON FEDOU
Publisher, 1929-44

C. B. STROHN
Interim Editor and Publisher

MacKenzie, publisher of the Courier at the time of its consolidation with the News, began his newspaper career in Elgin in 1898, when he became circulation and advertising manager for the News. In 1920, he became associated with the Courier, as publisher, continuing in that executive capacity with the Courier, and later with the Elgin Daily Courier-News, until his death in 1929.

Fedou, publisher of the Courier-News from 1929 to 1944, was a veteran of 40 years' service in the publishing field. He first was associated with the Courier, in the advertising department, in 1904, and three years later was promoted to manage the department, a position he held until 1916, when he entered the trade journal field in Chicago. Returning to Elgin in 1921, he again served in advertising executive capacities with the News, and later the Courier-News, until his appointment as editor and publisher, on August 28, 1929.

Strohn, first vice president of the Courier-News Publishing Co., served as interim editor and publisher of the newspaper during the illness and following the death of MacKenzie, remaining in the executive position until Fedou's appointment.

Long was appointed editor and publisher of the Courier-News on October 13, 1944, and continues in that capacity. He previously served the newspaper as its director of advertising, from July 1, 1935, until his appointment as publisher. Long's first work in the newspaper field was in the advertising department of the Aurora Beacon-News, from 1917 to 1921. Then followed a six-year span of service with the Elgin Daily Courier, after which he was director of advertising for the Danville Morning Press and the Illinois State Journal, in Springfield, before his return to Elgin for a second time, in 1935.

Kendall White, assistant to the publisher since July, 1949, began newspaper work in Elgin in 1920 as a member of the editorial staff of the Elgin Daily News. He continued in editorial work on the News, and the Courier-News, until his assignment to the display advertising staff of the Courier-News in 1947. Since then his duties have been principally advertising and promotion.

John E. Thompson, managing editor, started with the News as a reporter in 1914, and was promoted to city editor of that newspaper in 1917. In 1922, he left the News to become managing editor of the Courier and

OLD-TIMERS HEAD COURIER-NEWS DEPARTMENTS

Standing, left to right, Ralph L. Peterson, composing room foreman; George E. Pierce, pressroom foreman; Howard J. Jones, circulation manager; Alexander Clark, mechanical superintendent; S. G. Chambers, director of advertising. Seated, left to right, Kendall White, assistant to the publisher; Julius N. Johnson, auditor and business office manager, and John E. Thompson, managing editor.

has held that position continuously, first with the Courier and, from 1926, with the Courier-News.

S. G. Chambers has been on the advertising staff of the Courier-News since 1930, except for one year (1944), when he was director of advertising for the Daily Olympian in Olympia, Wash. He became advertising director of the Courier-News in 1945. Chambers' earlier advertising experience was with the Centralia (Ill.) Sentinel, the St. Louis Post-Dispatch, and the Dairymen's Journal, of East St. Louis, Ill.

Howard J. Jones was named circulation manager in 1924. Prior to that time, he was circulation manager of the News for three years.

Julius N. Johnson, auditor and business office manager, became associated with the newspaper in July, 1920. He was graduated from the University of Illinois in 1917 and joined the Courier three years later as cashier. Subsequently he was promoted to the auditorship.

George E. Pierce, foreman of the pressroom since February, 1939, came to Elgin from Des Moines, Ia. He learned the printing trade 35 years ago and, except for naval service during World War I, has been engaged in the printing trade continuously, working in Rockford and Chicago as well as in Des Moines, before coming to Elgin.

Alexander Clark, mechanical superintendent, and manager of the Courier-News Building, is the dean of the newspaper's employes, his service dating from March 1, 1912. He began on the newspaper as a printer's apprentice, later served as a journeyman and composing room foreman, and was promoted to mechanical superintendent in February, 1941, following the death of his father, Herbert Clark, who had held that position.

Ralph L. Peterson was made foreman of the composing room in February, 1942. He learned the printing trade following service with the Army in World War I and was employed in shops in Kansas City, Mo., and in Elgin, before becoming an operator for the Courier in June, 1921. He has been a member of the newspaper organization continuously since that time.

In March, 1926, Col. Copley purchased the present-day home of the Elgin Courier-News, the former Spurling Block at DuPage and South Spring Streets, in the heart of downtown Elgin. The Elgin landmark was promptly remodeled into what at the time was considered one of the finest combined newspaper plants and office buildings in northern Illinois. Prior to 1926, the Courier was located in the Odd Fellows Building on North Spring Street, and in earlier years, in smaller quarters on DuPage Street, just south of the present Courier-News Building.

Today's home of the Courier-News is of brick and terra cotta, and is of fireproof construction. It fronts 65 feet on DuPage Street, extends 133 feet along South Spring Street, and comprises six floors, one below ground level. The newspaper's pressroom, paper storage quarters, photographic and engraving departments, boiler room, and utility space are in the basement. Business, advertising and executive offices, the circulation department and mail room occupy the first floor, while the editorial department and composing room, the mat rollers and flat-cast stereotyping department take over most of the second floor. The three top floors are rented for general office purposes.

An interesting story is told of how Col. Copley came to buy the Spurling

BUILDING OCCUPIED BY ELGIN DAILY COURIER-NEWS

Block. The building was erected in 1892 by the late Gen. Andrew Spurling. During negotiations leading to the consolidation of the News and the Courier, Col. Copley was visiting in Elgin with the then publisher of the Courier, D. A. MacKenzie. The two were standing by a large window in the Elks Club, located over the Theo. I. Swan Department Store, across the street from the Spurling Block.

The discussion turned to the need for larger quarters for the merged newspaper properties and Col. Copley, glancing out the window, suggested the possibility of acquiring the spacious Spurling Building.

"I believe that's the place for us, Mac," he remarked. "Buy it if you can. . . ."

And shortly thereafter MacKenzie entered into negotiations with Ralph W. Hawthorne, manager of the building, for its purchase. The papers were signed and Col. Copley became the owner of the building on March 1, 1926.

It is no idle boast that the Elgin Daily Courier-News has been "A Good Neighbor and Friendly Servant Since 1874." This slogan is printed in each day's edition beneath the title line on Page 1, and in countless ways the newspaper strives to live up to its fullest meaning. Constantly its columns are devoted to the tasks of building a greater Elgin, a better, more progressive Fox River Valley community. This dedication of purpose has been manifest time and again and has won for the newspaper its most priceless asset, the abiding loyalty and friendship of the neighbors it serves.

The Courier-News, in fact, has become the clearing house for every deserving civic endeavor in Elgin and the Elgin region. Its readership depends upon the newspaper to point the way, to provide the leadership through its news and editorial columns to assure the success of every worthwhile community activity.

Thus for more than three-quarters of a century the Courier-News and the pioneer publications which preceded it have kept as a constant goal the determination to live up to the good name established for the newspaper by its founders.

In journalism a good name implies devotion to the public service, capacity to tell the news accurately, with clarity, and without bias, a purposeful editorial policy, and unflagging attention to expanding the benefits of a free press for the public welfare. The Courier-News never has swerved from these vital attributes of every good newspaper.

The Courier-News is a member of The Associated Press, Audit Bureau of Circulations, the Illinois Daily Newspaper Markets, Inland Daily Press Association and the American Newspaper Publishers Association. It also is served by The Copley Press Washington Bureau and is represented nationally by West-Holliday Co., Inc.

The Courier-News publishes every weekday afternoon except New Year's Day, Memorial Day, the Fourth of July, Labor Day, Thanksgiving and Christmas, or days observed as such. It employs 7-Point Regal No. 2 type face on an 8-point slug and prints on a Goss unit-type press consisting of four units, printing 16 pages each, and capable of producing 30,000 papers of up to 32-page size an hour. Press capacity for a single run is 64 pages.

In addition to its Goss press, which was acquired in 1939, the Courier-News includes six Intertypes and eight Linotypes in its inventory of mechanical equipment. Two of the Intertypes, incidentally, are the newest G-4-4 models. Other important mechanical units include a Ludlow type-casting machine, an Elrod strip material unit, a Goss giant mat roller and a Goss Model 45 mat roller, a Goss flat-casting box, two Delta band saws and a Goss flat-casting shaving machine.

Adhering to the adage that trifles make for perfection and perfection is no trifle, the Courier-News has given increased attention in recent years to serving the everyday needs of its readers. No request, however small, fails to receive a response from the newspaper, whether from a man in Coventry, England, regarding a birth record needed to prove his pension rights, from a Children's Museum in Fort Worth, Tex., asking to locate an old brass drum, or from a reader asking whether the president has a social security number.

In countless other ways the Courier-News serves, too. Its School Children's Shoe Fund has raised nearly $20,000 over the years and has provided more than 5500 pairs of shoes for needy, deserving children of school age.

The Shoe Fund was born of the depression years. Need for its ministrations was called to the newspaper's attention by the principal of an elementary school who learned that several children were staying away from classes because they did not have shoes fit for the rigors of winter. An appeal was sounded in the news columns and public response was immediate and wholehearted. Thus a most worthwhile community welfare cause came into being because of the interest of the press.

The Courier-News has played an important role in the promotion and expansion of the Kane County Fair, in the support of the program of the Elgin Community Chest Association, in the publicizing of the Boy Scout Big Timber Players "Hiawatha" pageant, in telling the story of public and private education in Elgin, in calling attention of all northern Illinois to the attributes of the Fox River Valley as a place in which to live and to make a living. Many hundreds of letters of appreciation bespeak the public's regard for the newspaper's continuing interest in these and all other constructive matters that are good for Elgin and the valley region.

Further, the Courier-News has found time to stress the "open door" policy in its own home. Here the latchstring always is out to visitors and particularly to the schools which are encouraged to schedule class visits to the newspaper plant. During a typical year, 35 groups, including 624 individuals, were guests on conducted tours of the newspaper.

Each year special attention is given to visits of teacher and student groups during the city's observance of Business-Industry-Education tours sponsored by the Elgin Association of Commerce. On these occasions the visitors meet with executives of the newspaper, are taken on carefully-planned tours of the newspaper plant, and are privileged to view the process of producing the newspaper. This program has paid dividends, in that each year more and more people come to understand their newspaper better and, perhaps, appreciate it more.

For some years the Courier-News has regularly been included on the workshop tours of Northwestern University's Medill School of Journalism. Dr. Charles L. Allen, associate dean at Medill, has been generous in his praise of the Courier-News as an example of progressive journalism in a typical community of Midwest America.

Indispensability of the local newspaper in telling the local news story as no other medium can possibly do has been emphasized in Courier-News promotion activities.

In this connection, an interesting analysis of the scope of the Courier-News coverage of the local story is provided by the continuing year-to-year check of the newspaper's contents. In almost every category the survey indicates the Courier-News is steadily expanding its reader services, is continually striving to do an even better job in telling the local news story, in word and picture.

In a recent year, for instance, the names of almost a million persons and places familiar to the Elgin region were published in the Courier-News. An actual day-by-day check of the newspaper for a full year disclosed this remarkable scope of local news coverage.

During a single year, the Courier-News printed the equivalent of 199 solid newspaper pages of local news pictures. All told 2755 local news pictures were used with 15,464 persons identifiable by name in cutlines beneath the pictures. Most of the pictures were taken by Courier-News staff photographers, and the engravings were made in the newspaper's modern engraving department.

During the same year, the Courier-News published 82,051 local news stories, 3898 of which made Page 1. Other interesting totals included 636 local editorials; 28,163½ column inches (167 solid newspaper pages) of feature stories; 22,307 column inches, or 133 solid newspaper pages of sport news; 29,796 column inches, or 177 solid newspaper pages of club, lodge and organization news; 143,795 classified advertisements, 6216 reader ads and 23,775 display ads.

The Courier-News is striving ceaselessly to do a still better job, to tell the news story and to tell it completely, to boost the fortunes of Elgin and the Elgin community, and to assure at all times that its columns will be open to both sides of every question, thus making certain that everyone may be heard, regardless of race, color, or creed.

That is the mission of the Elgin Daily Courier-News. That is the privilege of the newspaper which has been "A Good Neighbor and Friendly Servant Since 1874." That is the destiny which Col. Copley conceived for the Courier when he acquired it in 1910 and when he combined it with the News in 1926 to give Elgin one greater newspaper to render an even more effective public service.

JOLIET HERALD·NEWS

"A Paper for All the People All the Time"

JOLIET, SETTLED IN 1831, ORIGINALLY KNOWN AS JULIET

JOHN F. LUX
Editor and Publisher, Joliet Herald-News
Vice President, The Copley Pres

114

Joliet Herald-News

78 North Scott Street   Joliet, Ill.

T HE SIGN OVER THE DOOR of the handsome three-story building
that houses the Joliet Herald-News, in Joliet, Ill., bears the words,
"Herald-News, Founded 1839." A bronze plaque on the corner of the
building presents the genealogy of the newspaper, which has been in continuous publication since it was founded as the Juliet Courier 114 years ago.

The Herald-News has been officially recognized as a member of the
American Press Century Club, comprising newspapers which have reached
the age of 100 years. It marked its centennial in 1939 and issued a 172-
page special edition which served not only as a tribute to the enterprise of
the newspaper itself, but also as a solid measure of the esteem in which it is
held by Joliet and Will County residents.

The tiny settlement along the DesPlaines River that later was to become the modern city of Joliet was scarcely eight years old when a local
group began issuing the Juliet Courier as a weekly paper, April 20, 1839.
The first white families, from New York, Ohio and Indiana, had settled
in Joliet Township in 1831. In 1832, Chief Black Hawk led his Indian
warriors in a vigorous campaign against the encroaching settlers, and some
of them were frightened into returning east. The few who remained built
a stronghold, within the present city limits of Joliet, which they called,
through some quirk of humor, "Fort Nonsense."

Once the Black Hawk War had ended, settlers started coming into
Illinois in a gradually increasing stream, and many families which have

continued to live in Joliet down to the present day settled along the shady DesPlaines banks.

Two famous early explorers, Father Marquette and Louis Joliet, came down through the Great Lakes and the Mississippi Valley in 1668. They passed down the Mississippi as far as the Arkansas River, then started back upstream. Coming to the mouth of the Illinois, they proceeded up that stream and thus came into the DesPlaines Valley. Almost two centuries later, construction of the early-day Illinois and Michigan Canal was to link the water routes of the Great Lakes with those of the Mississippi basin, providing the forerunner of the modern-day Lakes-to-Gulf waterway over which millions of tons of barge freight now pass each year.

By 1837, the village of Joliet had grown large enough, so its citizens thought, to incorporate. A charter was duly obtained under the name of "Juliet," probably through a mixup in the spelling of the French explorer's name, possibly because of partiality, on the part of some of the residents, to the tragic heroine made famous by Shakespeare.

Founding of the Juliet Courier in 1839 was in part the result of a fortunate circumstance. As August Maue, authoritative Will County historian, relates it, a printing press had been shipped by mistake to a company at Ottawa, about 60 miles west of Joliet. When the makers of the press offered to sell it at a bargain price, 13 enterprising residents of Joliet (or Juliet) raised the money to buy it. O. H. Balch, who had edited a paper in Michigan and who understood the printing arts, became the first editor of Joliet's first newspaper.

In the first issue of the Courier, Balch put forth this sensible doctrine: "He will only state in general terms that he intends to publish a newspaper in which the principles of Democracy shall be enforced and vindicated, and in which the National Constitution shall be held up to view as the foundation of our Republican institutions and the bond of our Union and as the safeguard of our civil liberties."

Balch published a "true-blue Democratic" paper, adhering to the principles put forward by Thomas Jefferson. Nevertheless, the young weekly had a difficult time. Within a year, Balch gave way to D. L. Gregg, a brilliant young lawyer, who afterward served in the state legislature and as Illinois secretary of state. In 1843, the Courier was purchased by William E. Little, who changed its name to the Joliet Signal. Meanwhile the village charter of Juliet had been repealed by the legislature and the trustees had resigned. The community operated on an unincorporated basis until it was granted a new charter, this time under the name of Joliet, on June 19, 1852.

"The struggles of the pioneer publishers who operated the Courier and its successor, the Signal, can only be imagined since the records of their venture are fragmentary," remarks a modern historian. "When one considers that each word was set by hand, one realizes the production of a newspaper, even the four-page, six-column sheet of the day, must have been a laborious undertaking.

"The stage coach was the chief means of transportation and even national news was gathered in a fashion that resulted in some startling inaccuracies. As a result, the early editors confined themselves chiefly to political comment, with sprinkling of personal items and miscellaneous information.

"Martin Van Buren was president. Oxen were used to pull the plows. Most of the houses were built of logs and fences were made of rails. The I. & M. Canal had been started, but work had been abandoned after two years because of lack of funds. This work was resumed in 1845, when the state succeeded in making a loan of a large sum from England."

William Little, who had acquired the Signal in 1843, sold it within a year or two and there was a rapid turnover of management until May, 1846, when the paper became the property of C. and C. Zarley, sons of Reason Zarley, one of the first settlers of Will County. Later estabished as Zarley & Co., the firm continued to operate the paper for nearly 40 years.

Another Joliet newspaper, the True Democrat, was launched in 1847 by A. McIntosh. He sold it to H. N. Marsh in 1848, then bought it back in 1852. Joseph L. Braden, later a postmaster of Joliet, acquired the True Democrat in 1857.

Files of the True Democrat for 1849, when it was under the editorship of Marsh, show that it was a four-page standard-sized weekly, printed on rag paper of such excellent quality that it remains flexible and easily legible to this day. The front page included a "Business Directory," listing stores, service establishments and professional people. Departments were reserved for poetry, "Selected Yarns," "Personal Sketches," historical essays and foreign news. Page 2 offered local news items, brief "dispatches" from other parts of the nation, most of them at least six days old, and miscellaneous information. Pages 3 and 4 were devoted to commercial notices and a list of letters remaining uncalled for at the local post office.

That there was lively rivalry existing between the True Democrat and the Signal is apparent from an item in the October 18, 1849, issue of the former paper which said: "We regret that the Signal, in its notes of the Wilmington meeting, could not have kept truth on its side."

News was not lacking in that period either. This single issue of the True Democrat reports two rather serious mill fires, in one of which "the loss could not fall much short of $10,000, no part of which was insured." There was an account of the accidental death of a 2-year-old girl in a nearby community, when her clothes caught fire. This last sad item was captioned, "Distressing Casualty."

In a succeeding issue, the editor of the True Democrat hurled another barbed dart at his local rival. He noted: "The editor of the Signal says he is 'still as sound as ever.' We are happy to hear this, as even a slight falling off on the score of soundness would leave him in a deplorable condition."

Even at that time, more than 100 years ago, Editor Marsh appreciated the importance of timeliness in the news. Over a late listing of election returns in the November 8, 1849, issue he said: "We delay our paper to the latest possible moment, for returns from the different precincts, knowing the anxiety of our friends in the country to get the returns."

In addition to presenting the news, this early-day editor had a discerning viewpoint on the importance of "trading at home." He lauded the merchandise available in Joliet stores, in his November 22, 1849, issue, and remarked: "The idea that goods 'dear bought and far fetched' must be the cheapest, as well as the best, is productive of great mischief. The money paid to our own dealers goes more or less into the general circulation and, passing through the various channels of business, cheers and encourages the farmer, the mechanic and the laborer in its beneficient course."

Joseph L. Braden, who published the True Democrat through the Civil War years, finally was constrained by his admiration for Abraham Lincoln to change the name of the paper to the Joliet Republican. Later destined to become a semi-weekly and then a daily, the Republican announced the assassination of Lincoln to the startled residents of the community in 1865. Braden died in 1866 and James Goodspeed became the owner of the paper. Involved in politics, as were practically all the editors of the time, Goodspeed later served as postmaster of Joliet. He continued as publisher of the Republican for many years and the Joliet Republican Printing Co., a com-

DAILY AND SUNDAY CIRCULATION EXCEEDS 30,000

mercial printing establishment, still is operating in Joliet today, although it long since has ceased any connection with the newspaper field.

In 1870, the Joliet Record was founded by the Henderson brothers,

119

John, James and Daniel. Their office and printing establishment were in an upstairs location over the California Tea Co. store. It was Dan Henderson who developed the knack of making woodcut cartoons, believed to be the first used by any newspaper in Illinois.

The post-Civil War era witnessed the birth and death of several newspaper ventures. At one time there were five papers in Joliet, none with a circulation of more than 600. The Signal, running behind in this fiercely competitive era, eventually was sold to the Republican, operated at the time by Robert Mann Woods.

Woods had a distinguished Civil War record and was one of the most esteemed residents of the community. Only recently, when the staff of the Inland Press Association began looking up old records for a historical sketch, it was discovered that Woods was one of the three men who participated in organization of the Inland Press. Eventually Woods sold the Republican to the firm of Hayes & Fletcher and control of the paper changed hands several times until the circulation list finally was sold to the Joliet Herald.

The Joliet Record, founded by the Henderson brothers, continued operating until 1883. In the meantime, two other papers had been launched—the Joliet Sun, beginning in 1872, and the Joliet News in 1877. The News, a modest little publication, was begun by Charles Dutcher, but he sold it later to James H. Ferriss and Horace E. Baldwin. The Sun was the leading paper of the town at first, according to reliable accounts, but it faded and later was eclipsed by the News. It was owned and operated by Charles Hayes.

In the late '70's, a man named Styx MacDonald, who had a talent for writing rousing editorials, was running five editions of a paper called the Phoenix, each slanted toward the interests of a different community. The editions were distributed in Joliet, Peotone, Lockport, Plainfield and Frankfort. Perhaps this was not the first attempt at establishment of a "string" of weekly papers, all published from the same plant, but it certainly was among the early efforts of the kind in Illinois.

Will H. Stevens, circulation manager of the Record, maintained that his paper had a circulation of 980 at one time, with one-third of this total being in the community of Wilmington, 18 miles south of Joliet. Most of the other dailies had little circulation outside Joliet.

"The majority of the small advertisements of the time," according to one student of the period, "was traded out in merchandise. Most of the

COPY DESK OF HERALD-NEWS GOES INTO ACTION

Starting at the left, Glenn Whitney, city editor; Calvin Daniel Albrecht, managing editor; Robert Laraway, telegraph editor, and Harry Kelly, reporter. Leased wire teletype machines in background.

printers were paid in orders on stores and the average pay was $12 a week. Press dispatches were clipped from other newspapers. Reporters were scarce and the owners of the papers did their own news gathering. N. D. Dyer was the first big advertiser in Joliet. He signed a contract with the News calling for 150 columns of advertising, at a price of $150. Later a similar contract was signed by Dinet, Nachbour & Nicholas. These contracts put the News in control.

"Cylinder presses became the vogue and they were run by steam power. The average speed was 12 to 18 papers a minute.

"Early editors appear to have been a fiery lot, and a bit outspoken. Frequently, it seems, they delved too deeply into affairs that might be considered private. They often set themselves up as the moral judges of the community. As a result, they became involved in many battles and sometimes were punched for their efforts. But they persevered through good times and bad, and the records seem to show that hard times were the rule. One newspaper was sold, lock, stock and barrel, for $225. It would seem that few of them ran a great risk of libel suits, since a judgment would have been almost worthless."

The first issue of the Joliet Herald appeared November 18, 1904. It contained 24 pages, produced with considerable effort, and was regarded with awe by contemporary newspapermen. As one student of the period has noted, it probably represented a greater achievement than a large special edition or an election extra issued by the papers of today.

The Herald was published by the Joliet Printing Co., stockholders in which were a group of well-known business and professional men of the day. First president of the company was Col. John Lambert, who had participated in organization of the Illinois Steel Co. Illinois Steel was the forerunner of the present-day American Steel & Wire Division of United States Steel, and its establishment in Joliet did much to fix the destiny of the community as an important industrial center.

Other original stockholders were Frank H. Hall, William M. Cochrane, T. A. Mason, C. E. Woodruff, Dr. J. C. Flowers, C. B. Hayward, A. C. Dillman, Dr. H. W. Woodruff, George A. Ducker, John O. Barrett, Fred Bennett, A. E. Dinet, C. S. Witwer, Edward Corlett, E. E. Howard, Frank Kiep, Dr. P. G. Rulien, August Schoenstedt, J. J. Hamil, A. W. Fiero, J. J. Gaskill, James Smith, L. F. Beach, W. O. Bates, James W. Martin, Harry N. Hall, F. S. Lambert, H. B. Smith, E. R. McClellan, Thomas McHugh, C. G. Jones, W. H. White, Dr. E. J. Abell, John Stukel and Henry Hallenstein.

Frank H. Hall was the first general manager of the Herald and James Murphy the first editor. The Herald was launched with considerable flourish and represented a sizable financial investment, at least for that day. The stockholders had confidently expected the dividends to start rolling in at once, but it turned out that things weren't that easy. When the Herald continued in the red, not only for the first month, but for several months, the stockholders began to criticize the general manager and he sold his holdings to Col. Lambert and then resigned. Editor Murphy took over as general manager, but profits still remained nowhere in sight. Murphy resigned in 1906.

The man who succeeded Murphy was Archibald S. Leckie. The deficits continued, but by that time the stockholders had begun to realize that

ARCHIBALD S. LECKIE
Became General Manager of Joliet Herald in 1906

no quick fortunes were to be made in the newspaper business. They were vaguely hopeful that, if the paper could continue to operate for a period, it would become established in the community and eventually would achieve a profitable standing. Thus their original investment would be protected and they might expect some future return.

At any rate, Leckie was given a relatively free hand in management of the paper. When eight years had gone by with no sign of profit, many of the stockholders began to grow weary of the enterprise and offered to sell their stock. It was purchased in part by Leckie, who thus acquired a substantial holding in the paper. By 1928, Edward Corlett was the only original stockholder who still retained his interest.

Those who knew and worked with Leckie regarded him as an able executive and an editor with a singularly keen understanding of the value of news—particularly local news. His constant emphasis was upon the need for "covering" home-town and Will County affairs and this emphasis, it may be said, has been carried on and even intensified right down to the present time.

Col. Ira C. Copley acquired the Joliet Herald in 1913 and at the same time purchased the printing equipment and circulation lists of the Joliet News. On June 1, 1915, he consolidated the Herald and the News under the title of the Joliet Herald-News. The News had been published six evenings and the Herald had been issued five evenings and Sunday morning. The consolidated newspaper since that time has been published six evenings and Sunday morning. Far-sighted in this, as in other enterprises, Col. Copley realized that the interests of communities of the size of Joliet and Aurora could be served better by one strong paper than by two relatively weak ones.

The Herald-News continued under the management of Leckie until 1920. Meantime an energetic young man had joined the newspaper staff as office boy and had shown such ability in handling small assignments that he soon was writing sports. Later he was made sports editor, and the sports pages of the Herald-News had, in the words of a contemporary, "begun to sparkle." Featured in the sports department was a new column, written by this young and enthusiastic member of the staff. It was entitled "Dope De Luxe," and the writer was John F. Lux, later to become city editor, then publisher of the Herald-News. But a

EDWARD CORLETT
Herald-News Publisher, 1920-32

war was going on, and the promising young sports editor soon found himself in the muddy fields of France. Returning from service, he rejoined the Herald-News staff and, in 1920, was made city editor.

Following the resignation of Leckie in 1920, Col. Copley appointed Edward Corlett, well-known Joliet attorney, as publisher of the Herald-News. Corlett had been active in politics in Will County for many years and at one time served as mayor of Wilmington. He had managed Col. Copley's congressional campaigns in this county. Aside from the fact that he had been an original stockholder in the Herald, Corlett had little basic knowledge of the newspaper business. But he was a man of honor and integrity, with good business sense and a firmly-rooted interest in the growth of the community.

Through the 11 years that he served as publisher, Corlett attended faithfully and conscientiously to the business affairs of the paper. But he interfered little, if at all, in activities of the news department. Whenever a subscriber had a complaint concerning the handling of a news story, he listened attentively to the reader's tale of woe. Then he called in Editor Lux and anyone else concerned with the story to hear their side of it.

When he felt that the news department had handled the matter fairly, and without bias—which nearly always was the case—he stood firmly behind his staff, no matter what threats might be made.

For Joliet, the decade of the 1920's was an active and turbulent period. Prohibition had come to the nation and in the whole Chicagoland area lawless elements sought to capitalize on the opportunities for making a fast dollar through sale of illicit beer and alcohol. Star police reporter of the Herald-News during that period was a tall, quick-witted and resourceful Irishman named William M. Hart. Between them, John Lux and Bill Hart had scores of news sources, and they never hesitated to give the fullest possible publicity to efforts of Chicago hoodlums to infiltrate the community. By honest and accurate reporting, they constantly harassed those shady men who wanted to operate without benefit of attention from the press.

When a spectacular prison riot occurred at Stateville, partially as a result of administrative laxity that has long since been corrected, Bill Hart went into the prison yard, scene of some of the most dangerous fighting, and telephoned an account of the uprising to his paper from a guard's booth.

Corlett served as publisher until February 1, 1932. In the latter part of 1931, Col. Copley, at the meeting of publishers of the Illinois papers, suggested that certain changes be made in the interest of streamlining the production of the papers, such as reducing roll sizes and other economies. Corlett, whose business training had been in the field of law, suggested to Col. Copley that he (Corlett) was not qualified to carry out such program and that, inasmuch as he desired to give his full attention to the practice of law, he felt he should retire as publisher. Col. Copley urged that he continue as publisher, turning over these details to experienced news production men.

However, Corlett reiterated his desire to return to the field of law and Col. Copley acquiesced to his wishes, appointing Lux, who had a practical knowledge of the newspaper business, to the position of publisher. Lux has continued as editor and publisher since that time.

This account thus far has dealt only lightly with the physical aspects of publication of the Herald-News. Following the consolidation of the two papers in 1915, the office of publication was in the original Herald Building, now the site of the Marquette Hotel. Growth of the newspaper in circulation and advertising volume made it necessary to find new quarters. It was an interesting coincidence that a site for a new building was purchased at the corner of Scott and Van Buren Streets from the granddaughters of Charles Clement, one of the founders of the pioneer Juliet Courier.

The new three-story structure of buff brick and concrete went up rapidly and was ready for occupancy in 1924. The building is of "L" shape and contains approximately 40,000 square feet of floor space. Through a program of constant modernization and improvement which has been accelerated since the end of World War II, the Herald-News has kept pace with the newest mechanical developments and has put particular emphasis on equipment which would improve the appearance of the paper and speed up production.

The Herald-News press is a six-unit Goss, with a maximum stated capacity of 96 pages for a single run. The press was installed in 1947 in a completely new pressroom constructed at the rear of the original building. Modern stereotyping and routing equipment was installed at the same time, to reduce the time between rolling of mats and casting of page forms. The auto-paste spindles of the press are on the basement level, connecting conveniently to the basement paper storage facilities in the plant.

One of the units of the Goss press is designed for color reproduction, and as many as four colors can be handled on a single run of the paper. Increasing use of color has been noted in recent years and advertisers have reported almost invariably that they were well pleased, not only with the accuracy of the register and the excellence of reproduction, but also with the sales results achieved through color presentations.

In the composing room, modern equipment has eliminated many time-consuming operations and has greatly facilitated the handling of the extensive news and advertising linage carried by the Herald-News. There are 10 Linotypes and five Intertypes, some of the latter equipped with type fonts up to 36-point. This means that the bulk of advertising copy can be handled on typesetting machines.

The composing room also has three Monotypes, used to produce base material, strips and borders. Two Ludlows handle headline types from 42- to 96-point in size and provide fresh type for every purpose, thus assuring a clean, sharp impression. A new stereotype mat-rolling press was installed in 1950, as another move to improve printing results.

126

HERALD-NEWS BUILDING, ERECTED, 1924; REMODELED, 1946.

Printers of the Herald-News also have, handy for use, a Vandercook page proof press, a motor-operated Wessel galley proof press, four saws, one stripper and two mitering machines. There is a page storage elevator which aids in preparation for large papers, when some of the forms must be made up ahead of time. A motor-driven conveyor connects the composing room, on the third floor, with the dispatch room, on the first floor, and makes for speedy delivery of mats and ad copy.

The news room has been redecorated, and the entire ceiling covered with acoustic board. The display advertising department has been moved from the second to the first floor, the business office has been relocated in the space on the first floor formerly occupied by the pressroom, and the classified advertising department has been redecorated and rearranged.

As a result of these extensive changes, as well as other improvements such as the recent installation of a complete dispatch department for handling ad mats and proofs, the Herald-News has kept abreast of the latest developments in the mechanical field and the building has maintained an attractive, modern appearance. Fluorescent lighting has been installed throughout the plant.

Lux took over as publisher at a trying time, and he was called upon to make innumerable difficult decisions. He was guided in these decisions, as he had been in virtually every act since he joined the Herald-News, by a sense of acute loyalty to the newspaper and a desire to keep it functioning as a strong and influential news organ. Bill Hart was transferred to the advertising department, where he soon made his talent felt by bringing back into the paper a number of accounts that, for one reason or another, had discontinued regular advertising.

Within a short time, Hart was made advertising director, and the familiar "team" of Lux and Hart—perhaps better-known in Joliet than Rodgers and Hart—began to function again, this time in the field of advertising. By vigorous promotion and aggressive salesmanship, constantly stressing to Joliet merchants the importance of getting their message to prospective buyers in the most attractive form, Hart and his staff helped to bring the advertising volume of the Herald-News to new highs. When Hart was appointed publisher of the Aurora Beacon-News, January 1, 1952, the good wishes of the entire staff went with him.

If it is true that every good newspaper reflects the qualities of the community in which it is published, a glance through the pages of the Herald-News would give even a stranger some idea of what the city of Joliet is like.

The front page, with its stories of problems faced by the City Council, the school boards, the park district, the county board and other governmental agencies, as well as its report of projects being undertaken by the Association of Commerce, would tell the visitor, for instance, that Joliet is a city that has lately grown at an exceptional pace. Not only that, but leaders of the community are looking forward to a further period of tremendous progress, during which the population may well grow by leaps and bounds. Such growth brings its own special problems, and governing bodies are seeking to meet them in the best way possible; the problems and the measures adopted to cope with them make prime news for all those who live in the community.

On inside pages of the Herald-News, and often on Page 1, too, the visitor might read of innumerable activities sponsored by local organizations, of preparations for campaigns to support the Community Chest, the Red Cross, the Y.M.C.A., or some other worthy project, of new business and industrial developments, of building activity and of meritorious service by men and women of the Joliet area in the armed forces, either in the U. S. or overseas. He also would see many pictures of local persons in the news, of churches, homes or business structures being erected, and of oddities or human interest happenings that have attracted attention.

On the woman's pages, the stranger would see announcements of many weddings, past and future; reports of women's activities in countless clubs and organizations; pictures of brides, committee chairmen and leaders in cultural, music and civic groups; chit-chat about personalities and styles; "how-to-stay-young" and "how-to-make-it" articles, and numerous other items of interest to women readers.

In the sports section, there would be well-written accounts of high school and college athletic activities, local amateur sports, major professional sports—in season—and all of the other outdoor and indoor events that interest masculine readers. There would be a column of interesting comment on sports, special features on well-known coaches, managers and other sports personalities, "how-to-do-it" pieces on golf, bowling and such.

The advertisements throughout the paper, and in the classified section as well, would present a picture of busy trade and commerce, indicating that Joliet is one of the important business centers of Illinois, even though it is located almost within the shadow of Chicago.

Thus the pages of the Herald-News tell, in a general way, what citizens of the community know very well: that it is a thriving industrial city with remarkable geographical advantages, arising from the fact that Joliet is virtually at the crossroads of the nation, served by six railways, by the Lakes-to-Gulf waterway and by such important U. S. highways as Nos. 30, 66, 52 and 6 .

Biggest employers in the Joliet area for many years have been and are the American Steel & Wire Co. (2700 employes) and the E. J. & E. (Outer Belt) Railway (2500 employes).

The Carnegie-Illinois (now United States Steel Co.) coke works is also a major employer, along with wallpaper mills, the biggest horseshoe plant in the world (Phoenix Manufacturing Co.), roofing and refractory manufacturers, various machine and foundry companies, heavy chemical plants, a big oil refinery (Texas Co.) and a variety of machinery, tank and specialty factories.

The industrial picture changed sharply a little more than two years ago when the Caterpillar Tractor Co. of Peoria, after an extensive survey of the Midwest, selected Joliet as the site of a new branch plant to make road scraper units, wagons and other heavy equipment used in roadbuilding. Announced originally as an establishment that probably would employ 1500 persons at peak, the Caterpillar plant was up to 3600 by August, 1952, and the management had announced plans for an addition that would provide room for still further expansion.

Another change took place after the outbreak of hostilities in Korea and decision of the government to rebuild American defenses. The big Joliet arsenal, combining TNT manufacturing and shell-loading facilities, was reactivated and employment there passed 7000, as of August, 1952.

As might be expected, Joliet's housing facilities were overtaxed by these rapid-fire industrial developments, and a building boom of considerable intensity followed. Efforts also were made by the Association of Commerce to interest one or more big-scale housing developers in the construction of large projects, and it appeared probable that these efforts would bear fruit.

Joliet's city trading zone, as determined by the Audit Bureau of Circulations, includes 87,722 persons. The whole retail trading zone comprises 147,759 persons. Retail sales in 1951 exceeded $112,000,000, suggesting the standing of the community as a consumers' market.

Residents of Joliet like to speak of it as a "friendly, warm-hearted town," and there is plenty of evidence to back this up. The Community Chest, Red Cross and other fund appeals almost invariably have exceeded their goals over the last several years, as Jolietans opened their hearts and their pocketbooks to give generously to health, charity and character-building agencies. The number of clubs and organizations in the community, all bustling with projects of one kind or another, indicates the congenial nature of the people.

Although Jolietans come from varied national backgrounds, they have learned to work together and to pull together for the good of the community. A majority of home ownership is vested in the families living in them, making for a substantial citizenry. Levels of savings and insurance are high, indicating that most people who reside in the Joliet area are inclined to look to the future and to do what they can to prepare for it.

Joliet Junior College claims the distinction of being the first junior college in the United States, and administration of the school program has shown both vision and foresight over the years.

The Joliet Park District operates two golf courses and a swimming pool, and park and play areas available to Joliet residents compare favorably in size and equipment with those of any city under 100,000 in the United States.

Health facilities are good, with two hospitals available: One St. Joseph's, operated by the Sisters of the Third Order of St. Francis, and the other, Silver Cross, operated by a private board, but originally established through the efforts of the Order of King's Daughters. Silver Cross constructed a $600,000 addition a few years ago, using funds raised by popular subscription.

When the new Joliet Diocese was formed by the Catholic Church in 1949, Joliet was designated as the jurisdictional center and a subsequent campaign throughout the seven counties of the diocese raised more than $2,000,000 for construction of a beautiful cathedral. Ratio of Joliet residents who attend church is estimated at 10 to 1, considerably higher than that for the nation as a whole.

Thus it is that the casual reader of the Herald-News gets a fairly accurate impression of the community, just by looking through an average edition of the newspaper. Favored by location and served by water, rail and highway transportation, the city—many Jolietans feel—is destined to continue as one of the fastest-growing areas in the nation. As a Chicago newspaper writer noted, after a visit to the city, "Joliet is galloping forward to meet the future."

No account of Herald-News history would be complete without reference to the important role played by the newspaper for many years in every project for civic improvement. One of the most effective agencies in Joliet is the Herald-News Free Milk Fund, supported by contributions from hundreds of interested residents. Harry Kelly serves as volunteer treasurer of the fund, through which free milk is provided during most of the school year, on a daily basis, to all underweight children in the public and parochial schools. The program has been credited as a major contribution to community health, in that it has helped undernourished children to build up resistance to all forms of disease.

Other promotional activities of the Herald-News include the annual public links golf tournament, which has been operated for 26 years; the annual marbles tournament for schoolboys, and the annual cooking school, which attracts a capacity audience to the largest theater in town for three days each February. The newspaper always has strongly supported such campaigns as the Community Chest, the polio fund, the Red Cross, the

Tuberculosis Seal sale and the cancer fund. Generous space is given in the news columns to every activity of a civic nature. When a little Joliet girl became ill of an incurable disease and required expensive medication, a few years ago, readers of the Herald-News contributed $8000 within a period of a few weeks to provide for her care. The girl died before all the funds were used, and the money was returned to the donors—at least to those who were known—on a pro rata basis.

The news policy for many years has been to report, without fear or favor, every event that is considered of interest to the readers of the Herald-News. Emphasis now, as in the past, is on local and Will County coverage.

Col. Copley once said: "It is unwritten law among the Herald-News executives that we play the game 'on the square' and print no harmful gossip and no scandal except after one or the other has become a matter of court record, and then we print it no matter who is involved.

"One other and equally important item is our general policy of neighborliness. Friendliness with the people of Joliet and every other community where our newspaper is circulated is a careful rule.

"We get into no petty squabbles. We fight only on principle. Where there is a definite principle involved, if it is only a school trustee, we will fight. But where there is no principle involved, we are not going to make a factional organ out of our newspaper."

A brief history showing the uninterrupted publication of the Herald-News appears on bronze plaques at the front of the building. It reads as follows:

"Juliet Courier, April 20, 1839; Joliet Signal, 1843; True Democrat, 1847; Joliet Republican, 1862; Joliet Record, 1870; Joliet Sun, 1872; Joliet News, 1877; Joliet Herald, 1904. Since 1839 uninterrupted publication in Joliet, Will County, Illinois."

One of the favorite features of the paper for a quarter of a century or more has been a front-page column, "I See by the Papers," written by "Jack Thorne." Practically everyone in Joliet knows that Jack Thorne in reality is John Lux. The column is human, humorous and folksy by turns, with an occasional "scold" for some public official because of the condition of the streets or failure to keep traffic under proper control. One of Thorne's fictional characters, "The Girl on the Cass Street Bus," has become a local legend, and readers always look forward to a further report on the amusing

TEAMWORK KEYNOTE ON JOLIET HERALD-NEWS

Raymond Howk, national advertising manager; Glenn Whitney, city editor; John Raymond Hennessy, circulation manager; Calvin Daniel Albrecht, managing editor, and William Blackburn, classified advertising manager.

opinions of this gum-chewing, soft-hearted working gal, who ever seems to have something on her mind, even if it's only a new hair-do.

Over the years, Lux has moved carefully and patiently to build a spirit of teamwork and teamplay among all employes and all departments of the Herald-News. Lux characteristically is a pessimistic soul and often emits dire forebodings, but the obstacles he envisions usually never are encountered and when they infrequently develop he meets them head-on and conquers them with dispatch. In any emergency, there is a quick interplay of well-directed energy, with every man and woman springing eagerly to the task which seems necessary at the moment.

Department heads of the Herald-News include several individuals who never have worked for any other employer, except possibly the armed forces, and reflect the stable character of the entire staff as well as its solid roots in the home community. Eight department chiefs were born in the Joliet-Lockport community and have lived there all their lives.

Calvin Daniel Albrecht, managing editor; Glenn Whitney, city editor, and Robert Laraway, telegraph editor, make up a "team" which produces an interesting newspaper with local news the predominant factor. Albrecht came to the Herald-News on September 4, 1945, from the Elkhart (Ind.) Truth, where he had been employed for 17 years. Whitney came to the Herald-News on August 30, 1943, from the Ottawa (Ill.) Republican-Times. Laraway started as a cub reporter on the Herald-News. In addition to his duties as managing editor, Albrecht conducts a daily column on the editorial page, entitled "Home Town Musings," which has a wide readership. He takes an active part in all community activities.

Arthur Kramer, who started as an apprentice in the composing room in 1922, has been its superintendent since 1940. He devotes his time and attention to supervising the composing room and is an expert at typographical layout. He has instituted many innovations in production in that department.

Wilfred Burns, director of advertising, has been with the newspaper for 18 years, and Raymond Howk, the national advertising manager, is a veteran of 42 years' experience. John Raymond Hennessy, circulation manager, started as a carrier boy with the Herald-News and has been with the newspaper since 1936. William Blackburn, classified advertising manager, has been with the Herald-News since 1936. He has inaugurated many improvements in this department. Robert Delaney is acting foreman of the pressroom and started as an apprentice with the Herald-News in 1946. Miss Daisy Connolly is auditor and Clarence Layfield is superintendent of the pressroom and director of the dispatch department.

Miss Connolly has been with the Herald-News ever since the consolidation of the Herald and the News, in 1915. Prior to that time, she had been on the business staff of the News for seven years. Clarence Layfield, pressroom superintendent and director of the dispatch department, passed papers for the Herald-News before becoming a full-fledged employe on May 3,

TAKE ACTIVE ROLES IN PRODUCING HERALD-NEWS

Miss Daisy Connolly, auditor, started work with the Joliet News in 1908, and has been with the Herald-News since 1915. Others are, left to right, Robert Delaney, acting pressroom foreman; Wilfred Burns, director of advertising; Arthur Kramer, composing room superintendent, and Clarence Layfield, pressroom superintendent and director of dispatch department.

1923. He joined the pressroom staff at that time and was made superintendent in 1943. He had much of the responsibility of supervising the change-over from the old press, which was in the basement of the main building, to the modern Goss unit-type press, which was set up in a new pressroom at the rear of the plant. Under his direction, a capable press crew was developed. The pressroom, with its tile-lined walls and modern equipment, is one of the finest in the country.

If there has been a guiding principle that has served to bring the Herald-News and its predecessors through their more than a century of service to the community, it might be expressed in the phrase, "Look to the future." Joliet editors have had an infinite capacity for looking to the future.

Circulation of the Herald-News now stands at more than 30,000 daily and Sunday. More than two-thirds of the total circulation is concentrated in the immediate Joliet-Lockport area, with most of the remainder covering a trading zone that extends roughly about 30 miles from the city in all directions. With Joliet experiencing a tremendous period of industrial expansion, the Herald-News faces a new era of growth and service. And it is prepared, in every way, to meet the challenge.

Illinois State Journal

"The Journal paper was always my friend and, of course, its editors the same."
—*A. LINCOLN, June 18, 1864.*

ILLINOIS STATE REGISTER

"We want the Register to be the people's paper."—Excerpt from salutatory editorial in the State Register in 1881.

AIRPLANE VIEW OF SPRINGFIELD'S BUSINESS CENTER

J. EMIL SMITH
Publisher, Illinois State Journal and Register
Vice President, The Copley Press, and Editor, Illinois State Journal

138

Illinois State Journal

Illinois State Register

313 South Sixth Street   Springfield, Ill.

ABRAHAM LINCOLN'S PROFILE at the masthead of the Illinois
State Journal is a daily reminder to 52,000 subscribers in Springfield
and a dozen counties of central Illinois that the state's oldest daily newspaper still is a rock of Republican thought and action in the Prairie State.

"The Journal paper was always my friend and, of course, its editors
the same."

This quotation from Lincoln, whose body lies buried in Oak Ridge
Cemetery, reflects a kinship which began shortly after Simeon and Josiah
Francis published the first modest edition of the Sangamo Journal[1] on No-
vember 10, 1831.

In a monograph entitled "Lincoln's Association with the Journal,"
Audus W. Shipton, president of The Copley Press, quotes this paragraph
from the Journal of March 15, 1832:

"I am young, and unknown to many of you. I was born, and have ever
remained, in the most humble walks of life. I have no wealthy or popular
relations or friends to recommend me. My case is thrown exclusively upon
the independent voters of the country; and, if elected [to the state legisla-
ture], they will have conferred a favor upon me for which I shall be unre-
mitting in my labors to compensate. But, if the good people in their wisdom
shall see fit to keep me in the background, I have been too familiar with
disappointments to be very much chagrined."

The signature is A. Lincoln.

1—The newspaper first bore the name *Sangamon Journal*. It was discovered that a wrong-font *N* was
used in the title on Page 1 and, since the plant had only two *N's* of the correct font, decision was reached
to drop the final *N* from *Sangamon* and use it in place of the wrong-font *N* in *Journal*. Thus, on January
19, 1832, the newspaper became the *Sangamo Journal*.

Thus early in their careers—for the Journal was but four months of age, and Lincoln a youth of 23 years—did the association between the Journal and Abraham Lincoln commence.

In its 121 years, the Illinois State Journal has been published and edited by a procession of individuals who in their time lent particular flavor or personal flair to its columns, yet there is a constancy of purpose and philosophy running through its hundreds of thousands of pages which amounts to a transcendent personality.

Perhaps the man who best understood the whole sense of the Journal was the late John Early Vaughn, from 1893 to 1945 reporter, editorial writer and columnist for the capital city's morning daily. A tireless researcher, he wrote for many years a column entitled "Recalled to Life." Although the column continues on the editorial page of the Illinois State Journal each day, no one has been able to fulfill the promise of its title since Vaughn's death.

Writing in the massive Centennial edition of the Journal, published on Sunday, November 8, 1931, Vaughn masterfully condensed his knowledge of the paper's first century into a summary entitled "A Century in Springfield." This history has been drawn upon for the bulk of this article, adding to it an accounting of the first fifth of the second century.

SANGAMON JOURNAL
Started November 10, 1831

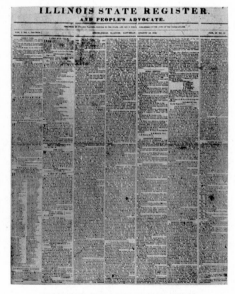

EARLY STATE REGISTER
Dated August 10, 1839

TOMB OF ABRAHAM LINCOLN, IN OAK RIDGE CEMETERY
Lincoln and the Illinois State Journal were closely associated

141

The story of the newspaper is the record of 121 years of continuous service—unswerving and never-questioned devotion to the community in which it was established, loyalty to the state which has been developed since it was given birth, and like loyalty to the nation.

Any institution which has endured for more than a century can well claim attention, particularly if its years have been spent in such work as that carried forward by newspapers. Those connected with the enterprise feel proud of their association with a newspaper, the history of which records so much that is commendable.

Founded when Illinois was on the frontier of the country's civilization, the paper was a factor in upbuilding one of the most valuable territories of which the Union boasts. It lived with, grew with and was the voice of the vigorous amalgamation of pioneer blood and spirit which was drawn into the Illinois country.

Infused with ambition and enterprise of the period which produced it, the paper for a century and a fifth has been representative of the people of Illinois, their character and their institutions. In no less degree has it represented the national sentiment so warmly nurtured in Illinois and so valiantly defended by Illinoisans.

The 121 years in which the State Journal has lived cover the most remarkable period in the history of the human race. What has occurred since the little paper made its appearance in the village of Springfield transcends not only all that preceded it in written history, but all that man's imagination theretofore conceived. Not in all the legends of the most romantic peoples are wonder-stories that compare with those in the Journal's files.

It has been the privilege of this newspaper to see the growth of the world's greatest experiment in colonization and government; to witness the supreme test of the republic's stability; to chronicle the amazing inventions that have followed the employment of steam and electricity; to tell the story, day by day, of modern man's remodeling of the world.

The chronicle, recording as fact one day what was unbelievable only a few short hours before, has not always been a pleasing kaleidoscope. Amid the wondrous marvels have been forbidding pictures. The glamor of man's high achievement halos the whole, but it does not altogether hide the tragedies of the Journal's first century.

The most deplorable, because the least excusable, of the black periods

ILLINOIS STATE CAPITOL IN SPRINGFIELD

intimately affected the newspaper. The rebellion, commonly referred to as the Civil War, which terminated in the assassination of Abraham Lincoln, took toll of the newspaper's capable men and visited upon it the loss of its best friend. Lincoln had sustained this relation to the newspaper from the day he made his first venture in politics and it printed the platform on which he made his initial race for the legislature.

In its long history, the Journal has recorded the progress of numerous wars. Aside from those between other nations, its files tell of the conflicts in which this country has been concerned, beginning with the Black Hawk War. The old papers are rich in incident glorious and tragic, affecting Illinois soldiers who participated in these struggles.

So, too, with politics. In the second year of its existence, the Journal was drawn into a national political contest. In none since that time has it been neutral. The advocate of internal improvements for the development

143

of the West, favoring a sound system of banking, a friend to the protective policy, its earliest political expressions committed it to a program it has consistently followed.

Of more vital importance, however, has been its adherence to the Union, its abhorrence of secession, nullification and other doctrines which threatened or threaten the integrity of the United States as a nation. Not since one of its pioneer editors wrote in praise of President Andrew Jackson's pronouncement against nullification in South Carolina has the Journal changed its attitude.

When, following the election of President Lincoln, the southern states began to talk secession and many northern newspapers were in doubt as to whether an effort should be made to stay them, the State Journal was unassailed with misgivings. Its course had been charted for it. Recorded in its old files is the essence of unanswerable argument against disunion. The Journal had only to be consistent to be right.

Again, in a business way, consistency has served the State Journal. When its editors first "set up their types" in the muddy little village which is now the beautiful capital of Illinois, they were keenly alive to their dependence on their neighbors. They had few resources other than their health and habits of industry. Money was scarce. Before the winter was over, they were advertising for cordwood and provisions in exchange for subscriptions.

The Journal never for a moment has forgotten the lesson of those lean months. Today it is one of the biggest newspapers in downstate Illinois, but it is still, first of all, the community newspaper. No matter what proportions it attains, it can have no desire to alter the relations with its neighbors. Its consistency may be provincial, but such is the character of the State Journal.

The Journal's first issue was given to its limited public on November 10, 1831. The outlook wasn't promising. During the previous winter, the settlers had passed through the experience of the Deep Snow, a visitation such as Illinois never before had known, and which not since has been repeated. Severity of the weather during the winter had denuded the Sangamo country of its game. Only the soft-padded wolves, which could travel over the snow and prey upon the helpless deer, remained.

With their chief supply of meat gone, the settlers were looking ahead to another long, hard winter. They couldn't be expected to become enthusi-

SANGAMON COUNTY COURTHOUSE IN SPRINGFIELD

astic over the Connecticut Yankee boys, Josiah and Simeon Francis, who had come up from St. Louis to print the Journal. They had witnessed the failure of others to start a newspaper in the village and they had no reason to believe the Yankees could succeed.

Springfield, itself, looked like a hopeless case at that time. It was an inland town, connected with the outside world by irregular stages and freight wagons. For many years the struggling young newspaper complained of miserable facilities which held up mails for days and weeks, and even months. The editors depended on eastern papers and letters for their news and these delays seriously affected the newspaper business.

Following the Black Hawk War, Gen. James D. Henry, sheriff of Sangamon County, went south for his health. During his absence, his friends entered upon a campaign to elect him governor. The Journal was foremost in the movement which spread rapidly. Gen. Henry was popular because

145

of his record in the Indian War and with great confidence the Journal predicted his success.

Then, one day, the editor received a letter from New Orleans, announcing Gen. Henry's death. The campaign had been made in vain. Gen. Henry had been dead a month when the news reached his friend. Such were the mail facilities connecting Springfield with the Gulf. It took longer to span the distance than was required to apprise Gen. Jackson of the Treaty of Ghent.

If the future capital of Illinois was an unpromising town, the outlook for what became its largest city was even less hopeful. When the founders

OLD JOURNAL BUILDING ON SITE OF PRESENT STRUCTURE

OFFICES OF ILLINOIS STATE JOURNAL AND REGISTER

of the Journal came west from their New England home, one of the brothers decided to locate in the vicinity of what now is Chicago. When he investigated the prospects, he turned back to La Porte, Ind. There was nothing in Chicago to furnish a hint of its future greatness. The early missionary work of the Journal included a campaign for the improvement of Chicago harbor. Numerous scathing editorials were directed against members of Congress who refused to vote for the improvement.

The Journal's interest in Chicago was inspired by its recognition of the economic possibilities in northern Illinois, and the prospect of attracting immigration from the East by way of the Great Lakes. Then, too, its editors were not favorable to controlling elements in St. Louis. Later, when St. Louis became a center of slave traffic, their antipathy became more pronounced; this despite the fact that St. Louis was their first western home. Perhaps familiarity with the Missouri metropolis was partly responsible for the young Journal's desire to see Chicago developed. It advocated construction of both the Illinois and Michigan Canal and the building of a railroad between Lake Michigan and the Illinois River.

In its zeal for improvement of the Illinois country, the newspaper was led into the advocacy of some projects which were impractical. The most notable of these errors was based on the assumption that the Sangamon River was a navigable stream—a delusion which to this day persists in Washington. Abraham Lincoln made his first campaign as an advocate of waterway connection between Springfield and Beardstown by way of the Sangamon. The Journal was for the proposal. Even when the *Talisman*, brought around from Cincinnati to test the waterway, was trapped by falling water in the river, the paper was not disposed to admit Lincoln was in error.

To Washington's indifference to the West and to the national administration's banking policies, the early editors attributed bursting of the internal improvement bubbles in Illinois. Fiercely they resented suggestions that Illinoisans were indulging in dreams impossible of fulfillment. They did not hestitate to print as prophecies what conservative enthusiasts regarded as wholly visionary pictures of the country's future. Before they had quit their pioneer venture in journalism, they had seen the realization of those dreams.

The Francis brothers disposed of the paper in 1855. The Journal, however, carried on in the spirit of its founders. It was, as under the first publishers, Lincoln's mouthpiece. During the tragic period leading to and during the Civil War, it reflected the Union spirit. Various able men contributed to its editorial columns, some of them interspersing their work with service in the field. The list included the brilliant Edward L. Baker and his associate in the publication of the paper, W. H. Bailhache; David L. Phillips, who owned an interest in the paper; Gen. Moses Brayman and others not regularly identified with the editorial staff.

In the period of reconstruction and for many years thereafter, the Journal had as its editor the scholarly Paul Selby. John Hay, secretary to President Lincoln and later secretary of state, did service at the editorial desk. Later came, as proprietors as well as editors, Clarence R. Paul, Lewis H. Miner, Harry F. Dorwin, S. Leigh Call and Will H. McConnell.

When the newspaper was purchased by Col. Ira C. Copley, on January 1, 1928, A. L. Bowen became the editor. J. Emil Smith, the present editor and publisher, succeeded him, and A. W. Shipton became the publisher.

The history of the State Journal is practically the history of the Sangamo country. It qualified for initial membership in the Old Settlers' Society, and its early editors are listed in the history of that organization.

Files of the newspaper, preserved in the Illinois Historical Library,

ILLINOIS STATE JOURNAL IN ITS 122nd YEAR

furnish the story of Illinois for more than a century. They tell, in detail, day by day, the history of Abraham Lincoln and are authority for the most important works on Lincoln. These files are in constant demand, too, by authors and others who are interested in American history.

149

"The welfare of Springfield, its institutions and its people will be the editor's first concern, coupled always with unswerving loyalty to the State of Illinois and the National Union."

This was J. Emil Smith's editorial pledge to Journal readers when he returned to the paper after 19 years in public life. Resigning his office as mayor of Springfield, Editor Smith resumed a career which he had started as a reporter in the 1890's. He exulted in the challenge of his new responsibility.

With Shipton publisher of the Journal, the team of Shipton and Smith began to function. The two men brought the Journal through the grim years of the depression, and to the threshold of a great journalistic adventure in the summer of 1937.

Returning from a tour of Europe, Editor Smith found Publisher Shipton eager to organize the Journal as an "all-day newspaper," thus entering into afternoon competition with the Illinois State Register, a paper founded in 1836 in Vandalia, then the state capital. The Register had moved north to Springfield in August, 1839, after Abe Lincoln's "Long Nine" had succeeded in leading the effort to relocate the capital on its present site.

[The "Long Nine" were the seven Whig state representatives and two Whig state senators representing Sangamon County during the 1836-37 session of the Illinois legislature. They were known as the "Long Nine" because all were tall, their aggregate height being 54 feet. Lincoln, the leader of the "Long Nine," headed a successful fight during the session to move the capital from Vandalia to Springfield. Legislation to that effect was approved February 28, 1837. Sangamon County was much larger in area at that time than now. It embraced the present counties of Sangamon, Menard, Logan and Christian. In 1839, Lincoln introduced in the legislature a bill that was enacted into law, dividing the area into four counties.]

William Walter was founder of the Register at Vandalia. Subsequent publishers included George R. Weber, a partner of Walter; Charles H. Lanphier, publisher from 1846 to 1864; E. W. Merritt, 1864-1877; Gen. John M. Palmer, 1877-1879, and Thomas Rees and Henry W. Clendenin during the half-century prior to Copley Press stewardship.

While the Register had fought alongside the Journal on many occasions of community interest, notably the successful effort to create Lake Springfield, the two papers were consistently on opposite sides of the political fence. The Register's history is as ardently Democratic as the Journal's is

Republican. Before, during and ever since Civil War days, each newspaper has strongly championed the views of the political party to which it has adhered.

Competition was intensified when, on Monday, September 20, 1937, the Illinois State Journal began to provide 24-hour news coverage in Springfield with five daily editions. The editorial, advertising and mechanical tasks involved were formidable, but, from the very first, the noon and afternoon Journals won wide acceptance, as had the morning newspaper for so many years.

To its previous Associated Press and Newspaper Enterprise Association dispatches were added the news and features of International News Service. Two Journal editorial staffs and extra shifts in the mechanical departments brought fresh news to the breakfast, luncheon and dinner tables of the Springfield area.

Five hectic years were to follow. The Japanese were assaulting Nanking as the all-day Journal began its career. To follow were the events leading up to World War II, and this country's entry into the global conflict after the Pearl Harbor attack on December 7, 1941. War put severe restrictions upon the two competitive papers. Manpower was in short supply, materials were equally scarce, and throughout the nation papers were merging in the face of these conditions.

The Journal's headlines told of the Royal Air Force's exploits in France, and of the Japanese massing for an attack on Australia, on the day a two-column box near the top of Page 1 made this crisp announcement: "Copley Press, Inc., Leases the State Register." The date was May 1, 1942.

Journal Publisher Shipton stated:

"Effective Monday, May 4, and for 15 years thereafter, the State Register Publishing Co. has leased to The Copley Press, Inc., its publishing rights in Springfield and environs. No change will be made in the policy of the paper."

High costs of maintaining competition thus had been resolved. The Register staff moved into Journal quarters, the Journal returning to the morning field exclusively and the Register remaining in the afternoon field.

This editorial comment in the Journal of Saturday, May, 2, 1942, set the stage for a new era of Springfield journalism:

"Springfield can be congratulated on the prospect of better news coverage and advertising service. It is still a two-newspaper city and the wholesome influence of competition is retained by the oldest rivals in the newspaper world. They have been at grips ever since Abraham Lincoln and Stephen A. Douglas contributed to the editorial discussions of pioneer America—Lincoln in the colums of the Francis boys' Journal and Douglas as an editorial contributor to the Register."

Among the executives to remain with the Register were Vincent Y. Dallman and Clarence Clendenin. Dallman, then collector of internal revenue at Springfield, was editor of the Register and has continuously served in that capacity. Under the managing editorship of the late Robert Stubbs, and currently under James Armstrong, a Register staff member since his cub days, the Democratic Register is among the best-edited newspapers in Illinois.

V. Y. DALLMAN
Editor, Illinois State Register

When the papers became common tenants at 309-315 South Sixth Street, John Ferguson was advanced from the state desk to his present position as managing editor of the Illinois State Journal. Robert Harris soon thereafter became city editor of the Journal, and the two men brought the paper through the difficult war years.

William F. Dagon, of the Journal advertising department, became advertising director of the Illinois State Journal and Register, and Walter Henkes, former Register advertising manager, became national ad manager for the coalition. Dagon and Henkes have continued in these positions, with George L. Pehlman as current display advertising manager; J. J. Slaven, classified manager; J. Paul Kienzle, circulation director, and George W. Thompson, auditor.

In a speech before 400 business and civic leaders at Hotel Abraham Lincoln on the evening of Friday, May 1, 1942, Col. Copley stated:

"Our prosperity and success are so closely linked with the prosperity

STAFF EXECUTIVES OF TWO SPRINGFIELD NEWSPAPERS

Front row, left to right, James Armstrong, managing editor of the Illinois State Register; Grover E. Shipton, assistant to publisher, Illinois State Journal and Register; William F. Dagon, advertising director, State Journal and Register. Back row, left to right, George L. Pehlman, display advertising manager, State Journal and Register; J. Paul Kienzle, circulation director, State Journal and Register; Walter Henkes, national advertising manager, State Journal and Register; John Ferguson, managing editor, Illinois State Journal.

and success of Springfield that it must be obvious that the interests of Springfield are our interests."

It was at that time that Journal Publisher Shipton won promotion to the presidency of The Copley Press, and J. Emil Smith became publisher of both Springfield papers as well as editor of the Journal. President Shipton, with a natural interest in the Journal and Register as one of the biggest brothers of the Copley family, and Editor-Publisher Smith, by the nature of his job and abilities, have continued working together to fulfill the Colonel's pledge. Grover E. Shipton, son of A. W. Shipton, is assistant to the publisher.

Helping to build and expand Springfield's trading area through superior newspaper coverage, the Journal and Register organization also is alive to civic responsibility.

Ten years after the leasing of the Register's publishing rights by The Copley Press, the political character and editorial integrity of Springfield's two historic newspapers remain as ever. And both papers are being served by a constantly improved physical plant and advertising as well as circulation staffs.

Mechanical modernization plans, formulated years before, were put into effect in 1952, and were centered around a new six-unit Goss Headliner press equipped with a color half deck. Colortrol, Tensionplate Lockup, centralized lubrication, high-speed and precise color-plate registration and printing are features of the Headliner. With the new press, the Journal and the Register can roll off the folder at a rated 54,000 papers an hour.

The Journal composing room has the latest in modern equipment consisting of 15 typesetting machines, two Ludlows and two material-makers. The typesetting battery is composed of five Intertypes and 10 Linotypes. Up to 30-point is set on the Intertypes, while sizes above 30-point are set on the Ludlows, thus giving approximately 100 percent all-slugged composition. In the casting department, the Journal has a Monotype machine for dashes, rules and borders, and an Elrod machine for casting of slugs and basing materials.

The ad room has three C & G saws, one mitering machine and one slug cutter, which are placed close to the work benches in order to facilitate ad composition.

Included in the stereotyping department are a Goss molding machine; two pony autoplates; a newly-installed seven-ton Kemp metal pot that can produce semi-circular plates for press cylinders at the rate of one a minute, and a three-ton job pot for ingots and advertising cuts.

The engraving department equipment includes a 24-inch Robertson camera with Grafarc lamps, a 24-inch Robertson printing frame, double-arc printing lamp, master etching machine and royal router, guillotine cutter, burning-in stove and plate cooler, power box and Delta saw.

Superintendents of the composing room, stereotype department and

THEY DIRECT DEPARTMENTS OF JOURNAL AND REGISTER

Front row, left to right, John A. Moser, night foreman of the pressroom; Herman W. Staab, superintendent of the stereotyping department; John L. Satterlee, building superintendent; Lee Doyle, superintendent of the pressroom. Back row, left to right, George W. Thompson, auditor, Illinois State Journal and Register; J. J. Slaven, classified manager, State Journal and Register; Milford C. Hunsley, superintendent, photoengraving department; Thomas F. Grady, superintendent of composing room, Walter G. Novack, day foreman of pressroom.

pressroom are, respectively, Thomas F. Grady, Herman W. Staab and Lee Doyle. Day foreman of the pressroom is Walter G. Novack and night foreman is John A. Moser. John L. Satterlee is building superintendent. Milford C. Hunsley heads the photoengraving department.

Open house for the present Journal Building was held on June 18, 1930. In honor of the occasion, the Journal published an Expansion edition of 100 pages, by far the largest newspaper which up to that time had been printed in Springfield. The building is of modern design. It occupies the site of an earlier Journal Building. The front is of pulsichrome terra cotta with a polished granite base. Entrance doors are of bronze. The center entrance door opens to a vestibule from which a marble stairway leads to the executive, editorial and advertising departments on the second floor.

Revolving doors at the back of the vestibule open into a large room used by the classified advertising and circulation departments.

A large, recessed plate-glass window is on either side of the center entrance. The one at the left looks into the classified advertising and circulation departments, and the one to the right gives a view of the new Goss Headliner press, and enables the public to watch the newspapers as they are being printed.

The counter and wainscoting in the classified advertising and circulation departments are veined, green marble quarried on the isle of Tinos, off the coast of Greece. The floor is of pink Tennessee marble.

The walls are severely plain, finished in a palm-modeled effect, and the ceiling and archways over the lobby openings are ornamented in low relief and richly decorated in antique gold and polychrome color.

The lighting fixtures were especially designed to match the architecture of the room and the ornamental bronze and glass match the ornaments of the plaster.

To the rear of this room are the accounting and statistical departments, private office of the circulation manager and mailing and delivery rooms.

The second floor contains the executive offices, display and national advertising departments, news and editorial rooms, the photography department, and headquarters for the papers' three wire services—The Associated Press, United Press and International News Service. The corridors are light and airy and are wainscoted with marble. The entire floor is marble terrazzo.

The third floor contains the composing, stereotyping and proofreading rooms, layout room for the art department, artist's room and engraving department.

According to the 1950 U. S. census, the population of Springfield within the city limits was 80,832, and of the Springfield metropolitan area, designated by the U. S. Census Bureau to include Springfield and Sangamon County, 130,649. This is a far cry from the pioneer days of 1831, when the

STATE REGISTER HAS SERVED CENTRAL ILLINOIS SINCE 1836

Journal's first issue was printed and the population of Sangamon County numbered about 13,000.

It also is in sharp contrast to the Lincoln era, when Sangamon County's population was 19,228 in 1850 and 32,274 in 1860. A rapid advance in the population of Springfield also has been marked in recent times. The census figure for 1930 was 71,864 and for 1940 it was 75,503.

As Springfield and Illinois have grown and developed, so also have the Illinois State Journal and the Register progressed. The two newspapers, oldest in the state, always have been closely identified with the basic interests of the territory they have served from stagecoach days to the era of the skyliner. Much has changed since November 10, 1831, when the state itself was only 13 years old, and the first Sangamo Journal was laid upon the rough-hewn doorsteps of Springfield; yet essentially the role of the Springfield papers remains the same—to bring the latest and freshest news and dispatches to the community, print the public record, and to offer leadership in the realm of ideas. This is the challenge of the future in Springfield.

The San Diego Union

"Forthrightness and Integrity"

EVENING TRIBUNE

"A Nonpartisan Newspaper"

SAN DIEGO, THE MOST IMPORTANT CORNER IN THE U.S.A.

159

WILLIAM SHEA
Associate Publisher and General Manager, Union and Evening Tribune
Vice President, The Copley Press

160

The San Diego Union

Evening Tribune

919 Second Avenue   San Diego, Calif.

THE SAN DIEGO UNION and the Evening Tribune are companion
newspapers. Although in many respects they appear to be twins in the
family of 15 newspapers in California and Illinois, they are not twins.

They complement each other, covering the morning and evening fields,
and are under the same management, the Union-Tribune Publishing Co.
The business operations are conducted by a single staff, but in the editorial
departments the staffs are separate and distinct and are highly competitive.
Thus, though they are companion papers, they are not friendly companions
from an editorial point of view.

The largest newspapers in The Copley Press, The Union (morning)
and the Evening Tribune serve the City of San Diego (population 434,924
in 1952) and San Diego County (population 688,748). More than 99
percent of the combined circulation is confined to the retail trading zone.

The Union traditionally adheres strongly to Republican lines, while the
Evening Tribune is independent in politics and editorially is designed to
please readers whose views differ from those vigorously expounded by The
Union. Thus the papers have different appeals. The Union is the paper
of business and professional people, farmers and other independent operators, of army and naval officers, and of the many thousands living in
retirement in San Diego County. Also it is widely accepted in educational
and cultural circles.

On the other hand, the Evening Tribune has a wider mass appeal and
is popular with thousands of workers in the aircraft plants and shipyards,
and others who, by the nature of their occupations, find leisure for reading

only in the evening, and by those who, by long custom, prefer an evening newspaper.

Again the papers are not to be classified as twins because of the wide divergence in age. The Union, a pioneer newspaper of San Diego and California, was founded on October 10, 1868, while the Tribune was established December 2, 1895. So The Union, the elder by 27 years, was in full vigor when the Tribune saw the light of day. Indeed, they are not even consanguineous, for the Tribune was owned and operated for almost six years in direct competition with The Union, until September 27, 1901, when the owners of The Union bought the Tribune. Since that time, the business of the two dailies has been conducted jointly.

In an historical sketch of the two newspapers, it seems proper to lay aside for a time the Tribune and revert to that Saturday in October of 1868, when the first issue of The San Diego Union was printed, carrying a nameplate in Old English letters similar to that used by The Union today.

The name *Union* was especially significant at the time, because, little more than three years prior to appearance of the paper, the United States had emerged from the great Civil War. Since by that war the Union of states had been preserved, it was fitting that Union should be adopted as the name of the new paper in San Diego, even though that name had been taken earlier by such California publications as the Sacramento Union (1851), the Union Democrat, at Sonora (1854), and the Grass Valley Union (1864).

As has been true with many of the leading newspapers in the United States, The Union was started on a shoestring, with a Washington hand press and the proverbial shirt-tail full of type. Indeed, Col. William Jeff Gatewood, who came to San Diego from San Andreas, a gold camp in Calaveras County, in Northern California, with his associate, Edward W. Bushyhead, to launch The Union as a weekly, apparently was skeptical of the possibility of success of the venture. In the initial number of the new paper, the publisher was listed in Column 1 of Page 1 as J. N. Briseno, identified by one chronicler as the office boy, but probably he was a printer.

The first issue of The Union consisted of four six-column pages. The pages were 15½ inches wide by 22½ inches deep; the type form 14 by 19½ inches, and the columns 14 ems wide. It was printed on rag paper. The front page carried, as advertisements, six professional cards, including one, presumably deadhead, of "W. Jeff Gatewood, attorney and counselor at law," and a four-inch advertisement for George Irving, a meat packer in San Francisco. He advertised "hams, bacon, shoulders, dried beef, etc." Perhaps he was angling for business from San Diego, the products to be shipped from San Francisco by steamer. Most of the front page was devoted to a short fiction story. Column 2 was led by a poem.

Despite their reluctance at the outset to be listed as publishers of The Union, Gatewood and Bushyhead, in a salutatory on Page 2 of the first issue,

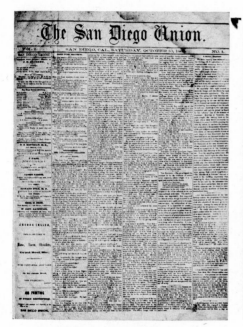

FIRST SAN DIEGO UNION
Issued October 10, 1868

EVENING TRIBUNE LAUNCHED
Vol. 1, No. 1, December 2, 1895

bubbled over with enthusiasm for San Diego and its people. Gatewood wrote in lofty language:

"It has become a custom among editors, when about launching a new paper into the reading world, to portray in glowing words a future of brilliant sunshine and a career of magnificent successes. The custom, in all probability, had its origin in the brain of some dreamer, whose hopes for the future were bright beyond any earthly realization, and whose poetic exuberancy was only equalled by his credulity. In departing from this custom, we might, with more veracity than cunning, frankly avow as our reason a total want of the poetic imagery and exuberant fertility required in creating or describing delusive visions for the gratification of those who 'listen with credulity to the whisperings of Fancy.'

"But it is not the mission of The Union to deal in fiction. Bright hopes may cheer its editor, when disappointments would chill his ardor—may beguile many a weary hour of some tediousness. The Union will be a faithful mirror, reflecting from its pages times of distress as well as of prosperity —hopes and fears, gloom and gayety and smiles and tears. A faithful chronicler of today, and a future reliable historian of the past. Along its columns shall grow the daily record of works, enterprises and improvements, that will linger upon the earth long after we and our dreams and hopes shall have been laid quietly beneath the sod. It must toil. In the grand struggle for the improvement of Southern California—in opening the way for the march of civilization—in leveling the hills—grading streets—developing the mines—tilling the soil—planting vineyards and fruit trees—in building wharves, docks, arsenals, forts and fortifications—in adorning the hills, beautifying the valleys and spreading the white sails of commerce—for the education and refinement of the present and future generations—to spread the doctrines of Christianity and inculcate pure morals, and towards the enlightenment and perfection of mankind it must and shall labor earnestly and unceasingly. Its world must be a world of stern reality.

"Its influence shall be used in urging the people to lay aside the animosities engendered within the last few years, and so sedulously fostered by the selfish political aspirants of the present day—to foster and encourage fealty to our political institutions—obedience to the laws of our country, and charity towards all mankind.

"To the taxpayers and citizens of San Diego County the editor promises a watchful care over county affairs, full and immediate exposure of all wrongs that may be perpetrated by officials, without 'fear, favor or affection.' We will use our best efforts to have the burdens of taxation lightened, if possible; suggest such retrenchments and reforms as may occur to us—give a history of the doings in the world outside, as well as in the different localities of the county; record the mineral developments, the agricultural and commercial improvements; labor for our mutual advancement and rejoice in our common success and prosperity.

"To the citizens of San Diego, we promise an earnest co-operation in all efforts to promote the welfare of the city. Cheering words of hope and kindness shall shower upon you 'as the gentle rain from Heaven upon the place beneath.'

"In our columns shall appear no vulgarity, obscenity, vindictiveness or personal abuse. We will pursue an open, fair, generous and just course with all—allowing no personal griev- ance of our own to find its way into these columns; unhesitatingly con- demning wrong wherever we find it, we will give credit where it is due; and, as we will act complaisantly towards all, we ask courtesy of all.

"The editor of The Union having, by contract, closed its col- umns against the expression of his own political sentiments, will not allow the subject a place therein, until such time as he can do so without violating his word.

"We have no further promise to make. We only pray that our lives may be spared to see the waters of our bay fretting beneath the burdens

WILLIAM JEFF GATEWOOD
Founder of The San Diego Union

a busy commerce—to hear the shrill whistle of the iron horse as it spurns the sands of the desert—toils over the mountains and shoots through the valleys in its flight from the Atlantic to meet in our harbor the rich cargoes from the ancient Orient—to see our bay surrounded by mammoth manu- facturing and mercantile houses, princely residences, domes and spires of churches and schools of learning—the streets teeming with a prosperous and industrious people, and our lovely valleys lifting to our genial skies flowers and fruits, in tints as varied and gorgeous as our incomparable sunsets."

The subscription price of the weekly was $5 a year, $3 for six months, or 50 cents a month. Single copies sold for a bit, or 12½ cents. Half-cent and 2-cent pieces were in circulation then, but the last half-cent coins were minted in 1857 and it is doubtful if many found their way to far-off Califor- nia, so it was strange that the paper was priced at 12½ cents a copy.

The advertising rate was $2 a square (10 lines or less) for the first

COTTAGE IN OLD TOWN WHERE THE UNION STARTED

insertion and $1.50 for subsequent insertions, and "to those who wish to advertise quarterly or yearly, a liberal reduction will be made." Advertising at the time was confined to announcements by business and professional men, and the wording of the advertisements seldom was changed. Thus, when an advertisement had been put in type, it usually ran for weeks or months without alteration.

The Union was launched in a vine-covered cottage in Old Town. San Diego was a mere village. The one-story building still is standing. It is situated at 2602 San Diego Avenue. Painted a bright yellow, it was occupied (June, 1953) by a real estate office. Near the front door is a plaque which reads:

Casa de Altamirano

Home of San Diego's

First Newspaper

1868   1871

First Frame Building

The term, "first frame building," evidently refers to the structure as having been the first to be built of wood in Old Town, earlier buildings

166

having been of adobe. An error appears in the legend, for The Union was not San Diego's first newspaper. The population of San Diego at that time probably was considerably less than 2000, for the federal census of 1870 gave the population as 2300, and listed 915 houses. However, in 1869, The Union placed the town's population at 3000, evidently an exaggeration. The Union, in its first issue, carried a report by the county assessor, John M. McIntire, who estimated the county's population as 3000. San Diego County at that time comprised the area of the present county, all of what now is Imperial County, and a part of the present Riverside County. San Diego County extended from the Pacific Ocean to the Colorado River.

The figure for the town is given as 731 in 1860 and in 1850 it was 640, including 240 in the military service.

Although Juan Rodríguez Cabrillo, a Portuguese, entered San Diego Harbor with two ships under the Spanish flag in September, 1542, colonization came 227 years later. Sixty years after Cabrillo's visit, Commander Don Sebastian Viscaino arrived in the harbor with two ships, on November 5, 1602, and gave the place the name of San Diego de Alcala. He took back to Spain word that San Diego was a good place for settlement, but Spain

PLAQUE MARKS BIRTHPLACE OF THE SAN DIEGO UNION

was occupied elsewhere, and the west coast of North America was neglected by what then was the world's greatest colonizing nation.

It remained for Fr. Junipero Serra, a Franciscan missionary, to found Misión San Diego de Alcala. Four expeditions, two by land and two by sea, set out from Mexico in 1769, under order of King Carlos III of Spain, to establish a settlement in Alta California. The paqueboat *San Carlos* sailed from La Paz, in Baja California, January 9, 1769, and arrived in San Diego Harbor on April 29. The *San Antonio* sailed from San José del Cabo February 5 and arrived on April 11. The two overland parties were headed by Don Gaspar de Portola, governor of Baja California, and Capt. Fernando Rivera Moncada. Father Serra was a member of the Gaspar de Portola expedition. He founded at San Diego the first of the string of California missions that extended northward to Sonoma. San Diego was made a presidio on July 1, 1774. Residents of the presidio in 1798 were reported as 173, comprising 70 men, 32 women, 44 boys, 27 girls and four Indians. Presumably the Indians were not counted in the total of 173.

For a half century, San Diego was a small settlement within the walls of the presidio, situated on a hill overlooking what later became known as Mission Valley. The site of the presidio now is the location of Presidio Park and on it stands the beautiful Serra Museum, built for the city by the late George W. Marston.

Mexico's successful War of Independence against Spain resulted in Alta California coming under the Mexican flag on April 20, 1822, but with little change in the tempo of San Diego. The presidio, however, had begun to decay and settlement spread to the flats, now known as Old Town, and in 1835 the presidio was abandoned. Under the Mexican régime, the pueblo's principal business was in the sale of hides and tallow to traders who called at the port. In 1831, citizens and soldiers in the settlement were said to have numbered between 400 and 500.

Early in the war between the United States and Mexico (1846-48), California fell to the American forces and the Stars and Stripes were raised over Old Town the afternoon of July 29, 1846.

Rich in historical background, under the flags of three nations—Spain, Mexico and the United States—San Diego did not seem ripe for a newspaper until 1851 when, on May 29, the San Diego Herald was founded by John Judson Ames, only 12 days after establishment of La Estrala de Los Angeles (The Star of Los Angeles), also a weekly and the first newspaper published in Southern California. Ames operated the Herald, a four-page, four-column sheet, until April 7, 1860, when he suspended publication and moved the printing plant to San Bernardino. After nine years, San Diego again became a town without a newspaper, and more than eight years passed before another paper was published in this, the oldest town in California. When that paper—The San Diego Union—was established it was destined to become, with the passing of the years, one of the outstanding newspapers of the West.

In the eight years following suspension of the Herald, the need for a newspaper in San Diego was apparent. But the town was small and isolated, and no doubt few men in California were qualified to operate a paper, or possessed the mechanical equipment to do so. In the absence of a railroad spanning the continent, printing equipment necessarily was brought around Cape Horn by ship from the east coast, or was transported laboriously by wagons across the plains and through the mountains. Thus facilities for producing a newspaper, however small, were not readily available.

In the 1860's, San Diego was growing, slowly but surely, and public-spirited citizens smarted at the lack of a newspaper to expound the county's resources and tell the world of its opportunities. Promotion by the printed word was essential in exploitation of the town and county, to the end that more settlers would be induced to locate in the southwestern corner of the United States and capital would be attracted.

In the spring of 1868, Philip Crosthwaite, a pioneer of San Diego even in those days, and a figure in political and business life, visited his sister, Mrs. Gatewood, at San Andreas, where her husband was publishing the Register. Crosthwaite painted such glowing pictures of San Diego and its future, and the community's need for a newspaper, that he induced Gatewood to visit San Diego and investigate the situation.

Gatewood came to San Diego, saw and was impressed. He returned to San Andreas. He decided to suspend the San Andreas paper and interested his foreman, Bushyhead, and Briseno in the San Diego project. Gatewood hastened overland to San Diego to lay the foundation for The San Diego Union. He particularly solicited subscriptions and advertising. Bushyhead followed by steamer from San Francisco with the printing plant, arriving September 19, 1868. The equipment was installed in the frame building owned by José A. Altamirano, adjoining the parsonage in Old

USS *CONSTITUTION* OFF SAN DIEGO, JANUARY 21, 1933
"Many an Eye Danced to See" Navy's "Old Ironsides"

Town. By October 3, they were sufficiently settled to issue a prospectus, setting forth that the first number of The Union would be off the press by October 10, and since that memorable day, more than 84 years ago, The Union has been inseparably bound with the life and growth of San Diego. As San Diego developed and expanded and became a metropolitan center, so also has The Union enlarged its facilities, extended its news coverage and increased its circulation until it has become a metropolitan newspaper.

Gatewood, in his prospectus, distributed under date of October 3, said:

"To the Public: On Saturday next, I will issue the first number of The San Diego Union. Those who wish to advertise will confer a favor upon me by sending in their advertisements as early next week as possible. In order to insure an insertion on the first page of the paper, the copy must be handed into the office by next Tuesday night. I presume that the business men of San Diego appreciate the advantages of advertising and will therefore accept with avidity the opportunity now offered them.

"I will be thankful for any local item of general or special importance,

170

AIRCRAFT CARRIER *KEARSARGE* IN SAN DIEGO HARBOR
Many an American Thrills at Sight of Navy's Air Might

and particularly request to be furnished with names of vessels arriving and departing from our harbor, and with all matters of importance to shippers.

"From those who purpose farming, I will be pleased to learn the character of crop they intend planting and the probable quantity of acres they will cultivate. I respectfully invite from all branches of business such communications as will tend to advance the multifarious interests of San Diego County, and promote the general prosperity of our citizens.

"Neither political tirades nor personal abuse will find place in the columns of The Union. As my object—and such is my agreement with my patrons—is to publish to the world the advantages of the harbor, climate and soil of this vicinity, I hope that no imposition, exaggeration or prevarication will ever be tolerated by those who may afford local information to The Union. In my humble judgment they need no such subterfuges, but the plain, unvarnished truth of our harbor, climate and soil is all that need be told, to insure the wonder and win the admiration of the world.

"As The Union is to be politically neutral, I know of no way by which

I can prevent the expression of my political predilections except by steering entirely clear of politics, therefore, The Union will maintain politically a wise and masterly silence.

"For the many favors I have received at the hands of the citizens of San Diego, I return my sincere heartfelt thanks, and only bespeak of them the same kindness, courtesy and consideration for my pet, to be born on next Saturday.

"WM. JEFF GATEWOOD."

While The Union in its early years took an active part in local controversial issues, it eschewed partisan politics for a time. This course probably was due to the fact that the nation not long since had emerged from the Civil War and no doubt some residents of San Diego were sympathetic with the Confederate cause, for the population of California came from all parts of the nation. Gatewood was a native of Kentucky and a Democrat. Since the Southerners were Democrats and most of the Northerners were Republicans, no useful purpose could be accomplished by the new paper in fanning the war-engendered flames which had not died down, even though armed conflict had ended.

As might have been expected, The Union encountered some economic difficulties and frequent changes in management resulted. The four-page weekly, published at the outset on Saturdays, carried what might be regarded as a fair amount of advertising, considering the size of the town, but the remuneration from advertising and circulation apparently was little more than enough to keep the paper in operation.

Indicative of the growth of San Diego and the enthusiasm of The Union's editor over the community's development was this editorial, which appeared February 27, 1869:

"One walks our streets without recognizing in everyone he meets an acquaintance. Our city is full of strangers. Each stage and steamer brings its daily and weekly installment of mankind, with a larger proportion of womankind than of yore. Our hotels are full to overflowing and considerable is said of building a new hotel. Not an eligible house [is] to be rented in town and not lumber to be got in town at one time to build a house, though we are blessed with three or four lumber yards.

"Material to make brick houses is scarce; it is but a few weeks since a large brick burner was obliged to leave unburned for a time a large brick kiln, the wood to burn the same being worth almost as much as the bricks when burnt. . . .

"Notwithstanding all the difficulties in obtaining material for building purposes, scarcity of mechanics, and high wages, it would be impossible to chronicle the advent of every new building that makes its appearance on our streets. General business prosperity seems to prevail and all goes merry as a marriage bell."

The paper by March, 1869, found need for more floor space for its operation. The issue of March 6 carried this announcement:

"Our subscribers may have to do without their usual paper next Saturday. We have made a large addition to The Union Building and will have to move our press into it this coming week. The columns of the paper also will have to be lengthened to accommodate the demands upon the paper.

"We have about concluded to change the publication day from Saturday to Wednesday. The change will be to the advantage of our subscribers, inasmuch as we will be able to give our local subscribers the latest news from our exchanges by the steamer of Tuesday and dispatch on Wednesday our papers to our subscribers up the country.

"We may as well also add that there is but little doubt but that the mails will be so arranged shortly that we can forward our papers every Wednesday morning toward Arizona and the eastern, western and southern states."

The next issue of The Union was dated Wednesday, March 17, and the column length was changed from 19½ to 21 inches. In that paper, Gatewood moved his name from Page 1 to Page 2 and the name of Briseno was dropped.

On November 4, 1869, publication day was changed from Wednesday to Thursday. "This change," the announcement read, "will enable us to get the Los Angeles and San Francisco news by Tuesday's mail and we can furnish more and later news."

Need for a courthouse was stressed in an editorial on April 21, which read:

"Public convenience requires a courthouse. Public convenience requires that all of the county offices should be within said courthouse, or near the same. . . . At present, the various offices of this county are scattered, each so far from the other that it is a great inconvenience to parties having business to transact therein, and, if not remedied, will be a serious public grievance."

Gatewood, the founder, did not remain long with the paper. On May 5, 1869, The Union said:

"The last steamer carried away the late proprietor and editor of this paper, Mr. W. J. Gatewood, who goes to Memphis to attend the great railroad convention to be held in that city on the 20th inst. Mr. G. is president of the San Diego, Gila & Atlantic Railroad Co., and attends the aforesaid convention as a representative of this company. . . ."

The next paper, May 12, listed Taggart & Bushyhead as publishers, for Gatewood had sold his interest to Charles P. Taggart, an attorney. In that issue, Gatewood wrote, under the heading, "Valedictory":

"We have sold this paper to Messrs. Taggart & Bushyhead, who will continue its publication and redeem the pledges we made when we started it.

"It is with feelings of regret that we bid adieu to our readers. We started The San Diego Union in the face of many obstacles, but by the kindness of the people of this county, they have all faded away, so that today we can say our enterprise has proved a complete success, in a pecuniary point of view, and we flatter ourselves we have made some friends.

"Mr. Bushyhead has been with us ever since the paper has started, and has done all the heavy work of getting out the paper. He is one of the best printers in the state. Mr. T. is a good writer, and has had some experience in the newspaper business. We commend these gentlemen to the patrons of The Union. We intend to live and practice our profession in San Diego, and will be glad to meet any of our friends when it is their convenience to call upon us."

Upon his return to San Diego, Gatewood resumed the practice of law, at which he was unusually successful, and about 1872 published another San Diego paper, the Daily World. A public-spirited citizen, he also was a picturesque figure. He wore a full beard. He is said to have had almost all the criminal legal practice in San Diego and usually was employed on one side or the other in important civil cases. He was a veteran of the U. S. Army in the Mexican War. He resided at Union and D Streets, and took an active part in affairs of the city and state. The San Diego historian, William E. Smythe, said Gatewood died March 27, 1888, on board the schooner *Rosita*, in San Diego Bay.

An adventurous type of man, Gatewood, prior to locating in San Diego, killed in a duel a man who had been one of his best friends. The duel was fought near San Andreas as the result of a political squabble. The man slain was Dr. P. Goodwyn.

The San Andreas Independent for September 17, 1859, carried this account of the duel:

"For several days past, we have heard suspicions rumored about town that a duel was in contemplation between two gentlemen residents here, but nothing was known publicly, as whatever arrangements were being made were kept secret. On Thursday night, however, it was pretty generally suspected that a meeting was arranged for the next morning between William J. Gatewood, Esq., and Dr. P. Goodwyn.

"We have reason to believe that the seconds—W. T. Lewis, (late state senator) and Major Glynn, for Goodwyn; and Capt. Pope and Martin Rowan, for Gatewood, left no honorable efforts untried to remove the cause of the quarrel without a resort to arms.

"Early yesterday morning, four or five carriages containing the principals, seconds, surgeons and a few friends left town . . . coming to a halt on the flat near Foreman's. Here they alighted and proceeded to measure off the ground. The agreement was to fight with rifles, distance 40 yards. Mr. Lewis, acting for Goodwyn, won the word; Capt. Pope, for Gatewood, the choice of ground. The preliminaries were all arranged and the parties ready for position at 7 a.m.

"The principals are reported to have appeared cool and to have exchanged courtesies at the moment of taking positions assigned by the seconds. The word was given thus: 'Are you ready? Fire, one, two, three.'

"At the moment three was about to be articulated, both sprung the triggers of their rifles. Dr. Goodwyn's hung fire and he lost his shot. Mr. Gatewood's shot struck Goodwyn in the abdomen, ranging obliquely and downward, passing out at the hip.

"Immediately upon Dr. Goodwyn's fall, Mr. Gatewood advanced toward him, extending his hand and remarking: 'Doctor, I am very sorry that this affair has terminated, so very sorry, indeed.' To which the doctor replied: 'I am glad to know that you acted like a gentleman.' Gatewood thanked him for his kind remark and left the field with his surgeon.

"Mr. Gatewood's carriage, which was a large vehicle, with room to accommodate the wounded man in a reclining position, was left for that purpose and Gatewood returned to town in the doctor's buggy. In about an hour, Goodwyn was brought in and conveyed to his room. He was in great agony and only survived some two or three hours, dying between 11 and 12 o'clock in the morning.

"Universal regret at the bloody affair and fatal termination is the sentiment that pervades the town. Both gentlemen are well known here and have lived in this place for years and have many warm friends. It also happens that the friends of one are the friends of the other. Everyone exonerates Mr. Gatewood from blame, and it is agreed upon all hands that the duel was throughout conducted upon the most humane and honorable terms known to the code. Perhaps no one more sincerely regrets its fatal termination than Mr. Gatewood himself.

"We are not informed as to the precise cause of the meeting, but heard that it originated before election. Angry words were passed by Dr. Goodwyn and were resented by a blow from Mr. Gatewood. A challenge was then sent by the former to the latter and the matter, we believe, was postponed until yesterday. . . ."

Taggart, the successor to Gatewood, greeted the readers with a salutatory, setting forth his aims as editor of The Union. He said in the paper for May 12:

"We do not believe in using many words in introductions. We never read long prefaces to books, no matter how well written, and we are decidedly opposed to making promises. In taking The San Diego Union, we have but little to say to our readers in the form of a salutatory, preferring to allow our acts to speak for us, and by them to be judged.

"When the paper was started, it was with the distinct understanding that the question of politics should not be discussed in its columns for one year. This promise, made by our predecessor, we intend to keep in good faith; but because we are neutral and noncommital on political questions, we do not wish it to be understood that we are to be so on others. If there is one person in the world that we dislike more than another, it is the man who is neutral—a yes, yes man. Having strong convictions, we intend to express them on subjects affecting the interests and welfare of this city, county, and part of the state.

"It shall be our earnest purpose to give to our readers the current news of the day, gleaned with care and judgment, and make The Union a live newspaper. We shall, at all times, advocate every measure which intends to aid the development of Southern California, publish all facts which throw light upon the resources of this section of the Golden State. We intend to speak the truth as we believe it. Whatever seems right and just to us, shall have our hearty approval, and whatever seems wrong shall be handled without gloves. We are in full and hearty sympathy with every person who has come here to make a permanent home and do something toward the development of our wonderful natural resources. For such we shall ever have a cheering word, and be ready to extend a helping hand to assist him in his laudable efforts.

"We have no narrow jealousies about New Town and Old Town, and hope that our vision will never be obscured by any such nonsense. The interest of one place is the interest of the other, and we ask the citizens of each to work harmoniously together for the common good. When we get 20,000 people here and the terminus of the Southern Pacific Railroad, with direct steam communication with China, Japan and the rest of the world, it will be time to discuss such issues. We ask to be judged by what we say and do."

In spite of the eagerness with which Taggart embarked on The Union and the glowing promises he made to the people, his journalistic career indeed was brief. He left the paper on January 1, 1870, less than eight months after he joined it. Taggart's shares in the business were bought by Frederic A. Taylor, of San Francisco.

Taggart bade farewell to The Union's readers in a lead editorial on December 30, 1869, in which he said:

"Hereafter this paper will be conducted by Mr. Frederic A. Taylor, late of San Francisco, and Mr. E. W. Bushyhead. It is no part of my intention to make even the usual valedictory apologies. Since my connection with The Union, it has been my endeavor, as far as professional engagements would permit, to make it a live paper, devoted to the interests of San Diego and this part of the state. Never did the prospects of the railway system and the general development of this county look brighter than now. If I have been instrumental in aiding in the consummation of this state of things, I am satisfied with the result of the past eight months of arduous labor.

"The Union is in a prosperous condition. The subscription list [is] daily increasing and the usefulness of the paper more and more appreciated. Mr. Bushyhead is one of the best men in this county, and his many friends will be glad to know that he is to continue in the paper. I most heartily commend The Union to my personal friends and ask a continuation of their patronage; assuring all such that, notwithstanding my withdrawal from the paper, yet my sympathies and occasional support in the way of contributions will be continued.

"To the many who have shown their kindness by cheering words of approval, I return my hearty thanks, and wishing all a Happy New Year, I am &c.,

"C. P. TAGGART."

The Union's page size was changed, on January 20, 1870, from six 14-em columns to seven columns of 13 ems.

But Taylor, like Taggart, remained with the paper only a few months. He sold his interest to William S. Dodge on May 12, 1870. Bushyhead, who had been a member of the firm since the beginning, continued as a partner.

In those days, factional strife existed between Old Town, the area in which the early Spanish settlement had been made, and New Town, a competing real estate development promoted by Alonzo E. Horton, who had arrived in San Diego in April, 1867. Horton, later affectionately known as Father Horton, bought at public auction from the town, through its Board of Trustees, for an average of 26 cents an acre, about 1000 acres in what now comprises the city's principal business district. Named Horton's Addition, the subdivision grew and prospered, and soon overshadowed Old Town.

Another newspaper, the Bulletin, was launched in New Town on August 21, 1869, and began to cut into The Union's meager business, for the Bulletin received considerable patronage because of its location and advocacy of the interests of New Town.

The Union and the Bulletin became bitter editorial enemies as well as business rivals. Of the Bulletin, The Union said editorially on January 27, 1870:

"From the date of its first appearance, it has been the special organ of Mr. A. E. Horton, and has been noteworthy only for the publication of some two columns per week of the most remarkable ungrammatical sentences under which typers have ever writhed. . . . Its circulation is trifling at home and, fortunately for the reputation of the place, but few copies have ever gone abroad."

Taylor and Bushyhead at that time were proprietors of The Union.

The same issue acknowledged a call on the editor by Horton, who was enraged because of The Union's editorial policy. Efforts to calm Horton failed. He discontinued his real estate advertising and settled his account with the paper. An editorial, headed "Stop My Paper, Sir!" read:

"The 'Father of New Town' honored our office with a call last Thursday morning, during which he took occasion to condemn, in a very severe manner, our remarks on the proposed location of the courthouse on Block 212, and the spirit of levity in which we commented on the proposition to organize a Chamber of Commerce in this city.

"We were sorry to see our good old friend manifest so much irritation as he did on this occasion, and, re-membering that 'a soft answer turneth away wrath,' endeavored to soothe his troubled mind; but our efforts were unavailing, and his indignation

ALONZO E. HORTON
The Union's Foe, Then Friend

finally culminating in the abrupt settlement of his account, and an order for the removal of his advertisement as a real estate dealer from our columns.

"We are obliged to Mr. Horton for the prompt payment of his little bill, as money is always acceptable in a newspaper office; yet we grieve to lose his valuable advertising patronage. We received the large sum of $40 per year for the insertion of his card, and the withdrawal of that sum from our regular receipts at this time will seriously embarrass our business.

"But really we cannot think the kind old gentleman is in earnest about this matter. He has probably become fretful from loss of sleep induced by his nocturnal cogitations on the location of the new courthouse. He will think better of it after a good night's rest, and, we doubt not, when he reflects on the situation in which we are involved by the withdrawal of his patronage, will reconsider his hasty action."

Gatewood, who by then had returned to San Diego, was attorney for the people of Old Town in a controversy over removal of the county seat from Old Town to New Town and The Union had supported their side of the battle.

New Town grew rapidly. By March, 1870, it boasted 1000 buildings and claimed 3000 inhabitants, whereas in 1867 there existed in the tract two or three houses and a dozen inhabitants.

The proprietors of The Union, realizing that the fight was futile, abandoned it in the midst of the battle, and also abandoned Old Town. The Union moved, lock, stock and barrel, to New Town and established its office at the southeast corner of Fourth and D (now Broadway) Streets. The first paper was printed at the new place on June 30, 1870. That location, now the heart of the retail district, then was quite apart. The only other buildings in the neighborhood were a Methodist church and the Era House, a hotel later called the Occidental. Horton's hotel was under construction across the street.

By this time Horton and The Union had buried the hatchet, for one of the inducements for The Union's move to New Town was the assurance given by Horton that the paper would have his exclusive advertising patronage.

In bidding adieu to its place of birth in Old Town, The Union said editorially on June 23 under the heading "Removal":

"The present number of The San Diego Union is the last that will be issued from the old office on San Diego Avenue. The paper will hereafter be published in its own new office, just completed, on the corner of D and Fourth Streets, nearly opposite Horton's New Hotel.

"The concentration of business in that part of the city; the nearness of access to the steamers, and the facilities thus afforded for the prompt receipt of news; the approaching establishment of a telegraph office in near proximity to our new location, all make removal imperative. We can publish a better newspaper, with more profit, in the new office than in the old one; the change, therefore, will be of mutual advantage to our readers and to ourselves. We have no narrow feelings about New Town and Old Town; the interests of one place are the interests of the other; both are within the limits of the City of San Diego. This small sort of capital may suit the owners of the Bulletin, who, unable to present a readable newspaper, strive to profit by stirring up local jealousy. We are for the interests of San Diego —not of any special part of it.

"We bid farewell to the old Union Building with regret. Here the first

THE UNION'S SECOND BUILDING, FOURTH AND D (BROADWAY)

number was printed, nearly two years ago, when the prosperous city which
we now behold was unbuilt, and when the establishment of a newspaper
was rather a hazardous experiment. Here The Union has grown with the
growth and strengthened with the ever-increasing strength of our city and
county, until it has become a firmly established and profitable journal, and
its circulation has risen from less than 500 to upwards of 900 copies. . . .

"Until within a few months, The Union has been the only journal
published in San Diego; and even since the establishment of another paper,
it has been universally recognized as the only readable record of local events.
The files of this paper are the faithful history of the city and county during
the past two years. . . .

"The Union has made a good fight for the people of this city through
good and evil report, and its earnest advocacy of the interests of San Diego

181

NEW TOWN WHEN THE UNION CAST ITS LOT THERE IN 1870

has frequently drawn upon it the abuse of journals hostile toward the place. . . ."

In its new location, The Union was housed on the second floor of a two-story 25-by-30-foot building owned by Taggart and Bushyhead. The upper story was "lighted by 12 windows, four in front, three on each side and two in the rear—those great desiderata in a newspaper office—light and air are attained in the greatest degree." Two rooms were on the first floor. One was occupied by the Board of City Trustees and the other by Taggart's law office.

In its next paper, June 30, The Union, in an editorial, "At Home," commented:

"The San Diego Union today greets its readers from its new office on D and Fourth Streets. Identified, as the paper has been from the very beginning, with the growth and progress of San Diego, its proprietors have a right to congratulate themselves upon their location in a splendid building, in the very center of our city.

"The Union is now 'at home' in its own house; that portion of the building occupied by the paper having been built especially for it, and with reference to the greatest convenience for a thriving newspaper office; and the builders have done their work well. For light, ventilation and space, The Union office has no equal in the state outside the cities of San Francisco and Sacramento.

"The publishers will keep pace with the times in the march of enterprise and improvement; and intend that The San Diego Union office shall continue to be, as it is now, the most complete newspaper, book and job printing office in Southern California."

The rival paper, the Bulletin, launched a daily on February 13, 1872, but the following July 13 the weekly ceased publication and the daily suspended on July 23.

The Bulletin's plant was sold to Gatewood, who, again engaging in newspaper work in San Diego, started the Daily World July 25, with a weekly two days later. The Union, which Gatewood had founded, by this time had become a Republican paper, whereas Gatewood was a Democrat. He was urged by local Democrats to establish a paper favorable to that political party. Briseno, who had been with Gatewood on The Union, joined him later on the World. Gatewood continued with the World until 1874, and about two years later the World was merged with the Daily News, which was founded in 1875, and lived until April 9, 1882, when it was purchased by the Sun, established July 19, 1881.

In the absence of telegraphic news service from the East, The Union carried a generous amount of local news, supplemented by clippings from California and eastern papers and mail correspondence from California towns and from Arizona. News from afar, brought to San Diego by mail transported by stage coach, post riders and ship, was days and often weeks old before it reached The Union. Much space was devoted to Arizona news, for The Union enjoyed considerable circulation in Arizona. The paper carried as filler short fiction, poems and miscellany, undoubtedly lifted from eastern publications. The news was well written but not in present-day journalistic style. Printers apparently took great pride in their work, and haste in production was not a requirement in setting up a four-page paper once a week.

The first telegraphic dispatches printed in The Union appeared in an extra, issued August 19, 1870, immediately the line was completed between Los Angeles and San Diego. A copy of the extra does not appear in the files that have been preserved, but the regular issue of August 25 carried on Page 1, under the heading:

"BY TELEGRAPH
The European War"
a series of brief dispatches on the Franco-Prussian War, bearing datelines

of London, Paris and New York, and dates of August 14, 15 and 16, and also an item under date of August 14, from Portsmouth, N. H., telling of the death there of Adm. D. G. Farragut. The war dispatches were jammed together in a single column, without benefit of subheads or dashes between them. The paper for August 25 also carried numerous war dispatches dated August 23 and 24. All were brief, for wire costs were high.

The Union, however, had $1000 credit with the telegraph company. In order to induce the Western Union to build to San Diego, a fund of $8000 was raised by San Diego businessmen, to be paid when the line was completed, with the understanding that contributors would receive credit for telegraph tolls in the amount of their contributions, provided the credit was used within three years. The Union contributed $1000 to the fund. The Western Union promised to complete the line

DOUGLAS GUNN
Editor of The Union, 1870-87

within three months. The Union for August 18 carried this story:

"The extension of lines of the Western Union Telegraph Co. was completed on Monday evening last, but the wires have not as yet been in working order. The operators are now on the line to rectify the causes of delay, and it is believed that communication will be open in a few days."

The wires apparently were in working order the next day, and in celebration of the arrival of the telegraph in San Diego the extra was issued. That the line was quickly built is evidenced by the fact that first mention of the telegraph company's proposition to build on a guarantee of $8000 was made in the April 14 paper.

In September, 1870, Dodge retired from The Union and was succeeded by Douglas Gunn, who had been a reporter and printer on the paper. Gunn, a man of ability and enterprise, became editor.

Dodge sang his swan song in the paper for September 20, when he said on the editorial page:

"In retiring from my connection with The San Diego Union, I thank the people for the support they have extended the paper and trust that they may continue to support it, and that it may hereafter, as heretofore, prove the champion of their rights under all circumstances."

Immediately following Dodge's farewell was an announcement by Gunn, who said:

"In assuming the editorial control of The San Diego Union, it is my purpose to so conduct its columns that it shall continue to deserve the confidence and command the respect of the public, as a reliable and perfectly independent newspaper."

Gunn is said to have been an extremely capable newsman and for four years he alone comprised the paper's editorial staff.

The Union, on December 8, 1870, made newspaper history when it printed in full President Ulysses S. Grant's message to Congress. The message had been received by telegraph at great expense. Set in agate type, the message filled almost three and three-fourths 13½-em columns 20¾ inches deep. In spite of the enterprise of the paper in presenting the full text to its readers, and notwithstanding the significance of the president's message, it was placed on Page 2, with an accompanying notice calling attention to the paper's unusual public service. On Page 1 was a long article headed, "How Beet Sugar Is Made at Alvarado." Said The Union in its modestly-displayed announcement of Grant's message:

"We give to the readers of The Union today the message of President Grant, delivered to Congress Monday, which has been especially telegraphed in full to this paper, the last page having been received yesterday morning.

"This is a piece of newspaper enterprise which has never before been attempted by any 'country paper' in the United States. We trust that it will be appreciated.

"The large space occupied by the message obliges us to lay over several communications and much editorial and local matter."

The Union apparently had difficulty with collections, for on December 22, 1870, this notice appeared as the lead on the editorial page:

"There are too many delinquent subscribers on our books. The circulation of the paper has increased until the press work is a heavy task, and we propose to lighten the labor of the pressmen by striking from our lists on January 1 the names of all subscribers then delinquent. We are determined henceforth to carry on as nearly as possible a cash business, not only as to subscriptions (which always are payable in advance) but also as to advertising and job printing. All persons indebted to this office are therefore requested to settle immediately."

It is significant that many of the projects vigorously advocated by The Union, virtually from its first issue, on through the years, largely are those supported by The Union today. Although much, very much has been accomplished, a great deal remains to be done, because of the tremendous increase in population of the city and county and the continuing needs. The early program included civic improvement, high cultural and religious aims, additional schools, good government, an adequate water supply, harbor development, greater sea commerce, industrialization, agricultural and horticultural expansion, more and better highways, especially eastward to Arizona.

Of paramount importance then, but off the list now, was the matter of railroads. The Union was full of railroad news and the paper strongly urged editorially that a transcontinental railroad be built to the Pacific by the southern route, to supplement the Central Pacific-Union Pacific, the first transcontinental railroad, completed in 1869. But it was not until September, 1883, that a railroad reached San Diego, and that was a branch line of the Atchison, Topeka & Santa Fe, from San Bernardino, and not a main line, of which San Diego long had sought to be the western terminus.

Bushyhead and Gunn were an aggressive team. Under their direction, the paper at least kept step with, and probably it set the pace for the growth and progress of San Diego. With the census of 1870 disclosing that the town had a population of 2300, the year had little more than closed when the progressive publishers laid plans for a daily paper, a costly and daring project, considering the size of the community. But they were men of enterprise and vision. They had unbounded faith in the future of San Diego.

Formal announcement of the daily was made in the weekly of March 16, 1871, with the launching of the daily set for March 20. Headed "The Daily Union," the statement read:

"On Monday morning next, March 20, we shall issue from this office the first number of the San Diego Daily Union. The paper will be regularly published thereafter every morning, Mondays excepted. Faithful to their promise that The Union should keep pace with the advancement of the city, its proprietors ordered, and received from San Francisco several weeks ago, the necessary material for the publication of a daily.

"The passage of the great Southern Transcontinental Railway Bill, fixing the western terminus of the road at the Bay of San Diego, at once inaugurates a new state of affairs in this city. The time has arrived when the conductors of a live newspaper must take a long step forward. Of course, we are aware that the publication of a morning journal is an enterprise involving some risk and very considerable expense; but we feel assured that the people of San Diego have an abiding faith in the future of the city, and that they are sufficiently wide awake to appreciate the fact that the establishment of a daily newspaper will add no slight degree to the importance of the place, and will result in direct benefit to every property holder and businessman in the community. We feel confident, therefore, that the Daily Union will be sustained.

THE UNION BECOMES DAILY
First Number, March 20, 1871

"We intend to give the public the very best paper, as to size, typographical makeup, news and editorial matter that the support extended to us will warrant. Our friends must not expect us to get out as extensive a journal as the San Francisco Bulletin just yet. We propose that the Daily Union shall pay for itself from the start—we do not intend to run into debt on its account one penny—and it will be enlarged and improved just as fast as its receipts will permit us to do so, and no faster.

"We shall give full local news—harbor and shipping items, law reports, proceedings of supervisors and city trustees, real estate movements, etc., etc.—from day to day; the cream of the telegraphic news of the world; correspondence and news summaries from the mining districts, Southern California and Arizona; a judicious selection of miscellaneous items, and brief editorials on the topics of the day.

"The paper will, for the present, be just half the size of the Weekly Union. We omit publication on Monday morning in order to avoid working on Sunday.

"The publishers of this paper must pay cash down for printing material; they pay for telegraphic news every Monday; they pay their printers every Saturday night; they pay their rent the first of every month. Nobody gives us credit; we do not want it, and do not intend to ask for it. Therefore the Daily Union will be conducted strictly on a cash basis; and, as we regard this of vital importance, we establish the rule at the outset, and make the announcement in advance of publication.

"Yearly, half-yearly and quarterly subscriptions must be paid in advance; weekly subscribers must pay up every Saturday. All transient advertisements must be paid for before insertion in the paper; regular advertisements must be paid every Saturday; advertisements two weeks overdue will be taken out. The cash system will work to mutual advantage of publishers and patrons. It is perfectly easy and practicable to pay a small sum every week; it may be practicable, but it is seldom easy to pay a larger sum at the end of one, two or three months. Our rules in this regard will be imperative in all cases, and will apply to the most intimate personal friends of the publishers with precisely the same force as to strangers. The Daily Union must be a cash paying and cash paid concern, or stop publication.

"We thus commend our enterprise to the citizens of San Diego; they have a direct personal interest in its success, and we look for such support as will enable us to publish a newspaper which shall reflect credit upon our young and rapidly growing city."

The daily was born on Monday morning, March 20, 1871. Thereafter no paper was printed on Monday for years. The daily was a five-column, four-page paper. Page 1 carried one column of advertisements, the second page, five columns; the third, three and a third columns, and the fourth, four and three-fourths columns. Many of the ads were mere business cards that seldom changed copy, much to the relief, no doubt, of the compositors who must have been pressed to set from the cases enough type to fill the paper. The publishers were encouraged by the public reception accorded the daily. They said in a "Good Morning" editorial:

"The Daily Union greets the good people of San Diego. A list of nearly 400 city subscribers, obtained since our announcement of the daily on Thursday last, and the advertisements already handed in, show that our anticipations were not unfounded, and encourage us in the belief that our enterprise will be sustained.

"As we have heretofore stated, no effort will be spared on the part of the publishers to make the paper worthy of the best support of the community.

"We submit the first number to the public with the confidence that it will meet a favorable reception, and with the promise that it shall grow with the growth of the city and shall be increased in size and made more complete in its several departments from time to time, as rapidly as the support extended to it will permit."

The weekly edition was omitted on March 23. The publishers and printers probably were overwhelmed by the added work of the daily and as a matter of expediency decided to forego the weekly for one issue. The weekly, however, was resumed on March 30 and its publication continued until May 21, 1925. In spite of the daily, the weekly lived for more than 56 years, to fulfill the needs of subscribers in isolated parts of the county not reached by regular daily newspaper delivery. Also it carried the delinquent tax list and other legal publications. News in the weekly largely was picked up from the daily editions.

The Union, then as now, was keenly interested in economy in government. Said an editorial of May 4, 1871:

"A recent official statement says: 'The cost of the occupation of Alaska by the United States is $10,388 a month, besides supplies, and is divided as follows: Army, $3900; Navy, $3500; revenue cutter, $2200, and custom-house, $700.'

"Now there does not seem to exist the slightest necessity for the monthly expenditure of $7400 set down to the Army and Navy. It is a simple waste of public money. Alaska does not need the presence of either troops or war vessels. Why does not the government spend that $7400 a month in Arizona? The money would do some good there."

The daily was well received by other newspapers, as is evidenced by the following comments:

Sonora Union Democrat—"Since passage of the Texas Pacific Railroad Bill, the people of San Diego have been filled with enthusiasm regarding the future of their town. Bushyhead and Gunn have commenced publication of a daily paper, the first number of which has come to hand. The Daily San Diego Union shows vim and business."

San Francisco Figaro—"We have received the first number of the San Diego Daily Union. It is a bright and sparkling little paper, and will do much to promote the interests of its section."

Watsonville Pajaronian—"The San Diego Union is now issued as a daily. It is a neat and entertaining journal and presents every indication of prosperity and influence."

Stockton Independent—"We have received the first number of the San Diego Daily Union, which was issued on the 20th instant. The proprietors, Bushyhead & Gunn, have heretofore issued The Union weekly, but the new impetus given the new city by the passage of the Texas Railroad Bill has led them to enter upon the publication of a daily. This number comes to us bristling with San Diego energy and glistening with San Diego news. The town evidently is wide awake and The Union has a fine prospect ahead."

Santa Cruz Times—"The first number of the San Diego Daily Union, a spirited and well-filled local sheet, has reached us. It claims a circulation of 400 to commence with, and is especially devoted to the immediate interests of the place of its publication."

Napa Register—"The San Diego Union is now issued daily. It is a sprightly, wide-awake little sheet, and its publishers, Messrs. Bushyhead & Gunn, deserve success."

Tucson Arizonian—"The daily San Diego Union has been received at this office. Its many columns of advertisements speak volumes for the enterprise of San Diego, while its several columns of choice reading matter reflect much credit upon its editors. The Union is beyond question a success."

The daily subscription price was $10 a year, $6 a half year, $3 a quarter. The paper was delivered in New Town and Old Town for 25 cents a week. Cost of the weekly was $5 a year, $3 for six months and $1.50 for three months.

Public transportation was by horse-drawn stage or ship. An advertisement in 1871 of the United States Mail Stage Line between San Diego and Los Angeles gave this schedule:

"Leave the Horton House, San Diego, every day (Sundays excepted) at 5 a.m. Leave Cosmopolitan Hotel, Old Town, 6 a.m., arriving at San Juan Capistrano at 7 p.m., and remaining overnight, leaving San Juan at 4 a.m., arriving in Los Angeles at 1 p.m. the following day. Fare through, $10.

"The very best Concord stages run on this line and the stock cannot be excelled on any stage line in the Pacific slope."

THE UNION'S OFFICES, SIXTH AND F STREETS, 1878-1901

The advertisement of another stage line read:

"San Diego, Arizona City and Tucson U.S. Mail Line. Tri-weekly four-horse coaches running between San Diego and Tucson. Time, five days. Fare to Arizona City, $40; Tucson, $90; Ralston, $125, gold coin."

Steamship lines advertised passage to New York and San Francicso. One advertisement read:

"Pacific Mail Steamship Co. Fare for New York via Panama: Cabin, $100; steerage, $50. San Diego to San Francisco: Cabin, $15; steerage, $8."

The cost of living was a small fraction of what it is today. The establishments that advertised in The Union no doubt were among the better places in the town.

The U. S. Restaurant advertised beef stew or mutton chops, 12½ cents; tenderloin or porterhouse, 25 cents; broiled chicken or quail, 37½ cents; sausage, bacon or ham, 12½ cents; two eggs, boiled, fried or on toast, 12½ cents; braised beef, mutton or pork, 12½ cents.

THE UNION'S NEW PRINTING MACHINERY.

R. HOE & CO.'S LATEST IMPROVED DOUBLE CYLINDER PRINTING PRESS.

PRESS, INSTALLED IN 1888, WAS TERMED 'PRINTING MARVEL'

The Union House offered board and lodging at $6 a week, board at $5 and single meals, 25 cents. The advertisement said a corral was maintained "opposite the house for the accommodation of animals."

The Union said editorially on October 5, 1871:

"Three years have passed since the first number of The San Diego Union was issued. In that time a city of more than 3000 inhabitants has grown up on the shores of this bay, and the population of the county has quadrupled. This is progress. The figures speak for themselves. We commence the fourth year with a determination to keep The Union in the front in the advance of Southern California."

In the first year of daily publication, the paper spent about $1200 for telegraphic news and the next year $2000. Bushyhead and Gunn worked hard to make the daily successful. Finally, in 1873, Bushyhead retired from the business and Gunn paid him $5000 for his interest. The paper soon afterward was doubled in size, for times were booming in San Diego. Then came the panic of 1873 and the paper, along with general business, was hard hit. Gunn said later he was editor, reporter and the entire staff, doing the work of several men in order to keep The Union going.

Business conditions improved within four years and The Union prospered also. On June 1, 1878, The Union moved to a building at Sixth and F Streets, which was much nearer the center of town. By 1880, San Diego's population had reached 2637. The figure of 3000, given for October, 1871, apparently was inaccurate. It was customary for newspapers of the day to exaggerate population and circulation statements. In 1881, a steam printing press was installed and the paper again was enlarged. Gunn retired

UNION-TRIBUNE'S NEW GOSS HEADLINER PRESS

August 3, 1887. He later was elected mayor and served in that office in 1889-91. Gunn died November 28, 1891.

San Diego experienced a boom lasting 18 months from 1886 to the winter of 1887-88, during which real estate prices rose to fabulous figures, and many new buildings, business and residential, were constructed. Trading in town lots was so feverish that often a lot bought one day would be sold the next at a large profit. Brass bands, barbecues and excursions were utilized by promoters to further stimulate enthusiasm for their offerings. In little more than a year, San Diego's population rose from 8000 to 21,000.

The "Great Boom," as it was known, resulted from the general business prosperity of the country, and it collapsed as quickly as it started. Overnight, San Diego real estate prices tumbled, property became a drug on the market, and fortunes were wiped out. The Union prospered during the boom, and suffered when it ended. Apparently many who had come to San Diego during the boom left when the crash came, for the federal census of 1890 gave the population as 16,159.

With retirement of Gunn in 1887, the paper's ownership passed to The San Diego Union Co., which had been formed for the purpose of acquiring the growing daily. Col. John R. Berry, who for two years had been city editor, became manager, and his associates in the company were William Collier and J. Russell Smith.

Several months afterward, Hosmer P. McKoon acquired an interest in the paper and subsequently E. W. Morse and Bryant Howard entered the company. A white paper famine occurred early in 1888 and for a time The Union was printed on dirty white, yellowish, green and pink paper. A double-cylinder Hoe press and feeders were installed in May, 1888.

The press, with a capacity of 5000 papers an hour, was regarded as a printing marvel of the day. The Union held open house and hundreds of people viewed the press in operation. The Union for May 10 reported that "the folders at each end of the press attracted the most attention and the guests stood watching the whole sheets pass in and come out all folded and cut. 'Wonderful, wonderful,' they said, and it is wonderful. . . .

"The expressions of pleased surprise at the elegance and perfection of the new machinery and the completeness of The Union's new establishment would, if written out, fill a book. They were to be heard on all sides as the crowd departed, each carrying away a copy of the paper with a description of the press as a souvenir."

In June of that year, John C. Monteith bought a block of stock in the company and became business manager. Later in the year, Howard M. Kutchin assumed the post of business manager and shortly afterward became editor, but served only until June, 1889.

The Daily Bee was bought in December, 1888, and on January 1, 1889, was consolidated with The Union, which to this day carries on the editorial page the legend: "The San Diego Union and Daily Bee."

The Daily Bee had been established in 1887. The following announcement appeared in The Union:

"It is the purpose of the publishers to make of The San Diego Union and Daily Bee one of the very best papers on the Pacific Coast, and it is not in the spirit of boastfulness that it is claimed to be better equipped to perform that promise than any paper San Diego has ever had, or probably ever will have. . . .

"Devotion to the interests of San Diego city and county will be our paramount mission, accompanied by a hearty interest in all portions of Southern California and the peninsular region, with which we are so closely allied.

"The paper will continue to be unmistakably Republican. No ardent partisan need entertain apprehension on that score. But it will not be an 'organ' and will be the master of its own conscience and conviction. . . . So The Union and Bee hails its old and new friends on this 'glad New Year' and hopes that we may mutually live long and prosper together."

Edmund F. Parmelee, business and advertising manager of the Bee, became business and advertising manager of The Union under the consolidation, and later was advertising manager of The Union and Tribune, filling that position until 1928, when he was named advertising counselor of both papers. Parmelee died February 9, 1937, after 48 years of service to the papers.

Early in 1890, Berry severed his connection with the paper and went to Ohio, but returned to San Diego within a few weeks and again took charge of the paper, and Andrew Pollock became associated with him. Later that year, Berry was named collector of the port and The Union was sold to John D. and A. B. Spreckels, of San Francisco, widely known California financiers and businessmen. They were represented at that time by E. S. Babcock. Thomas Gardiner, one of the founders of the Sacramento Union and of the Los Angeles Times, was made manager and Eli H. Murray, editor. Gardiner, who also later had the title of editor, remained with the paper until his death, June 10, 1899. In the decade 1890-1900, San Diego was practically at a standstill populationwise, for it gained only 1541 inhabitants, the total being 17,700.

The published announcement of the deal was somewhat confusing, for it did not disclose the Spreckels brothers as purchasers of The Union, but gave the buyers as Gardiner and Murray. The record discloses nothing of Murray's activities after the initial announcement, which read:

"Yesterday, August 1, 1890, the controlling interest and management of The San Diego Daily and Weekly Union passed into our hands. It is certainly gratifying for us to know that we are not coming among those to whom we are altogether strangers, as, to some extent, we are known to nearly every person in the community.

"We have few promises to make and these you may depend on being faithfully kept. In entering upon our new duties, we do so with a full knowledge of the watchful care and responsibility attached thereto and we will earnestly endeavor to perform them to the full satisfaction of every unbiased patron of the paper and to whom we must now appeal for help to assist us and creditably serve them.

"THOMAS GARDINER,
"ELI H. MURRAY."

For 38 years, the Spreckels interests owned and operated The Union and for 27 years the Tribune. Their business enterprises spread over San Diego and San Francisco and extended to Hawaii. While the brothers

JOHN D. SPRECKELS
Acquired The Union in 1890

were partners, John D. Spreckels devoted his attention largely to San Diego, where he made his first investment in 1887. Among the Spreckels properties in San Diego were office buildings, hotels, the transit system, the Coronado ferry and the San Diego & Arizona Railway.

The newspapers, operated as business entities, now were adequately financed and were in a favorable position for expansion. A member of the editorial staff during the Spreckels régime recalls life on The Union and Tribune was like that of a big family, and no one ever was fired, except for intoxication, and only when that was frequent. Spreckels was fond of both papers.

The pay scale was low and the hours were long. A day's work of 14 hours was not unusual. In order to compensate for the low salaries, members of the editorial staff were allowed to earn side money by writing publicity stories for theater and other commercial interests, political candidates and sports events. Also, members of the staff wrote for papers in other cities.

Being a part of a great business empire, the papers were operated in a manner favorable to those interests. There were so many "sacred cows," one old-timer said, that the staff was constantly alert as to what not to print. Unfavorable news was banned in connection with any of the Spreckels enterprises, the ranking personnel connected therewith and members of their families.

On June 19, 1899, nine days after the death of Gardiner, James D. MacMullen arrived from San Francisco to fill the vacancy. He had been managing editor of the San Francisco Call, also owned by the Spreckels interests.

"MacMullen was a fine man," said a staff member who worked for him. "He took an exceptional interest in politics."

Another associate of MacMullen said that "because of his nearsightedness, he had the appearance of being austere, but those who had the privilege of working with him knew he had a heart of gold. While he would brook no foolishness, he was always kind, considerate and tolerant of those who worked for him.

JAMES D. MacMULLEN
Editor-Manager, 1899-1933

"He was one of the few old-school newspapermen who had gained his knowledge of the business the hard way in the early days in San Francisco. His thorough understanding of the newspaper business was reflected in the papers. His untimely passing [April 2, 1933, at the age of 74 years] was not only a great loss to the papers, but to San Diego, in the growth and development of which he played a large part."

At one time, Spreckels and E. W. Scripps, the publisher and then owner of the San Diego Sun, had some differences of opinion as members of the county highway commission, on which they and A. G. Spalding, of sporting goods and baseball fame, served. That started a newspaper fight in which

THIRD AND BROADWAY OFFICES OF UNION-TRIBUNE, 1901-07

The Union printed some caustic cartoons of Scripps. All this was amusing and exciting at the time, but long since has been forgotten.

While MacMullen had the title of managing editor of the two papers, he actually was general manager and his word was law.

The Union made remarkable progress during the Spreckels régime. The owners were able to make improvements in staff and equipment on a long-range basis, for the paper no longer found it necessary to depend upon immediate returns to meet current costs. Competition was keen and price-cutting was not uncommon. Rivalry for city and county legal publications sometimes resulted in the successful bidder accepting the work below cost of production. On May 19, 1896, The Union (weekly edition) was awarded the county tax list at 10 cents a square, while the Sun bid 17 cents; Vidette, 22 cents; Record, 22 cents, and Tribune, 50 cents.

A notable step forward was taken May 8, 1895, when The Union installed its first Linotype. Prior to that time, all type for the paper had been hand set. The Union and Evening Tribune now have 28 typesetting machines. On August 5, 1895, the paper started printing on a Hoe Presto press.

The Union in 1895 comprised eight pages daily and Sunday. The first page was devoted to telegraph. Inside pages consisted of local news, editorials and extensive correspondence from various Southern California cities. The correspondence was run under trick standing hands, such as "Pasadena Pointers," "Redlands Rumors," "Santa Ana Sorts," and "Los Angeles Locals." There was a great amount of miscellany and many fashion articles were used. Woodcuts and casts of line drawings were employed for illustrations. Photoengraving had not come into use until 1890, and presumably was not available in San Diego in 1895.

Advertising consisted mainly of business cards without listing competitive prices. Safety bicycles, which recently had appeared on the market, were extensively advertised, as were patent medicines, known in newspaper parlance as "quacks," and which were declared by their manufacturers to cure every ailment to which mankind is subject. Four columns of classified were the rule and legal advertising patronage was generous. As late as 1901, the paper comprised eight pages daily and Sunday.

The Morning Call, a rival publication, formerly the Vidette, breathed its last on March 8, 1900, and the plant was bought by The Union for $2500.

BUSINESS OFFICE OF THE UNION ABOUT 1900

The Evening Tribune, started by T. D. Beasley and F. E. A. Kimball, December 2, 1895, was bought by the Spreckels interests on September 27, 1901. The business of the Tribune was consolidated with that of The Union. The Tribune since has been continued as an afternoon paper.

Growth of The Union and acquisition of the Tribune necessitated larger quarters. The plant was moved on November 30 and December 1, 1901, to the old Horton Bank Building on the southwest corner of Third and Broadway, a block west of the site of the paper's first building in New Town. The structure was renamed The Union Building. In 31 years since The Union had cast its lot with New Town, D Street, or Broadway, had been transformed from a dusty road to a busy paved thoroughfare lined with business structures.

Frank B. Goodman, a young newsman from Colorado, joined The Union on November 4, 1902. He subsequently was transferred to the Tribune, of which he became editor. He has been a counselor for the company since 1948.

In less than six years the papers had outgrown The Union Building, so the owners decided new and much larger quarters were necessary. The publications on March 6, 1907, moved temporarily across Broadway to the Burnap Building. A new Hoe 16-page press was put in operation March 26. The old Union Building was torn down and work started on a new home for the papers, a six-story structure, which was the first reinforced concrete business block erected in San Diego. It was completed January 28, 1908, and was immediately occupied by the papers. The business office was located on Broadway, with the editorial and other offices on the second floor, while the composing room and presses were in the basement. This building now is known as the Land Title Building. A double-width Hoe press was installed in March, 1914.

Between 1900 and 1910, San Diego's population more than doubled, increasing from 17,700 to 39,578. With continued growth of the city and the newspaper business, more space was required and The Union Building Annex, four stories and basement, was erected in 1914 on Second Avenue. The mechanical departments, editorial rooms and most of the offices were transferred to the annex, but the advertising and circulation departments remained on the Broadway side. The two buildings were connected. The papers operated under this housing arrangement until 1951.

Clarence A. McGrew joined The Union staff as city editor December 1,

UNION BUILDING, COMPLETED IN 1908, AND ANNEX, 1914

1915. He had come to San Diego January 1, 1908, to be editor of the San Diego Sun. A graduate of Harvard, McGrew, who had some newspaper experience while in college, went to the New York Sun in 1897 and, after seven years there, was on the New York Times for two years, then came to California to be editor of a new newspaper in Berkeley. When the depression of 1907 came, the Berkeley venture folded and he went to the San Francisco Bulletin. He left that paper to come to San Diego. He was appointed editor of The Union in 1933 and, on January 5, 1951, became editor emeritus. He was named editorial consultant in 1953.

The city continued its rapid growth, and the newspapers grew and prospered accordingly. In 1920, the city's population was 74,361 and in 1930 it had climbed to 147,995. Under MacMullen's direction the papers expanded into the metropolitan class. It was generally understood, however, that the papers functioned in the Spreckels interests, as John D. Spreckels worked toward development of a "dream city." The newspapers were used to mold public opinion in favor of his varied enterprises.

During this period, San Diego took on new aspects. The drastic change had begun from a place of retired folk, tourists and geraniums, to a city whose economy eventually became geared to naval operations and industrialization. The U. S. fleet was transferred from the Atlantic to the Pacific in 1920, and, with exception of the battleships, was based at San Diego.

Airplane manufacturing began in the mid-1920's. The packing of tuna had started somewhat earlier. These activities brought an influx of population and additional payrolls.

Further increase in business necessitated acquisition in July, 1927, of a Hoe unit-type press, initially with three units, to which units were added through the years, making a total of eight.

John D. Spreckels died June 7, 1926, at the age of 72, after a long and distinguished career. His brother and business partner, Adolph, died in San Francisco two years previously, June 28, 1924. He was 67 years old. For a year and a half after the death of John D. Spreckels, the papers were operated by the estate.

Col. Ira C. Copley bought The Union and Evening Tribune, includ-

ADVERTISEMENT OF 1901
'Only Giraffe . . . in the World'

ing the Union Building Annex, on January 21, 1928. Col. Copley was no stranger to San Diego. His first visit to the city was in 1881, when he arrived on a side-wheel steamer from San Francisco. On another sojourn in San Diego, in 1891, he is quoted as having said, as he read a copy of The Union:

"This is the best newspaper in a town of the size in the country. I should like to own it."

The Colonel's parents, Ira B. and Ellen Copley, established residence in San Diego in 1890, having come from Illinois. His father died here in 1893 and his mother and three sisters resided here thereafter. The mother and two sisters died in San Diego and the third sister, Mrs. Edyth C. Lamb, died in Los Angeles in May, 1948.

SELLING SPECIAL EDITION OF THE UNION IN 1926

Col. Copley had been a member of the Cuyamaca Club since 1907.

Not long after he bought The Union and Evening Tribune, Col. Copley purchased the John D. Spreckels home in Coronado, remodeled it and occupied the property during his frequent stays here, although he maintained his legal residence in Aurora, Ill., until his death.

Purchase by Col. Copley of The Union and Evening Tribune was announced under a seven-column streamer on Page 1 of The Union, January 22, 1928. The story, carried in Column 8, was accompanied by a three-column portrait of the Colonel. In the story, the purchaser outlined his policy for conduct of the papers. The story read in part:

"Sale of The San Diego Union and Evening Tribune by the J. D. & A. B. Spreckels Investment Co. to Col. Ira C. Copley, of Aurora, Ill., ... was completed yesterday noon and Col. Copley is now the owner of both newspapers.

"Col. Copley was the guest of honor last night at a dinner given at Hotel del Coronado by William R. Wheeler, former assistant secretary of the Department of Commerce and an old-time friend of the Colonel. Mayor Clark and others prominent in the civic life of the city were guests at the dinner and welcomed the new owner of The Union and Evening Tribune. Before that occasion, Col. Copley outlined his plans for the two newspapers.

" 'I plan no change in personnel or policy at present,' said Col. Copley, 'and I hope there will be no changes. I have just one thing to say about the papers. They are going to deliver the goods. I think they have been doing that, and I want them to keep on doing it. I have always looked upon The Union and Tribune with admiration. I had hoped for a long time to be able to buy The Union and Tribune and the opportunity came at a psychological moment.

" 'These papers are not to be personal organs of myself or anyone else. I have no political ambitions. I have no connections with any public utility anywhere and no connection with any other business than the newspaper business anywhere. There will be no connection of any kind between the papers and the San Diego Electric Railway Co. [The Spreckels interests also operated the street railway company.]

" 'It shall be the purpose of the papers to present the news on the basis of its honest news value. They will have neither enemies nor friends in that respect. No newspaper has ever been really successful that has not delivered the goods in an honest and constructive way, and it is my desire to have these papers continue their constructive and honest presentation of the news.

" 'The papers will continue to be Republican in their policy,' but not narrowly so. He expressed the belief that strong party government is necessary in national affairs, but that it is out of place in local affairs, and that The Union and Tribune will take no part in petty factional disputes in the city. . . ."

When the Colonel bought the papers, the people did not realize what his wide experience, background and acquaintance all over the world were to mean to San Diego. His acquisition of the papers brought about a decided change in them and their policy. He had but two things to sell—news and advertising. There were no special interests to serve. The taboo subjects disappeared overnight and the papers began doing the job that has brought them to their present high position in the community, state and nation.

Col. Copley had many ways of determining what the people thought about his papers. One noteworthy example came the day he stopped and asked a lad, who was selling a New Year's number in the street, if the product he was selling was good. The boy, who did not know the Colonel,

TYPICAL FRONT PAGE OF THE SAN DIEGO UNION, 1953

replied: "Do you think I would be wasting my time selling the papers if I did not think they were good?"

The Colonel bought 10 papers, paying 25 cents each for them, and addressed them to friends. Just after he left, a man from the circulation

205

department happened to pass by and remarked to the boy: "Did you know that man to whom you just sold those papers was Col. Copley?" The boy answered: "Why did he pay me 25 cents each for the papers when he could get them for nothing at the office?"

Buying his own papers on the street and asking pertinent questions of the news vendor was characteristic of the Colonel. At another time, however, the Colonel did not offer to pay, but ended up doing so. He stepped to the circulation counter in the front office and requested two papers. A boy on duty handed the papers to him and the Colonel started to walk away.

"That will be 10 cents," the boy called after him.

The Colonel hesitated, then said to the youth:

"I am Col. Copley."

"Oh, an employe?" said the boy. "In that case, the price will be 6 cents." [Employes were accorded a 3-cent rate.]

Highly amused, the Colonel handed the youth a dime, saying he guessed he could afford it, and departed.

Col. Copley neither asked for nor received favors from anyone. A striking and amusing example occurred when he and his brother-in-law, F. Karl Lamb, were arrested for crossing Fourth Avenue in the middle of the block. It probably was the first time the anti-jaywalking ordinance was enforced. The arrest occasioned about as much excitement as a fire, for a large crowd gathered.

The policeman who issued the tickets was greatly embarrassed and very apologetic when he learned one of the men arrested was Col. Copley, but his uneasiness was quickly dispelled when the Colonel told the officer he merely was doing his duty. The Colonel posted bail at the police station, something that some in the crowd evidently did not think would happen, for the remark was made: "It won't cost them anything, for he owns the newspapers." This impression was dispelled by a front-page humorous story in the Tribune which related the incident and stated that the Colonel and Lamb had posted $1 bail each.

Because reference frequently is made to The San Diego Union as The Union, confusion sometimes arises between it and labor unions. Such mis-understanding occurred at Coronado Cabanas, where the son of one of Col. Copley's friends was learning the hotel business. The young man was serving salad at a luncheon. Col. Copley stopped to chat with him briefly and, after the Colonel had departed, the head of the commissary department of the hotel, who recently had met with representatives of a labor union, asked the young man: "Who was that man to whom you were talking?" When the reply came that it was Col. Copley of The Union, the commissary chief admonished: "If I catch you talking to any more union people, I will fire you! I have trouble enough without you stirring up more!"

In addition to recognizing his editorial responsibility to the community, Col. Copley was keenly aware of his civic obligations and was a liberal contributor, both through the company and as an individual, to worth-while civic movements and charities. He particularly was interested in the Salvation Army, to which he made generous contributions.

Recognizing that any appreciable increase in San Diego's population was dependent on an adequate water supply, the Colonel employed engineers conversant with water development to conduct an investigation, as a result of which the newspapers' water policy was formulated. He ever was ready to discuss water with those who were particularly familiar with the situation and he did everything possible to assist in developing additional supplies. While he did not claim credit for the impounding systems that were constructed after he became owner of the newspapers, it is acknowledged that he did much to bring about this development.

Evidence of Col. Copley's belief in the growth of San Diego was his purchase of the Casa Loma Hotel, on the site of which he contemplated erecting an elaborate newspaper building. Circumstances that developed made it impossible for him to carry out the program. However, he was much interested in the project. Whenever his friends from a distance came to San Diego, he took them to the site of his proposed building.

Under Col. Copley's ownership, with the staff inspired by his masterful leadership, the papers made great strides editorially, in advertising, typographical appearance and in circulation. He was proud of The Union and Tribune and derived a great measure of satisfaction in the knowledge that they ranked high among the newspapers of California. It was a matter of deep regret among the executives of the papers and of all employes that the Colonel, because of his extensive and widespread business interests, could not spend more time in San Diego. All recognized that he not only was a man of keen mentality and rare executive ability, but an employer who had at heart the welfare of those who produced the papers and contributed notably to their success.

Shortly after Col. Copley bought the papers, William R. Wheeler was elected, on February 3, 1928, president and treasurer of the Union-Tribune Publishing Co. Wheeler had been assistant secretary of commerce and labor during the administration of President Theodore Roosevelt, who in 1908 referred to him as "one of the strongest men in public life." Wheeler remained with the papers until his death, February 17, 1935, at the age of 75.

Col. Copley induced Lester G. Bradley who, for many years, had been a banker in San Diego, to give up that business and join the papers. On July 1, 1932, Bradley joined the Union-Tribune Publishing Co., with the title of resident vice president of The Copley Press.

LESTER G. BRADLEY
Chairman of the Board

On April 13, 1933, following the death of James MacMullen, Bradley was elected a director and chairman of the board of directors of the Union-Tribune Publishing Co. On February 27, 1935, he succeeded Wheeler as treasurer. On March 13, 1935, he was elected president of the Union-Tribune Publishing Co. and Col. Copley was elected chairman of the board of directors. On June 11, 1942, Bradley became a director of The Copley Press, retaining his position as a vice president, and he still occupies both positions with the parent company.

On February 1, 1946, Bradley became publisher of the San Diego newspapers, and continued as president, treasurer, and publisher until June 14, 1950, when he was elected chairman of the board of directors of the Union-Tribune Publishing Co., to fill the vacancy in that office which had existed since Col. Copley's death.

Walter J. Schneider joined the papers on October 1, 1932, as controller. He had been identified with the F. W. Kellogg papers since October 1,

TOP EXECUTIVES AND THEIR SECRETARIES
William Shea, Phyllis Donley, Grace Israel and James S. Copley

1924, and after their purchase by Col. Copley continued in the general office of the Southern California Newspapers, Associated, until his transfer to San Diego. Schneider was named vice president and controller of the Union-Tribune Publishing Co. September 27, 1944, and on February 1, 1946, was elected vice president and business manager.

Arthur K. Whyte, who had been publisher of the Santa Monica Outlook during Col. Copley's ownership of that paper, came to San Diego in April, 1932, and, a year later, on April 13, 1933, became publisher and manager. After almost 14 years of service to the papers, he resigned on February 1, 1946. Whyte died in Los Angeles, March 6, 1950.

The longest record of service on the papers was held by William V. O'Farrell, circulation manager, who died October 30, 1941, at 65, after 53 years of employment. He started as a carrier boy for The Union, June 10, 1888. He was made circulation manager in the 1890's and in 1901, when the Evening Tribune was acquired, he took on the added duties as circulation manager of that paper. During his long service with the papers, nearly every businessman in San Diego who had resided while a youth in the city worked for O'Farrell at one time or another.

Circulation was his one aim in life and when anyone canceled his subscription, O'Farrell made it his business to learn the reason before the day ended. He was a "fighting Irishman," and woe unto the person who made a disparaging remark about the papers in his presence.

Lionel C. Ridout, assistant secretary and personnel director, had been with the papers more than 36 years when he died, July 30, 1947, at the age of 61. Ridout accepted a "temporary" job as payroll clerk, March 28, 1911, and later was auditor. He was made assistant secretary of the company, October 8, 1930.

ARTHUR K. WHYTE
Publisher-Manager, 1933-46

Edward T. Austin, who had been an editor on the Sun and also had extensive newspaper experience elsewhere in California, in Ohio and Oklahoma, was named editor-in-chief of The Union and Tribune in 1937, and in 1944 was appointed by Col. Copley as executive editor of The Copley Press. He continued to hold the San Diego position also, and resigned from the organization in 1949.

The San Diego Sun, started July 19, 1881, by Mrs. Charles P. Taggart, wife of one of the early co-owners of The Union, suspended publication November 24, 1939. The Sun had a succession of owners until 1921, when E. W. Scripps acquired control. Subsequently it became a member of the Scripps-Howard Newspapers.

Notwithstanding the depression of the 1930's, the papers remained in a favorable position, due in a marked degree to the city's growth. In 1940, San Diego's population totaled 203,341. Boomed by wartime activity of the armed forces and aircraft production, the civilian population soared to 362,658 in 1946, but dropped to 334,387 in 1950. Following outbreak of the Korean War in 1950, airplane production increased rapidly and, together with naval expansion, brought the population to 434,924 in 1952.

J. C. Safley, who had been editor of the Glendale News-Press, and who was city and news editor of the Hollywood News from 1928 to 1931, became managing editor of The Union and Tribune-Sun on December 2, 1940. It was a newly-created position. In September, 1943, the job was split. Safley retained the managing editorship of The Union, and Thornton Boulter, city editor of The Union, who had been with that paper since 1927, was appointed managing editor of the Tribune-Sun.

James S. Copley, son of the Colonel, was elected a director and assistant secretary of the Union-Tribune Publishing Co., January 20, 1947. He previously had filled various positions on other Copley papers, notably at Culver City and Glendale, with time out for service in World War II as a naval lieutenant.

William Shea, a veteran of The Copley Press, came to the San Diego papers May 1, 1948, as general manager. He previously was publisher of

J. C. SAFLEY
Editor, The San Diego Union

THORNTON BOULTER
Editor, Evening Tribune, 1951-53

the San Pedro News-Pilot and prior to going to San Pedro was editor and publisher of the Culver City Star-News. Shea was promoted to associate publisher July 1, 1950, and also continued as vice president and general manager. Later he was elected a vice president and director of The Copley Press.

ALEX DE BAKCSY
Assistant to General Manager

Col. Copley's death in Aurora, Ill., November 2, 1947, after a brief illness, cast a pall of gloom over the entire Union-Tribune personnel. Only a few weeks prior to his passing, the Colonel had been in his San Diego office and appeared to be in normal health.

It was realized at once that in his death a great leader had passed from the newspaper scene. Col. Copley had builded solidly and on a firm foundation and the San Diego properties, which had been near and dear to him, were far better newspapers in every way than they were when he acquired them in 1928.

The owner, who had gone, to return no more, left a great heritage, and those charged with the responsibility of carrying on the two San Diego newspapers, guided by his precepts and inspired by his lofty journalistic ideals, turned courageously toward the future, with a strong determination that the publications should advance to still greater public service and achievement.

Following the Colonel's death, James S. Copley assumed a more active part in operation of the papers, and on June 4, 1950, became president and publisher of The Union and Tribune.

Alex De Bakcsy, who joined the advertising department October 3, 1949, was appointed assistant to the general manager April 17, 1950.

The name and good will of the San Diego Daily Journal were acquired by the Union-Tribune Publishing Co., on May 27, 1950, when the Journal suspended.

PROBLEMS OF NEWSPAPER BUSINESS UNDER DISCUSSION

E. L. Schellenberg, circulation manager; Hugh R. Morick, controller; Walter J. Schneider, business manager, and Albert L. Vogt, credit manager.

Under the Spreckels régime and during the Copley ownership up to this time, the Tribune had been a staunch Republican newspaper. A change in policy was announced in 1950. The Evening Tribune henceforth would be an independent newspaper. It also started printing columns written by commentators of a more liberal turn of mind than had characterized those whose contributions had been carried heretofore.

It is the policy of the Union-Tribune Publishing Co. to make sharp distinction between The Union and the Evening Tribune in the handling and display of news. The Union is inclined to conservatism in writing and in makeup, while the Tribune is forceful in appearance, particularly in its street editions. Both newspapers are clean publications and good taste is a keynote in text and pictures.

Editorial changes were made January 5, 1951, whereby Thornton Boulter, Evening Tribune managing editor, became editor, and Newell Jones, city editor, assumed the managing editor's post. Simultaneously, J. C. Safley was named editor of The Union and Richard F. Pourade, who had been city

ADVERTISING EXECUTIVES HOLD CONFERENCE

Francis D. Ide, retail advertising manager; Kenneth Flood, advertising director; John T. Mulkey, manager of general advertising, and Worth Wright, classified advertising manager.

editor, was appointed managing editor. Pourade was made associate editor of The Union on January 1, 1953, at which time Russell P. Johnson became associate editor of the Tribune.

Executives, department heads and assistants of the two daily newspapers (as of June 1, 1953) are James S. Copley, publisher; William Shea, associate publisher and general manager; Alex De Bakcsy, assistant to the general manager; Walter J. Schneider, business manager; Karl J. Bauman, assistant to the business manager; E. Robert Anderson, consultant.

Kenneth Flood, advertising director; Francis D. Ide, retail advertising manager; John T. Mulkey, manager of general advertising; Worth Wright, classified advertising manager.

Hugh R. Morick, controller; Albert L. Vogt, credit manager; Roderick MacRae, personnel manager; Harold A. Huff, auditor.

J. C. Safley, editor of The Union; R. F. Pourade, associate and managing editor; Eugene F. Williams, executive news editor; Mil Chipp, news editor; Malcolm Donnelley, city editor; Lon J. Smith, Sunday editor.

NEWS AND EDITORIAL SUBJECTS CAREFULLY CONSIDERED

Eugene F. Williams, Union executive news editor; Richard F. Pourade, Union associate and managing editor; Clarence A. McGrew, editorial consultant of The Union; L. L. Sisk, Evening Tribune executive news editor, and Russell P. Johnson, Evening Tribune associate editor.

Russell P. Johnson, associate editor of the Evening Tribune; L. L. Sisk, executive news editor; Thomas R. Evans, news editor; Guy Ryan, city editor.

E. L. Schellenberg, circulation manager; Melvin L. Ellison, assistant to the circulation manager; Dennis T. Thompson, Union circulation manager; Chester C. Donnan, Evening Tribune circulation manager; W. Ernest Shohoney, country circulation manager; James Reading, circulation promotion manager. N. L. Hazelip, chief photographer; Paula Kent, promotion director; Louise Fahrney Doane, chief telephone operator.

Bertram G. Burke, production manager; Kenneth L. Gregg, production consultant; Lawrence Hendricks, composing room superintendent; Harry Lindsay, stereotyping superintendent; Matt Spratt, pressroom superintendent; Harry E. Swift, assistant pressroom superintendent; Verl Snyder, mailing room superintendent.

In addition to the foregoing, Lester G. Bradley is chairman of the

MECHANICAL DEPARTMENT HEADS CHECK THEIR PRODUCT

Lawrence Hendricks, composing room superintendent; Bertram G. Burke, production manager; Kenneth L. Gregg, production consultant; Matt Spratt, pressroom superintendent, and Harry Lindsay, stereotyping superintendent.

board of directors of the corporation. Other directors are A. W. Shipton, Richard N. Smith and Thomas H. Beacom.

Clarence A. McGrew is editorial consultant of The Union. Counselors for the company are Frank B. Goodman, Herbert Frey and John A. Kennedy.

Except for the first six years of its life, the history of the Evening Tribune has been virtually that of The Union for, since September 27, 1901, the ownership and business operations have been identical. The only variation has been in the editorial department personnel.

Founded December 2, 1895, by T. D. Beasley and F. E. A. Kimball, The Evening Tribune was a six-column, four-page paper. It carried Associated Press dispatches from the start and printed more local news on Page 1 than was customary at the time. That page usually was reserved for telegraph. Editorial comment, in the form of pungent paragraphs, appeared for several issues in the first column of Page 1. The lead paragraph of the first paper read:

EVENING TRIBUNE GIVES FULL COVERAGE IN AFTERNOON FIELD

"Young ladies should heed the fact that 1896 is a leap year and also that there will not be another leap year until 1904, eight long years."

B. L. Muir, a real estate dealer, was The Evening Tribune's first subscriber. Said the paper in its first number:

217

"B. L. Muir, the enterprising San Diego real estate dealer, has the honor of being the first subscriber to The Evening Tribune, handing in his name upon the first announcement of the paper. Mr. Muir is a man who always stands in the front rank of any movement looking to the advancement of the city's interests."

Muir carried an advertisement more than a half column long. In the early issues, advertising patronage was negligible. The paper printed six days a week, omitting Sunday.

From the outset, The Evening Tribune threw barbs at the other San Diego papers—The Union and the Sun. In their "Salutatory," Beasley and Kimball said:

"With this issue we begin publication of an evening journal, in accordance with a long-cherished desire to wield a more powerful force for the advancement and upbuilding of San Diego. Profiting by costly experience in the past and the lessons derived therefrom, the publishers feel that in this enterprise there is no such word as failure. This experience, being supplemented by a well-equipped printing plant and a thorough understanding of the city's needs, assures the establishment of what San Diego has so long needed, an independent newspaper fearlessly advocating the business interests of this city and its people.

"Thousands of persons in the East are looking towards Southern California as their future home, many of whom would come to this county, yet hesitate by reason of misstatements published in local papers, largely for the attainment of selfish ends. It will be the aim of the Tribune to truthfully depict the advantages of this section, without needlessly enlarging upon purely local and temporary disagreements. In the past we have had abundant proofs (some of which may be adduced later) of the injury done by the circulation of false reports concerning our city and county; and if in the future San Diego desires to speedily attain the position she is destined in time to occupy, there must be more united action in presenting her claims to the world. No one need hesitate to send the Tribune to eastern friends for fear of 'hurting the town.'

"The Tribune will be clean, bright and progressive, and for that reason will be the newspaper for the home. Believing in the fundamental principles of the Republican Party, the Tribune will advocate those principles, exercising the right of a free press to criticize a failure to live up to their spirit and intent as interpreted by us.

FIVE-STORY UNION-TRIBUNE BUILDING, FINISHED IN 1952

"The Tribune congratulates itself on having secured a contract for the Associated Press dispatches, and can assure its readers that its telegraphic service will be superior to that of any afternoon newspaper ever published in San Diego. Special efforts will be made to render the presentation of local news complete and attractive.

"KIMBALL &
"BEASLEY."

Continuing its digs at the established papers, The Evening Tribune commented editorially:

December 6—"Many of our readers have commented on the excellency of the Tribune telegraphic service. It is no idle boast, but a fact that cannot be contradicted, that this paper possesses the most complete service ever furnished an afternoon paper in San Diego, and the public are not slow to appreciate that fact."

December 10—"It is a well-known fact that the local papers have suppressed in the last few years more live news than they have published. The Tribune gives all the news."

December 13—"The Union comes out this morning with an editorial, 'Rule or Ruin.' Whose ruin?"

December 16—"The public are learning what it means to get fresh news, not clipped from other papers."

December 17—"The Tribune's dispatches come from the wires and are not faked from morning papers."

December 23—"For years the columns of The Union have been used as a channel to voice the grievances and ventilate the spite of one man. Citizens whose views did not coincide with his have been lampooned, abused, libeled, and the strangest thing of all is that many of the men thus assailed have continued to furnish that paper moral and material support."

The distinguished newspaper service of Howard Thornton Boulter, 45, editor of the Evening Tribune, ended with his death on April 24, 1953. Although confined by illness to his home for more than a year, he continued, until shortly before his death, to direct the editorial department of the newspaper by telephone. Boulter had joined The San Diego Union, June 16, 1927, as a reporter. He was widely known in national newspaper circles and took an active part in studies conducted by the Associated Press Managing Editors Association.

San Diego is a magic city. Endowed by nature with a salubrious climate, and with diversified sources of income from the land, the sea and the sky, San Diego boasts a growth and accomplishments that have been phenomenal. The Union and Evening Tribune, in their public service through the many years in the dissemination of news, in their helpfulness to business in carrying merchandising messages to the people, in their high ideals, their improvement, enlargement and progress, have kept pace with the achievements of the city and county.

To the end that the role of the two newspapers in the culture, economy and well-being of the region they serve may be enhanced, the Union-Tribune Publishing Co. completed in 1952 a new five-story building of reinforced concrete. Combined with The Union Building Annex, which was remodeled to conform with the new structure inside and out, the building has a frontage of 200 feet on Second Avenue and 150 feet on E Street. Total floor space is 75,000 square feet. The building, planned for efficiency in newspaper operation, is a striking addition to downtown San Diego. A garage on First Avenue, between E and F Streets, has floor space of 25,000 square feet.

Purchase of the six-story Security Title Insurance Co. Building, at 940 Third Avenue, by the Union-Tribune Publishing Co., was announced February 17, 1953. The structure, with a frontage of 50 feet, extends 100 feet back and is separated from the Union-Tribune Building on Second Avenue by a lightwell. The buildings will be co-ordinated in order to provide more space for the expanding newspapers.

During the last three years, the mechanical departments of the two newspapers have been greatly enlarged and completely modernized. Much new equipment has been added to permit greater and more efficient production.

News is set on 19 typesetting machines, including three that are tape-operated. There are four perforators with transmitters and reperforators for tape operation. Nine machines are used in the ad alley, which also is equipped with two Ludlows, one Monotype for rules and borders, and an Elrod for making type base and rules.

Included in stereotyping equipment are two Goss molding machines, one a new Giant model; a seven-ton metal pot and a three-ton pot; three flat-casting boxes; two heavy-duty vacuum-back Pony Autoplate machines, and much other equipment.

A new eight-unit high-speed Goss Headliner press, with two pairs of folders, was installed in the summer of 1952. It represents the latest in press engineering and is capable of producing a 64-page newspaper with color at a speed of 52,500 copies an hour. It will print a 96-page newspaper

FLEET OF TRUCKS DISTRIBUTES UNION AND TRIBUNE

with color at 26,250 papers an hour. The newspapers are produced complete in from one to eight sections. Two more units have been ordered for the press. They will permit simultaneous production of two 80-page newspapers.

The press is equipped with a Goss Tensionplate Lockup system, by which twisting and distortion inherent in the older type of lockup of stereotyped plates are avoided. The device consists of a series of fingers mounted flush with the periphery of the cylinder. By turning a wrench, the fingers rise up and engage pockets milled in the under surface of the plate. The fingers exert a pulling effect on the plate that tends to draw it down to the cylinder, at the same time applying tension to the head and tail of the plate, which makes the plate hug the cylinder tightly.

The new method makes for smoother running of the press and better printing, and virtually eliminates danger of the plate slipping off the cylinder while the press is running.

A Cline full-speed paster enables newsprint rolls to be changed at full speed of the press merely by pressing a button. Newsprint rolls are mounted on reels, each reel holding three rolls. One roll is in running position and two are in reserve. The reserve rolls are prepared for splicing by applying a solvent-sensitive gummed tape to the surface of the paper. As the running roll approaches the end, the new roll is brought into contact with the sheet of paper running from the expiring roll into the press. The expiring sheet presses against the new roll and starts it turning. When the new roll reaches the speed of the press, the pressman pushes a button, which causes a spray of solvent to impinge on the new roll. This makes the splicing tape adhere to the running sheet. At the same time, a serrated knife strikes the sheet behind the splice, cutting off the old roll.

Much valuable time thus is saved, for, under the old system, it was necessary to stop the press whenever a roll of paper was consumed.

The newspapers are carried by automatic conveyors from the pressroom to the mailing room, where they are counted and bundled. The mailing room has been entirely mechanized. A Wallastar wire-bundling machine compresses the papers into bundles under two tons of pressure, binds the bundles with wire and welds the two ends of the wire. Equipment also includes a Saxmayer rope-tying machine and five Girard semi-automatic wire-bundling machines. From the bundling machine, the papers go down a chute to the loading dock, where they are placed on trucks for delivery.

A fleet of seven trucks and 65 automobiles hauls the papers to all parts of San Diego County, for distribution to carriers, who make house-to-house delivery. The trucks and cars travel 1,750,000 miles annually.

The Union and Evening Tribune have full 24-hour service of The Associated Press, United Press and International News Service. The Copley Press Washington Bureau supplies both papers with coverage in the national capital and the papers maintain a state bureau, with special service from Sacramento during sessions of the legislature. In addition, The Union receives wire dispatches of the Chicago Tribune Press Service, the New York Times News Service and Reuters, Ltd.

With 750 full-time employes, a modern building, a gigantic press, the latest models of other mechanical equipment, world-wide news coverage and a combined daily circulation of 175,000 and 145,000 Sunday, The Union and Evening Tribune have come a long way since 1868, when three men produced The Union on a Washington hand press in a cottage in Old Town and the circulation was a few hundred.

THE MOST IMPORTANT CORNER IN THE U.S.A.

SAN DIEGO
CALIFORNIA

Southern California
Associated Newspapers

THE GOLDEN HORSESHOE MARKET

CLARK F. WAITE
Chairman of the Board, Southern California Associated Newspapers
Director, The Copley Press

226

Southern California
Associated Newspapers

Culver City, Calif.

FOR THE REAL HISTORY of the Copley newspapers—their service to their communities, their states and their nation, and their part in the lives of the citizens and families in those communities—the stories of the member newspapers must be consulted. Each newspaper is a vigorous social organism, intimately concerned with the progress and development of the individuals and groups which give life and character to a city and a region, and thus each newspaper has a fascinating story to tell.

All enterprises, even newspapers, nevertheless have their prosaic aspects—their legal existence, their property management—work-a-day activities that keep them healthy, but make no history. Since the story of the newspapers carrying on the traditions for community service set by Col. Ira C. Copley will be found elsewhere in this book, this chapter will tell the history of a corporation that makes possible the orderly management of one group of the Copley newspapers.

Southern California Associated Newspapers is the name of a California corporation, a wholly-owned subsidiary of The Copley Press, Inc. This corporation owns and operates the eight daily newspapers of the Copley organization published in cities in Los Angeles County. Offices of SCAN are at 4044 Lafayette Place, Culver City. For many years the offices were at 510 South Spring Street, Los Angeles.

SCAN is a present-day successor to the group of newspapers formerly controlled by the late Frederick W. Kellogg. Kellogg was a dynamic news-

227

paperman who, before coming to Southern California, had built up and operated newspaper properties in Omaha and San Francisco, as publisher of the Omaha News and later publisher of the San Francisco Call. His wife was a member of the noted Scripps newspaper family.

Kellogg founded the Pasadena Post in 1920. He chose Pasadena for his first Los Angeles County venture because it was close to his home in Scripps Park, Altadena. He brought with him to Pasadena men who had worked on the San Francisco Call, including Walter Cook, now business manager of the Glendale News-Press; Carleton Wright, at present with the Glendale News-Press, and his son, William Scripps Kellogg. He also brought to Pasadena a man who had worked for him as a mechanical employe as far back as the Omaha days, Charles Rhumland, later circulation manager of the Post and mechanical superintendent of the Glendale News-Press. An early employe of Kellogg in Southern California was Walter J. Schneider, who joined the organization October 1, 1924. Schneider now is business manager of The San Diego Union and Evening Tribune.

Starting with the Pasadena Post in 1920, through the first few years of that decade the elder Kellogg built up his suburban newspaper holdings in the Los Angeles metropolitan area, with additions and deletions, until he formed a holding company, Kellogg Newspapers, Inc., in 1926. By that time the following corporations, each of which published its own newspaper, were included in the group: Alhambra Publishing Co. (Post-Advocate); Culver City Publishing Co. (Star-News); Glendale Printing & Publishing Co. (Glendale Press); Hollywood News Publishing Co.; Pasadena Post Publishing Co.; Daily Breeze Publishing Co. (Redondo Beach); San Pedro Printing & Publishing Co. (News); Santa Monica Publishing Co. (Outlook); Venice Publishing Co. (Vanguard).

Kellogg printed at the Pasadena plant a newspaper known as the Monrovia Post. In reality, it was a replate of the Pasadena Post and was distributed in Monrovia with that paper.

Commercial printing plants were operated in three cities, under separate corporations. They were Glendale Press Job Printing Co., Post Printing & Binding Co. (Pasadena), and Santa Monica Bay Job Printing Co.

In addition to these suburban properties, Kellogg had been closely associated with the Earl interests of Los Angeles, which controlled the Los Angeles Express, an afternoon metropolitan daily. In June, 1925, Kellogg entered into an agreement with the Express under which his suburban

ALDEN C. WAITE
President, Southern California Associated Newspapers

dailies and the Express were circulated together at a combined subscription price. This agreement still was in force at the time of the purchase of the Los Angeles County group of newspapers from Kellogg by Col. Copley early in 1928, and the agreement remained in effect for about a year after the sale.

F. W. KELLOGG
Founder, Kellogg Newspapers

Kellogg continued to take an interest in the progress of the newspapers he founded, showing helpful co-operation with all Copley personnel until his death. He died on board a steamship in the Pacific Ocean on September 5, 1940, a day before the ship was due to dock at Yokohama.

William Scripps Kellogg received his early newspaper training from his father while still attending Stanford University, and, after being graduated from there, on the San Francisco Call. Upon sale of the San Francisco property, Bill, as he was known to all, became associated with his father on the Pasadena Post, where he rose to become circulation manager and later, under the Copley ownership, to the position of publisher of that newspaper.

After the Pasadena Post was sold to the Prisk interests in February, 1932, Bill became publisher of the Glendale News-Press, a position he held for eight years, during one of the greatest periods of growth of both the City of Glendale and of the News-Press, bringing to the newspaper those same forceful, hard-working qualities that characterized his father. During this period, Bill made many important contributions to the community of Glendale and to trade organizations in the newspaper business. He was president of the California Newspaper Publishers Association for a full term. In addition, he headed the Los Angeles Metropolitan Unit of the CNPA for a number of years.

Under his leadership, the Glendale News-Press developed into one of the four or five most important dailies in the county outside the City of Los

Angeles. Bill's editorial knowledge and business genius were manifest in the improvement of the property from an editorial as well as mechanical standpoint. Bill Kellogg resigned from the Copley organization in the fall of 1940, because of the death of his father. The elder Kellogg left an active and developing estate which needed the full-time attention of the only son. Among the properties was La Jolla Beach and Tennis Club, which the son has continued to operate.

Negotiations for the sale of Kellogg Newspapers to Col. Copley were begun late in 1927, with an official transfer date of January 1, 1928. At that time the name of the holding company was changed to Southern California Newspapers, Associated (SCNA).

The corporation sold the Glendale Press to Col. Copley on February 15, 1928, and he merged it with the Glendale News in a transaction which left him a 60 percent interest in the merged News-Press, with the 40 percent remaining in the hands of the McClure interests, which had published the News. Col. Copley then sold the majority control of the combined paper back to SCNA.

On March 6, 1928, the San Pedro News was merged with the San Pedro Pilot, forming the News-Pilot, with SCNA holding 60 percent, and 40 percent remaining in the hands of Clark F. Waite and his family interests, former publishers of the Pilot. The San Pedro Printing & Publishing Co. still is a separate corporation, subsidiary to Southern California Associated Newspapers.

The San Pedro Pilot, corporately the Pilot Printing & Publishing Co., was owned by Clark Francis Waite and his late wife, Ruth Massey Waite, jointly owning 60 percent, and his brothers, Julius A. (Dude) Waite, 20 percent, and the late Arthur L. Waite, 20 percent.

After the consolidation of the News and the Pilot, the members of the Waite family continued to own the same proportions of the minority 40 percent of the combined property. The death of Ruth M. Waite resulted in ownership of her holdings passing to her two children, Mrs. Marjorie Wanglin and Alden Clark Waite. Mrs. Wanglin's death in 1949 left her husband, Byron Chase Wanglin II, as a minority stockholder, and Arthur L. Waite's death in 1945 left his stock in the hands of his widow, Mrs. Lila Waite. These minority stockholders today represent the only minority ownership of any Copley newspaper outside the estate and holdings of the heirs of the late Col. Copley.

On February 28, 1929, SCNA sold the stock of the Hollywood News Publishing Co. to Col. Copley, who personally held that newspaper until its sale to the Hollywood Citizen, on October 31, 1931. The San Fernando Valley News was published as an adjunct to the Hollywood News for circulation in San Fernando Valley.

SCNA acquired the Monrovia News on March 1, 1929, from C. C. Howard, merging it with the Monrovia replate of the Pasadena Post, and thereafter published it locally in Monrovia as the Monrovia News-Post.

On September 15, 1931, SCNA acquired the Glendale Evening Herald, which was operated about seven months and then was liquidated.

During April, 1932, SCNA traded the 100 percent ownership of the Santa Monica Outlook for the 40 percent McClure minority of the Glendale News-Press, thereby becoming sole owner of the Glendale property. Upon acquiring the Santa Monica Outlook, Samuel G. McClure took with him to that newspaper his son-in-law, Jacob D. Funk, who had been publisher of the Glendale News-Press. Jake, always a friendly and humorous as well as an exceptionally able man, is kindly remembered, not only by all Glendale News-Press personnel who worked with him, but by the members of the entire SCAN organization.

Funk brought to the News-Press a sound business judgment, a keen interest in the welfare of the community and an honest love of people. He still is well known to all in the organization because of his activity in the California Newspaper Publishers Association, of which he served a term as president, and for co-operation with SCAN newspapers in solving problems common to the suburban newspapers of Southern California.

The publisher of the Outlook at the time of the change in ownership was Arthur K. Whyte, who had been successively composing room foreman, advertising manager and business manager, before becoming the publisher upon the resignation of Robert P. Holliday from that position. Whyte was sent by Col. Copley to San Diego, where, a year later, he became publisher of The Union and the Evening Tribune and held that position until his retirement a few years before his death, which occurred March 6, 1950.

Holliday, energetic editor, as well as publisher, under the Kellogg and the Copley ownerships, resigned as publisher of the Outlook to become publisher of William Randolph Hearst's San Francisco Call-Bulletin, a position he held until he left the newspaper to purchase a majority interest in the M. C. Mogensen Co., which became the present West-Holliday Co., newspaper publishers' representative. It still represents the Copley newspapers. Holliday attends the annual Copley conference each year as one of the organization.

On February 27, 1932, SCNA sold the Pasadena Post to Col. Copley, who immediately sold it to the Prisk interests, owners of the Pasadena Star-News. In addition to the SCNA properties mentioned, Col. Copley had acquired, as a personal holding in 1928, the Long Beach Sun, morning and Sunday daily, which, although not a part of the SCNA corporation, was operated with the SCNA papers until its sale, late in February, 1932, to the Prisks, publishers of the Long Beach Press-Telegram as well as the Pasadena Star-News.

During November and December, 1934, a series of corporate changes was made to simplify the structure of the Los Angeles County group, in which individual operating companies, including SCNA, but excluding the San Pedro corporation, were liquidated. Col. Copley, as the sole stockholder, received all of the assets and operated all of the businesses personally until March 1, 1935, when a new company, the present Southern California Associated Newspapers (SCAN) was incorporated. It took over from Col. Copley all the present newspaper properties of the corporation except the Burbank Daily Review.

In the spring of 1950, the officers of SCAN were approached by Harvey Ling, representing himself and the other stockholders of the Review Publishing Co., of Burbank. Burbank, a municipality of 78,577 population, according to the U. S. census of 1950, adjoins Glendale, and the commercial interests of the two cities in many ways are entwined. Ling offered the Review for sale, pointing out the obvious importance of the area to the Glendale newspaper. Transfer of title of the Burbank Daily Review and its mechanical equipment to SCAN from the Review Co. was made on May 1, 1950. The Burbank News was acquired January 1, 1952.

From the time of the merger of the News and Press in Glendale, in 1928, until his resignation on September 15, 1931, the general manager of the Los Angeles County group was Samuel G. McClure. He was succeeded by Clark F. Waite, who served as general manager until the new corporation was formed in 1935, then as president until February, 1948, when he was named chairman of the board to succeed Col. Copley in that position, following the death of the owner in November, 1947. Alden C. Waite at the time was named president, which position he now holds.

The late Samuel G. McClure had come to Glendale during the 1920's from Ohio, where he had been a successful daily newspaper publisher. In Glendale he bought the Evening News from the Cowan interests, and was publisher of that newspaper until the consolidation of the News with the Press, following purchase of the latter newspaper by Col. Copley.

McClure was an active civic leader, serving on many committees and in numerous organizations in Glendale, and for several years was Glendale's representative on the board of the Metropolitan Water District. His services on that board were so outstanding that, after his acquisition of the Santa Monica Outlook and removal of his home to the beach city, Santa Monica appointed him to the same board as its representative.

Clark F. Waite served as publisher of the consolidated News-Pilot in San Pedro until Col. Copley assigned him to assist in the management of the Hollywood News during 1929 and 1930, after which time he was appointed publisher of the Long Beach Sun. Following sale of the Sun, Waite was appointed general manager of SCNA, and when the present SCAN corporation was formed, he became president.

Alden C. Waite, like his father, Clark F. Waite, grew up in the newspaper business. He was born in Santa Ana in 1907, when his father was business manager of the Register. Alden, after a paper route period on the San Pedro Pilot, worked summers and after school as an apprentice, starting when 13 years old, and then worked successively through the various departments of the newspaper, throughout his school years. Upon being graduated from Pomona College in 1928, he became secretary of the Seismological Research, at Pasadena, at that time a joint project of the Carnegie Institution of Washington and the California Institute of Technology, now exclusively a department of Caltech. Coincidentally with this job, he became a part-time reporter for the Pasadena Post, covering scientific and educational institutions for the Pasadena area.

Resigning from the Seismological Research in the autumn of 1929, Waite, together with his brother-in-law, Chase Wanglin, started the Westwood Hills Press, both a publication and commercial printing business. Waite was editor and also was in charge of the plant. The Westwood Hills Press was sold in July, 1937. In 1936, prior to the sale, and following the death of Henry James, chief editorial writer for the SCAN papers, Alden was appointed to fill that position. He held that job until 1940, when W. S. Kellogg made arrangements to have Waite transferred to Glendale as editor of the Glendale News-Press, the date to await the transfer of J. C. Safley to San Diego as managing editor of The Union and Tribune-Sun. Before the change took place, Kellogg had resigned as publisher at Glendale, and was replaced by H. C. Burkheimer, formerly publisher of the Alhambra Post-Advocate. Upon learning of Safley's leaving, Burkheimer hired Waite as editor at Glendale.

Alden was appointed publisher of the Alhambra Post-Advocate on January 1, 1944, and he continued in that position until April 19, 1946, when he went to the SCAN offices as assistant to the president, Clark F. Waite.

Traditionally, publishers of SCAN papers also are vice presidents of the corporation, as is Rear Adm. Robert Henderson, USN, ret. Directors, in addition to the chairman, the president and Henderson, include representatives of the owners and of

REAR ADM. ROBERT HENDERSON
Vice President, SCAN

The Copley Press, Inc., sole stockholder of SCAN. They are James S. Copley, vice president of SCAN; A. W. Shipton, vice president of SCAN; C. C. Weiland, assistant secretary of SCAN, and C. V. Anderson, assistant treasurer of SCAN.

Adm. Henderson was born in Albany, N. Y., on October 15, 1878, and grew up in New England. He was appointed to the U. S. Naval Academy in 1898. He was graduated from the academy in 1902, and served the early part of his adult life, through World War I, as an officer in the Navy.

While the admiral is a vice president of SCAN, his activities are not confined to the subsidiary corporation. He has been for many years manager of the Copley conventions, has handled both the personal and corporate holdings of real estate in many cases for the Copley family and the newspaper organization, was an active assistant to the publisher of the Long Beach Sun from the acquisition of that paper by Col. Copley until its sale, and for many years was one of the chief officials of SCAN in its labor

OFFICE STAFF, SOUTHERN CALIFORNIA ASSOCIATED NEWSPAPERS

Left to right, Fred W. Robbins, Adra Smith, Richard Schwenker, Kathleen Ford, Robert C. Menely, Mary S. Guiroff, Carl V. Anderson, Patricia J. Smith, Frank J. Pfeiffer, Maxine E. Wasson, William A. Ahlgren.

negotiations and employe relations. Internal publications of the Copley organization, such as the frequently revised directories, the biographical book, and like productions, are under his editorship.

Carl Victor Anderson, assistant treasurer and chief auditor of SCAN, is a product of the Aurora area, being a native of nearby Batavia, Ill. He began his business career in 1922 with the Western United Gas & Electric Co., a Copley property, and worked there for four years. In 1926, he was employed by the Pure Oil Co., of Chicago, where he remained until coming to California in 1928. He was with the Huntington Land Co. and the National Guaranty Life Insurance Co. until 1937, then rejoined the Copley organization in Los Angeles as accountant and auditor.

(James S. Copley and A. W. Shipton receive full mention elsewhere, as do Richard N. Smith, C. C. Weiland and D. F. Hartman.)

SCAN has maintained for more than 20 years a news bureau in the Civic Center in Los Angeles. The bureau covers the federal, state, county and city buildings and courts for the eight SCAN newspapers. For many years chief of the bureau was Garber Davidson, who left to join The Associated Press in 1945. His position was filled by August M. (Gus) Borio, from the staff of the Glendale News-Press. Borio had been on the News-Press since 1933. Prior to that time, he was with the Los Angeles Express. He is a graduate of the University of California and is considered by newsmen as one of the best reporters in the Civic Center. Assisting him is Robert Hill, formerly of the Alhambra Post-Advocate. The bureau gives thorough coverage for SCAN newspapers and on frequent occasions, upon request, for other Copley newspapers.

Malvin (Mal) Quinn, the ambassador of good will of the plants and general office, has been inter-office messenger for SCAN and associated newspapers for more than 20 years. He started in 1930 his daily trek calling at SCAN plants, the offices of advertisers, West-Holliday Co., and other places upon request, riding a motorcycle through the ever-increasing traffic of Los Angeles County. Within a few years the load necessitated graduation to an automobile, which he drives an average of 4000 miles a month. Mal is perhaps the best-known man in SCAN to other SCAN personnel, and each newspaper considers him as part of its local staff. He was born in Philadelphia, but completed his schooling in Los Angeles. The SCAN general office in Culver City is Quinn's headquarters.

The present group of SCAN newspapers, representing the best among suburban dailies, includes the Post-Advocate, at Alhambra; Burbank Daily Review; the Evening Star-News, Culver City; Glendale News-Press; the Daily News-Post, Monrovia; the Daily Breeze, of the South Bay cities of Redondo Beach, Hermosa Beach, Manhattan Beach and Palos Verdes Estates; the San Pedro News-Pilot, and the Evening Vanguard, of Venice.

ALHAMBRA

ℌost ℌdvocate

"San Gabriel Valley's Daily Reading Habit"

DIVERSIFIED INDUSTRIES MAINSTAY OF ALHAMBRA'S ECONOMY

BARTON HEILIGERS
Editor and Publisher, Post-Advocate
Vice President, Southern California Associated Newspapers

Post-Advocate

11 South Stoneman Avenue   Alhambra, Calif.

ALHAMBRA FIRST FELT the impact of printer's ink on November 5, 1887, when G. W. Rice founded The Alhambra. This was 16 years before Alhambra incorporated as a city. Little is known of Alhambra's pioneer publication, except that its business office was located in the Alhambra Hotel, at the corner of Boabdil (now Main) Street and Garfield Avenue. It was printed by a firm that called itself the Alhambra Publishing Co. The Alhambra was four pages in size and was distributed on Saturdays.

In the issue of The Alhambra for December 24, 1887, an article entitled, "Alhambra—Its Past and Present," gives the first really accurate picture of the city that has now grown to be the seventh largest in Los Angeles County and the sixteenth largest in California. The article read in part:

"Twenty years ago, the San Gabriel Valley, or what is now Alhambra, was one barren plain from the Sierra Madres to the ocean. Save a few Mexican camps, a person might travel for miles without seeing a single dwelling. The inhabitants were mostly Spanish and raised little except for home purposes.

"The only important ranches under cultivation at this time were those of Mr. B. D. Wilson, the founder of Alhambra, Col. Kewen, George Stoneman and Mr. Wolfskill.

"Some of the ranches contained many thousand acres, and over them roamed vast herds of cattle, sheep and horses.

"The first vineyards, orange, lemon, lime and olive orchards exten-

241

(THE ALHAMBRA.

EARLY ISSUE OF THE ALHAMBRA (1888)

sively planted were on the ranches of Wilson, Wolfskill, J. De Barth Shorb, Gen. Stoneman and Col. Kewen.

"The first residence in Alhambra was built in 1875. It was a small redwood shanty with a lean-to in true California style.

"There are no saloons and, as the town is about to incorporate [it actually took until 1903], none will be allowed within the limits of the incorporation.

"With no rum shops, it will be an excellent place for parents to rear their children. For a person wishing a home in the country where the larger towns are wished to be reached, there is no place so convenient as Alhambra."

This was Alhambra's first newspaper. And despite the community's humble beginning with its dirty streets and its scattered few dwellings, it spoke out with enthusiasm and with optimism.

This forefather of today's streamlined and modern Post-Advocate told, in its issue of January 7, 1888, how land was now selling at $125 an acre and pointed out with considerable pride that land in nearby Pasadena was bringing only $100 an acre. It told how the first school was opened on October 25, 1886, with an attendance of 28 pupils. They were great days but most of them are lost forever, as no additional issues of The Alhambra can be found.

Alhambra's second publication was called the Alhambra Review. The only issue on record is dated February 21, 1891. Its publishers were listed as the Misses O. L. and C. E. Eddy. The lead editorial was on the problem of "It will not be too long before we shall have to decide whether we want to raise fruit or bugs."

The Alhambra Review didn't survive much more than a year, while The Alhambra lasted probably six or seven years. There are no records to support these statements. There is no question, however, but that they were the pioneer publications of the Alhambra community.

H. E. Lawrence founded the Alhambra Advocate in October 8, 1898, and from then on Alhambra's journalistic records are complete. The Alhambra Advocate was a forerunner of today's Post-Advocate. The Alhambra Advocate was published every Saturday by the Advocate Publishing Co., at Garfield Avenue and Main Street. On Page 1 of the first issue appeared an article entitled "Introductory," which read in part:

"Herewith the Alhambra Advocate. The cause for its appearance should be plain to even the ordinary observer, especially if he reads the paper. There is no town in the country with half the population and advantages of Alhambra but what has a local paper and it is surprising that any local quill should have forsaken this place for fields that could not be fairer and promise of the future more plain.

"But the facts are that our predecessor found his business in the city [Los Angeles] increasing so rapidly that he could not devote the necessary time and attention to The Alhambra, which we understand was a creditable publication.

"The time has now arrived, however, when it is necessary for Alhambra to be heard outside her own bailiwick, and a local paper is the proper medium for advocating her interests, hence this publication. . . .

"The editor would be thankful for brief local contributions of newsy character which may be left at Dr. Elwood's drug store, where a box will soon be placed for their reception."

Thus the Alhambra Advocate was born and at a time when Alhambra had no newspaper serving the community. For as Lawrence pointed out, the press of outside business had forced The Alhambra publisher to "forsake this place." Alhambra, however, never again was to be without a newspaper.

On April 28, 1900, Lawrence introduced a second publication to his Alhambra readers. It was called the Valley Vista and served Sierra Madre, El Monte, Lamanda (East Pasadena) and Alhambra. It was published in Sierra Madre.

The dual arrangement didn't last long for, on June 23, 1900, the Valley Vista was consolidated with the Alhambra Advocate to become the Alhambra Advocate and Valley Vista. It offered its readers and advertisers complete San Gabriel Valley coverage. Subscription rate was $1.25 a year. Lawrence's newspaper had thrived so well that, in 1906, its circulation was listed as 600 paid. Alhambra was a bustling community of 1500 persons. On May 1, 1907, the Advocate and Valley Vista began publishing twice a week.

The Advocate and Valley Vista, under Lawrence, continued as a semi-weekly without interruption or competition until the fateful year of 1908. This was the beginning of a turbulent period in Alhambra newspaper history.

Lawrence labored under some political difficulties. One of them came with the establishment, on May 9, 1908, of the Alhambran, a competitive weekly, founded by Maj. E. A. Routhe. For the first time, Alhambra became a two-newspaper city. In his first editorial, Routhe said:

"The Alhambran, in making its bow to the public, desires to say that it has a special mission, viz., to promote and foster the growth and interests of Alhambra and Southern California.

"Under the axiomatic rule of 'first things first,' the Alhambran will aim to reflect the real and true life of the city. The conditions here are metropolitan in many respects, all must admit. The City of Alhambra has passed the unconventional period of its existence and must keep abreast

ALHAMBRAN-ADVOCATE
Early Weekly Newspaper

FIRST POST-ADVOCATE
Papers Merged February 11, 1924

with other residential points adjacent to Southern California's greatest center if it is to take rank with the best or even assume to be even better than that which may now be considered to be the best. This paper will aim to give all the local news in the best form possible. It will have views of its own on all topics of public interest, whether political, religious, moral, social or municipal. In politics it will be Republican. The editor cast his first vote for Abraham Lincoln."

Routhe's ideal was the development of the kind of newspaper that every editor hopes to create, but few attain or retain. It was the organ for the expression of opinion and support of all measures that the editor believed good for the city. Advertising was of secondary importance. The Alhambran was printed on high-grade paper with light, attractive type faces. Editorials were placed on the first page of every edition.

But the inevitable happened. The friction among political parties and conflicting civic groups did not cease with the advent of Routhe into the publishing field. Friction, in fact, increased.

"There would have been war," said one early resident of the city, "if what had to happen didn't happen."

A group of representative citizens bought the Advocate and the Alhambran, and merged them under the name of the Alhambran-Advocate and Valley Vista. Routhe's publishing venture thus was short-lived and, on August 21, 1908, the new Alhambran-Advocate came into being. Political harmony was restored in the city and, with one party in complete ascendancy, all major differences were laid aside.

The owners of the merged weeklies leased the Alhambran-Advocate to William E. Willis. Willis formerly owned the Redlands (Calif.) Review and came to Alhambra from Redlands. Willis continued to live in Alhambra for the remainder of his life and died on July 1, 1947. His widow, 82, still resided in Alhambra in 1952. Routhe was named editor of the merged publication under Willis. The association lasted only five weeks.

Comparative peace prevailed in Alhambra for the next three years. The newspaper prospered under Willis. All news was local.

In 1911, competition again reared its head. S. W. Doty and Frank V. Stump established the Alhambra News. The News also was a weekly and was published by its two owners for one year, at the end of which, in 1912, Stump sold his interest to Willis of the Alhambran-Advocate.

It was another year, however, before the two papers consolidated. Willis continued to operate the Alhambran-Advocate and at the same time retained a half interest in the News.

The double role did not continue long, for early in 1913 W. G. Gilstrap, later publisher of the San Gabriel Sun, purchased Willis' interest in the News. And within a few weeks the Alhambran-Advocate changed hands again.

C. H. Randall, who afterward became a councilman in Los Angeles, bought the Alhambran-Advocate and thus were touched off several rapid changes of ownerships. Randall purchased the paper in 1913 from the group of citizens who had acquired it in 1908, Willis having only leased the newspaper.

Randall kept the Alhambran-Advocate only a short time before he sold it to J. J. Conrad. Conrad, who proved a cautious publisher, sold the newspaper to J. F. Mitchem, with A. W. Armstrong as editor.

Under Mitchem's ownership, Alhambra was given its first daily. The masthead read: *The Alhambran-Advocate and Valley Vista.* The first daily edition was published at 206 West Main Street on Monday, June 23, 1913. With little fanfare and a terse statement to his readers, Mitchem commented editorially:

"The Advocate, always first in line of progress, has acted upon the

PIONEER ON WEST COAST IN TELETYPESETTING

suggestion of the Chamber of Commerce and a daily paper in Alhambra is now a fact.

"It is the intention to make the Advocate conservative and yet progressive; newsy, but not sensational, at all times a consistent and energetic booster of Alhambra.

"This paper does not wear the collar of any political boss and it will be free and untrammeled to fight for those principles which shall be for the best interests of the whole people."

Subscription rate for the new daily was 25 cents a month. Along with the daily, Mitchem continued to publish the weekly Alhambran-Advocate and Valley Vista.

Mitchem didn't remain in the publishing field long, however, and on July 9, 1913, sold his interests to the owners of the weekly Alhambra News, Will G. Gilstrap and S. W. Doty, and again the rival papers were merged.

In a brief story in his July 9 issue, Mitchem said: "This is to announce that, on this date, the Alhambran-Advocate has been sold by J. F. Mitchem and his associates."

Gilstrap and Doty thus became the sole newspaper owners in Alhambra. They formed the Alhambra Publishing Co. and continued to publish the paper under the name of Daily Alhambran-Advocate. They also continued to publish the weekly Alhambran-Advocate and Valley Vista, but changed the name to Alhambran-Advocate and Alhambra News.

In 1914, Earl Brininstool, one of the editors of the Los Angeles Express, bought a half interest in the Daily Alhambran-Advocate, retaining that interest for one year, and then, on February 1, 1915, sold his share to B. N. Marriott.

Marriott, who later became postmaster in Alhambra, purchased the other half interest in August, 1917, from Gilstrap and Doty and thus became sole owner of the Daily Alhambran-Advocate and weekly Alhambran-Advocate and Alhambra News. At that time, the population of Alhambra was 6000.

After acquiring full ownership, Marriott dropped the *n* from Alhambran in Alhambran-Advocate. On January 1, 1918, he discontinued the daily and published the Alhambra News on Tuesdays and the Alhambra Advocate on Fridays. Discontinuance of the Daily Alhambra Advocate was announced on December 31, 1917, in a Page 1 statement, which read as follows:

"After carefully studying the matter for several months past and going thoroughly into all phases of the situation and conditions here, the Advocate management has reluctantly come to the conclusion that a daily newspaper is not justified in Alhambra at the present time and under the present war conditions.

"The difficulties of publishing a daily in Alhambra are greater now than ever before and we feel that we can give our patrons and readers better results and much better satisfaction and service in another way. Therefore it has been decided to discontinue the Daily Advocate after tomorrow until altered times and conditions justify its revival." The editorial was signed by Marriott.

On Monday, November 5, 1923, Marriott resumed daily publication with an eight-page edition, and with offices at 117 West Main Street. The city had grown to 20,000. Subscription rate was $2.50 a year. In a Page 1 announcement, Marriott said.

"The Alhambra Advocate today begins its second period of service for Alhambra as a daily. This is being done in response to a strong demand on the part of many businessmen and citizens who feel that they need a daily service and urged the Advocate to supply this want."

Individual ownership was near an end for the Alhambra Advocate, however, and on January 16, 1924, Marriott sold his newspaper to the F. W. Kellogg interests.

In 1921, the Kellogg Newspapers had started the Alhambra edition of the Pasadena Evening Post, which was published daily in connection with the Pasadena paper. Its editor was Clayton I. Ward, who eventually served as editor of the Post-Advocate.

Announcement of the sale of the Alhambra Advocate to the Kellogg interests was made January 7, 1924, by Marriott, who wrote:

"The Alhambra Advocate, which has been controlled and managed by B. N. Marriott for the past nine years, yesterday was sold to F. W. Kellogg, E. S. Kellogg and their associates.

"It is with great regret that I announce my retirement from active newspaper work in Alhambra, after this long period of service here, but poor health, the too strenuous work of running a daily newspaper, as well as other important considerations, make this the logical and sensible thing to do.

"Mr. Kellogg and myself both have the same views with regard to the local newspaper field—that, while for a long time there has been strong demand from merchants and readers for a local daily newspaper, the field here is not yet large enough and strong enough to properly support two daily newspapers, and that one strong, well-managed and well-financed paper will better cover the field and give merchants and readers the best service.

"Alhambra has a great future and I believe it is destined to be one of the big cities of the Southland. . . . Its growth will be greatly augmented by the union of the Alhambra Post and the Alhambra Advocate."

A contest was held to select a name for the new publication, with $500 going to the winner. In the meantime, from January 17 to February 11, 1924, the Post and Advocate printed separate issues. Winners of the name contest were Mrs. W. A. Robare and Ralph A. Ruebel, who split the prize money. Both suggested the name of *Post-Advocate*—a combination of the old and the new.

On February 11, 1924, the masthead *Alhambra Post-Advocate* appeared for the first time. The paper was published in its new plant at 25 South Garfield Avenue. It was circulated with the Los Angeles Express and had an initial press run of 5100. E. S. Kellogg was publisher and general manager. Editor of the Post-Advocate was Clayton I. Ward, who served in that capacity for 28 years.

In his column on Page 1 of the first issue, entitled "Comments As We Pass Along," Ward said in part: "A newspaper can have a mighty big part in the development of a community like this, and can help in a hundred ways to mold the structure of civic life along the right channels. If this kind of newspaper work isn't worth while, we don't know what is. And this is the kind we propose to do. . . ."

The first issue of the Post-Advocate comprised 22 pages, with an eight-column format. Single copies sold for 2 cents. Home delivery was 50 cents a month.

On February 15, 1928, announcement was made of the purchase of the Post-Advocate and other Kellogg newspapers by Col. Ira C. Copley. Thus began a golden chapter in the growth and development of the Post-Advocate. The announcement read:

"Through an agreement consummated today, F. W. and E. S. Kellogg have sold the entire list of Kellogg newspapers, including the Alhambra Post-Advocate, to Col. Ira C. Copley, of Aurora, Ill.

"The transaction embraces the following papers: Alhambra Post-Advocate, Pasadena Evening Post, Monrovia Evening Post, Glendale Daily Press, Eagle Rock Daily Press, Burbank Daily Press, Hollywood News, San

FRONT BUSINESS OFFICE OF POST-ADVOCATE

Fernando Valley News, Sawtelle Evening Tribune, Santa Monica Evening Outlook, Venice Evening Vanguard, Culver City Star-News, Redondo Daily Breeze, Hermosa Daily Breeze and San Pedro Daily News.

"Col. Copley has also purchased the Glendale Evening News and has merged it with the Glendale Press. After today, the consolidated paper will be known as the Glendale News-Press.

"The Glendale papers and the Hollywood News are transferred to the new owner at once. The other Kellogg papers, including the Alhambra Post-Advocate, will remain under the direction and management of the Kellogg interests until they are taken over by Col. Copley on September 1, 1928.

"When all the newspapers pass under the control of Col. Copley, they will be known as Southern California Newspapers, Associated. Samuel G. McClure, one of the owners of the Glendale News, will be the president and general manager of that corporation.

"E. S. Kellogg, now general manager of the Alhambra Post-Advocate, will be president of the Alhambra Publishing Co., and a considerable stock-

251

holder in that company, and will continue as general manager of the newspaper when the change becomes effective September 1.

"F. W. Kellogg, whose vision and energy founded and developed the properties that have borne his name, will become, on September 1, vice president of The Copley Press, the corporation which owns Col. Copley's newspapers in Elgin, Aurora and Joliet, Ill., and will be the holding company for the stockholders of The San Diego Union and Tribune of San Diego, Calif., the Illinois State Journal of Springfield, Ill., and probably other properties.

"Col. Copley has been the successful owner of newspapers in Aurora, Elgin and Joliet for many years. He also was the controlling owner of large public utilities in that section. More than two years ago, he sold all his public utilities and now has no interests except his newspapers, to which exclusively he proposes to devote his time and energies.

"In this connection, it is important to say unequivocally and with emphasis that neither Col. Copley, nor any of those associated with him in the ownership and management of his newspapers, have any interests except those embraced in the newspaper business.

"The Copley newspapers in Illinois have been noted for years for their high quality, their broad spirit and fairness to all classes and interests, and their faithful service to the communities in which they are published. The same principles will control and animate his newspapers in California."

The Post-Advocate then was published at 47-51 South Garfield Avenue. On September 1, 1928, the formal change of ownership took place. A Page 1 box read:

"With today's issue of the Alhambra Post-Advocate, E. S. Kellogg becomes president and general manager of this newspaper.

"Today marks the consummation [of the sale] of the Alhambra Post-Advocate by F. W. Kellogg to Col. Ira C. Copley.

"The only changes contemplated by the new management are those involved in producing a larger and more complete newspaper.

"No change will be made in the personnel and the Post-Advocate will continue to vigorously support those things inaugurated to benefit this city and community."

A major change, however, soon was in the making when, on November 6, 1928, it was announced that the Post-Advocate planned to sever all ties with the Los Angeles Express, as of January 1, 1929. An announcement to Post-Advocate readers said:

"It is with great pleasure that the Alhambra Post-Advocate herewith announces the discontinuance of its combination circulation arrangement with the Los Angeles Evening Express, to take effect on or about January 1, 1929.

"That is, on or about that date the Post-Advocate will be delivered alone to its subscribers—there will be no other paper accompanying it.

"In other words, the Alhambra Post-Advocate has reached a point in its career when it is complete in itself and no longer requires a Los Angeles newspaper to supplement its news or features."

Subscription rate was 50 cents a month.

Yes, the Post-Advocate finally had grown up. Now it was ready to stand on its own feet in one of the most competitive newspaper fields in the entire world.

Even bigger and more important decisions were in the making, most important of which was the one to erect a new and modern $300,000 earthquake-proof building at 11 South Stoneman Avenue. But before the project reached the blueprint stage, E. S. Kellogg announced his retirement.

A news story on May 3, 1930, said that Kellogg, publisher and general manager of the Post-Advocate since it was established on February 11, 1924, had resigned to take a rest and to travel in the East.

Named to succeed Kellogg was E. F. Elfstrom, who came to Alhambra from the Hollywood News, where he was in charge of national advertising. The change in publishers was put into effect on May 5, 1930. Elfstrom began his newspaper career as private secretary to E. W. Scripps, founder of the Scripps-Howard Newspapers.

Under Elfstrom, the Post-Advocate moved into its new home, where the newspaper still is published, and marked the occasion with a 70-page souvenir edition on September 8, 1930. The dedication of the Post-Advocate Building was one of the largest and most colorful community celebrations in Alhambra history.

Elfstrom remained at the helm of the Post-Advocate until May 7, 1934, when he resigned to become general business manager of the John P. Scripps Newspapers.

Named to succeed him was H. C. Burkheimer, advertising manager of the Post-Advocate. Burkheimer joined the Post-Advocate on February 1,

E. F. ELFSTROM
Publisher, 1930-34

H. C. BURKHEIMER
Publisher, 1934-40

1931. Prior to that time, he was promotion manager of the Hollywood Citizen.

Burkheimer served as publisher and general manager until October 1, 1940, when he left the Post-Advocate to become publisher of the Glendale News-Press. P. E. (Pete) Ritcha, advertising manager, succeeded Burkheimer as publisher and general manager, while Barton Heiligers, now publisher of the Post-Advocate, was promoted to advertising manager.

At Glendale, Burkheimer succeeded William S. Kellogg, who had resigned to devote his entire time as executor of the estate of his father, F. W. Kellogg.

Ritcha, the new Post-Advocate publisher, joined the newspaper on August 8, 1935, in the capacity of local advertising manager. He came to Alhambra from Long Beach, where for two years he served on the advertising staff of the Press-Telegram and Sun. He broke into the newspaper field in 1917 on the Porterville (Calif.) Messenger. A year after joining the Post-Advocate, Ritcha was named general advertising manager.

Ritcha continued as publisher until his untimely death on December 21, 1943. He was only 51 years of age. Death struck swiftly and painlessly after he had retired for the night following a happy evening with his wife, Adelaide, and son, Hal. Death was attributed to a heart attack.

In a by-line article written by Clayton I. Ward, on Page 1, December 22, 1943, a eulogy, which captured the sentiments of his fellow workers, was extended to Ritcha. The article read in part:

"We at the Post-Advocate always thought of him as 'Pete.' From copy boys to department heads, he was 'Pete.'

"He always had time to listen to our troubles, no matter how trivial they were. He was a big man, of boundless human sympathy. He was sincerely interested in every one of us. . . ."

The vacancy created by the death of Ritcha was filled on January 1, 1944, by the appointment of Alden C. Waite as publisher and general manager of the Post-Advocate. He came to the Post-Advocate from the Glendale News-Press, where he had been editor.

Alden Waite, the son of Clark F. Waite, was born in Santa Ana and is a graduate of Pomona College. He at one time was a co-publisher of the Westwood Hills Press.

Under Waite's régime, the newspaper dropped *Alhambra* from its

P. E. RITCHA
Publisher, 1940-43

CLAYTON I. WARD
Editor, 1924-52

masthead and became known as the Post-Advocate. This was done on April 19, 1945, in recognition of the continued growth of communities adjacent to Alhambra and the desire of the newspaper to serve all of Western San Gabriel Valley as simply the Post-Advocate.

Waite served as publisher until April 19, 1946, when, in a major three-way administrative switch, he was promoted to the position of assistant to the general manager of the Southern California Associated Newspapers, and Barton Heiligers was named to succeed him as publisher. Frank B. Plaisted succeeded Heiligers as advertising manager.

Heiligers still serves the Post-Advocate as publisher and general manager. Under his leadership, the newspaper has taken its greatest strides and today holds an unusually strong position in the field of civic accomplishment.

Heiligers was born in Findlay, O. His first newspaper job was that of proofboy in the advertising department of the Hollywood Citizen. When Burkheimer came to the Post-Advocate in 1931 as advertising manager, Heiligers was not long in following him. Again he held the unexalted job of proofboy in the advertising department of the newspaper that in 1946 he was destined to publish.

Heiligers did not remain long as proofboy, however, and soon was promoted to display advertising salesman. In 1933, he left the Post-Advocate to become advertising director of the North Hollywood Sun-Record. Later he was on the advertising staff of Variety and in 1935 joined the Monrovia News-Post as an advertising salesman.

In 1936, he returned to the Post-Advocate display advertising department and, on October 1, 1940, was promoted to advertising manager. At the time he was only 31 years old.

Under his leadership, the Post-Advocate has won numerous national awards in the fields of advertising and journalistic excellence.

Death struck at the ownership of the Post-Advocate on November 2, 1947, when Col. Copley died at the age of 83, thus relinquishing the reins of The Copley Press to his son, James S. Copley, who continues to build and expand the Copley newspapers.

In an editorial in the Post-Advocate, on November 4, 1947, following the Colonel's death, he was quoted as saying: "Strive always to please yourself, and if your heart is right, you will please more people than if you tried to please everybody."

The Post-Advocate, from its inception as a daily, has had only three

POST-ADVOCATE'S MODERN BUILDING

men at the helm of its editorial department. Clayton I. Ward devoted most of the active years of his life to building the Post-Advocate to its present position of community leadership. He served as its first editor and was associated with practically every civic movement until illness forced his retirement on July 26, 1946. Until his death, on February 2, 1952, his name was carried in the Post-Advocate flag as editor.

On Ward's retirement, active control of the Post-Advocate newsroom fell upon the shoulders of Gilbert Fletcher, who was named managing editor. He resigned on October 29, 1948, to accept a position with the Los Angeles Times.

Warner Jenkins succeeded Fletcher as managing editor and continues in that capacity at the time of this writing. Jenkins first joined the Copley organization as a mailer on the Redondo Daily Breeze in January, 1932.

DON'T DELAY THE PRESS STARTER, BOYS!

Kneeling, left to right, Barton Heiligers, editor and publisher; Larry Benjamin, mechanical superintendent; Sam Valentine, stereotyping foreman; James Richardson, head pressman. Standing, Warner Jenkins, managing editor; Andrew J. Davidson, auditor; Cornelio Baca, display advertising manager; Jack Hathaway, classified advertising manager; S. W. Hensler, circulation manager.

He broke into the editorial field on the same newspaper as a cub reporter in 1936.

Cornelio Baca is display advertising manager and Jack Hathaway is classified advertising manager. Andrew J. Davidson is auditor; S. W. Hensler, circulation manager; Larry Benjamin, mechanical superintendent; Sam Valentine, stereotyping foreman, and James Richardson, head pressman.

Approximately 150 industries of varying sizes maintain plants in Alhambra. These firms employ more than 6000 workers, with an annual payroll in excess of $15,000,000. Small areas of industrially-zoned land are available, but no large tracts remain. Of the 6000 employed, about 30 percent reside in Alhambra.

Significant in the industrial composition of the community is its diversification. There are two foundries, an oil refinery manufacturer, machine and tool shops, a mattress factory, lumber companies, manufacturers of food products, welding plants, cabinet shops, small steel plants and others.

Many manufacturers hold defense contracts, but none relies upon them completely. Such diversification of industry means that collapse, temporary or permanent, of a single industry would not deal a death blow to the city's economic structure.

Property taxes from Alhambra industry and business make up 45 percent of the total collected in the city. Alhambra has a tax rate of $1.655 on $100 assessed valuation. It is the third lowest tax rate among Los Angeles County's 45 incorporated cities.

The Post-Advocate is printed on a Hoe press with 48-page capacity. It has a maximum speed of 50,000 newspapers hourly.

The composing room contains 10 line-casting machines, which include three teletypesetter-equipped Linotypes, two Intertype mixers for ad composition, one model 22 Linotype for heads and four for general and straight ad matter.

One of the teletype-equipped machines is the Mergenthaler Blue Streak Comet that sets editorial straight matter and classified ads at the rate of 12 lines a minute. The Comet also can be operated from a tape-controlled signal. Three teletype perforators punch all straight matter and 90 percent of classified for the teletype-equipped Linotypes. Other equipment includes three metal trimmer saws, one Elrod slug-casting machine for manufacture of the shop's own base and rule material, and one Ludlow for large head type and figures as well as text in ads.

A makeup table system is employed. Making up on turtles has proved impractical because of cramped quarters in the composing room. Two 12-foot makeup tables, designed by Benjamin, mechanical superintendent, are used also for storage space. A Morrison slug-stripper saves 75 percent of the time usually needed to make up angle type or boxer ads.

The Post-Advocate was one of the first newspapers on the Pacific Coast to pioneer in the field of teletypesetting. Perforators first were installed in 1948 and in the subsequent five-year period the Post-Advocate has seen dozens of other newspapers follow its lead to embrace teletypesetter operation.

In the words of Publisher Heiligers: "We look to the future with faith and confidence. The greatest chapters in the history of the Post-Advocate are yet to be written. Those of us who make up the flesh and blood of this newspaper dedicate ourselves to make those chapters synonymous with the communities we serve in the best tradition of those who marched before us."

BURBANK  REVIEW

"The Oldest Daily Newspaper in the San Fernando Valley"

BURBANK BUILT ON SITE OF PASTURES AND VINEYARDS

HUGH B. BAUMBERGER
Editor and Publisher, Burbank Daily Review
Vice President, Southern California Associated Newspapers

Burbank Daily Review

220 East Orange Grove   Burbank, Calif.

THE BURBANK DAILY REVIEW is the latest addition to The Copley Press. Purchased May 1, 1950, from Harvey R. Ling, it is a unit of the Southern California Associated Newspapers. Improvement of the newspaper was started immediately. During the first few months of the Copley ownership, the Review was under the direction of Carroll W. Parcher, editor and publisher of the Glendale News-Press, operating from the Glendale office. On September 1, 1950, Hugh Baumberger was appointed publisher of the Review.

Rapid strides have been made by the Review since its acquisition by COPRESS. Notable gains have been recorded in circulation and advertising. The news content has been greatly enlarged and improved and mechanical equipment has been augmented.

The Review is keyed to keep pace with the rapid growth of the community it serves. Burbank, according to the 1950 census, had a population of 78,577 and the Chamber of Commerce estimated it at 85,000 in the summer of 1952.

The town of Burbank was laid out on the historic Spanish land grant of Rancho la Providencia. This great rancho, which consisted of 17,000 acres, was divided among the Spanish heirs who had a legitimate claim at the time the U. S. government settled the rancho claims throughout this area. As a result of this action, Dr. David Burbank, a congenial and well-loved early-day settler, obtained the title to 4000 acres of Rancho Providencia. He, with others, began to make plans for the city that later was to be named after him.

In 1886, Dr. Burbank sold his land holdings to the Providencia Land,

Water & Development Co. The town of Burbank came into being the following year, on May 1, 1887, and was advertised with descriptive phrases, such
as "Land and ocean, mountain and valley, sunshine and shade, offer here
their choicest benefactions to prolong the lives of the feeble and enhance
the enjoyment of the robust."

The Burbank San Fernando Valley News, whose namesake was consolidated with the Burbank Review in 1952, had its inception in 1886, about
the time the City of Burbank was laid out. Its early editions recorded the
transactions leading up to the founding of the city.

It was not until 19 years later, on June 23, 1905, that the residents of the
then sleepy little town first read the Burbank Review. Published every Friday
by E. M. McClure and J. F. Boughton, the tiny four-column, four-page newspaper carried in its first issue the following announcement:

"With this, the initial number of the Review, the publishers present
to the people of Burbank what they believe to be a representative of the
town and community in a business and social sense. The substantial response
to business propositions, and the many cheering words of encouragement
from the citizens of Burbank, lead us to believe that the greater majority of
our citizens are fully alive to the need of a representative local paper for
this section. The publishers are experienced newspapermen and will devote
their entire time in endeavoring to promote the general welfare of the citizens
and the prosperity of the community. We have no favors to ask, but will
naturally expect the people to give the paper the support which it may
deserve!"

With that announcement, the Burbank Review was launched into an
uncertain field in a town of less than 1000, completely overshadowed by
Los Angeles, and offering little more than salubrious climate and fertile soil.

The Burbank Review, in its first issue, was dedicated to the good of
the community. Over the years since the founding of the weekly newspaper,
through nearly a half century of continuous publication, the Review has
campaigned for many projects of civic betterment.

Among them was the fight that many communities in the vicinity of
Los Angeles had carried on over the years and lost—that of opposing hydra-
headed schemes that popped up for the annexation of Burbank to the City
of Los Angeles. The Review and loyal local citizens fought annexation at
every turn, not once but several times, and won each time. As a result,
Burbank is the "queen city of the San Fernando Valley," in that it has

THE VALLEY NEWS
Established in 1886

FIRST BURBANK REVIEW
Founded June 23, 1905

prospered under its own corporate government as the largest incorporated city in the valley and one of two cities throughout the broad valley that have remained separate from Los Angeles.

In the early days of settlement and booming development of the valley, many communities sprang up, each with an old and distinguished history. All but Burbank and San Fernando have disappeared in the melting pot of a sprawling metropolitan conglomeration that extends for many miles from Los Angeles Civic Center. Names harkening back to early-day settlements, such as Lankershim, Van Nuys, Monte Vista, Cahuenga, Calabasas, Canoga Park, Reseda and Chatsworth, today designate communities in name only, for politically these communities are parts of a great metropolitan city miles away.

Following the real estate boom of more than a half century ago, about 60 communities in Los Angeles County were being promoted by speculators. Many towns folded because they were not promoted on a sound basis. Others, like Burbank, took hold and became solid communities because, as it was stated in one of the issues of a Burbank newspaper in the late 1890's, "Burbank is noted for its solid growth and for not having a brass band and promoters selling land," as was the common practice of the day.

McClure was publisher of the Review until December, 1911, when he relinquished control to H. E. Lawrence. Lawrence changed the format to six columns and increased column length from a small to medium-sized tabloid. Burbank was incorporated as a city in 1911. After the death of Lawrence, his wife took over the management of the newspaper and continued to publish it as a weekly until 1916. Mrs. Lawrence, in January, 1953, was residing in La Tuna Canyon, near Burbank, and was 96 years old.

On October 14, 1916, the names of Samuel M. Green and C. M. Brosius appeared on the masthead of the Review as publisher and manager, respectively. Green was replaced by Charles E. Salisbury as publisher on February 23, 1917, and a year later Brosius became both editor and publisher.

Meanwhile, Burbank was undergoing a change which marked the beginning of an era of development so overshadowing in its importance as to make other periods of growth seem petty. By 1916, a city hall had been built and a fire truck had been purchased. The high school was given additional equipment to care for its enrollment, which totaled 100. By this time, also, the population had passed the 1500 mark by a considerable margin. Manufacturing rapidly was becoming the outstanding activity of the community, and agriculture was passing.

The enterprise of the community, as reflected in later issues of the Burbank Review, was shown by the aggressiveness and initiative characteristics of local businessmen when they sought their first major factory. It was the Moreland truck factory, which was preparing to move from Los Angeles to Alhambra. Hearing of the plan, a group of Burbank businessmen hastily gathered and called on Watt Moreland, who at that moment was in conference with representatives of Alhambra. The deal apparently was wrapped up for Alhambra. Unable to impress the receptionist that time was of the essence, the leader of the Burbank delegation went out and bought a box of candy and presented the girl at the desk with this bit of bribery for an immediate interview with Moreland. The Burbank delegation succeeded in gaining an audience, offered a tract of land free for the motor truck plant, and soon the Moreland concern forgot Alhambra and located in Burbank. This incident was the forerunner of many more successful efforts to persuade industrial concerns to establish plants in Burbank.

Following the opening of Burbank's industrial régime by the More-

BURBANK DAILY REVIEW BUILDING

land Motor Truck Co., which established its 25-acre plant in 1917, other large concerns came to Burbank in the ensuing 10 years. Among them were the Andrew Jergens Co., Libby, McNeill & Libby, Empire China Co., First National Pictures, Inc., and 23 others, whose combined products number more than 60—all bearing the stamp "Made in Burbank."

Pages of the Burbank Review disclose that the industrial boom continued and to this day it has failed to stop. Four reasons given in the Review for the location of so many industries in Burbank are:

1—The ideal location—the reason the townsite was chosen in the first place by the Providencia Co. Situated on accessible high land at the junction of the valley and coast lines of the Southern Pacific and at the southeasterly entrance to the great San Fernando Valley, Burbank, with its extensive switching facilities and its broad boulevard connections, offers to industry the shortest average cost distance to a nearby consuming market numbered in the millions.

2—The abundance, cheapness and softness of its water. Recognizing the Burbank water as especially adapted for steam engine use, the Southern Pacific Railroad early chose Burbank water for its locomotives.

3—The community's proximity to supplies of natural gas, crude oil and electric power.

4—Its offer of ideal living conditions within walking distance of the industrial zone. Here the manufacturer may enjoy the quiet of home atmosphere in an exclusive residential district, and yet be within the sound range of his own factory whistle. Backing this point, the Alderman Industrial Survey was quoted as saying: "The keystone of Burbank's industrial peace and sustained attraction of the highest types of workers are conditions that afford mutual opportunities to both employers and employes. Burbank offers more and better homesites for the average worker nearer to its industrial zone and possesses more industrial sites situated along railway lines

HARVEY R. LING
Review Publisher, 1920-50

than are available at any residential-industrial suburb of equal distance from the center of the metropolitan population."

The Burbank Review grew with the city. Early in 1919, J. B. Welch and A. P. Welch purchased the growing weekly newspaper. J. B. Welch became editor and A. P. Welch business manager. Their tenure was brief. They were succeeded by W. P. Coffman, who took charge on May 2, 1919, and continued as editor and publisher until November, 1920. With the exception of a few years, when he served as postmaster, Coffman has continuously worked for the Review. At the present (1953), he can be seen at his composing room post, where he works on a part-time basis.

On November 1, 1920, the Review was purchased by Bert R. Greer and Harvey R. Ling. Ling became publisher and held that title until May 1, 1950.

Under Ling's management, the Review showed steady early develop-

LOCAL NEWS GETS BIG PLAY ON PAGE 1

ment. First step was absorption of the Pathfinder, another weekly. Additional issues of both the Review and Pathfinder were printed each week. Later, two more issues of the Review were introduced and eventually the two issues of the Pathfinder were absorbed by the Review, which became a six-day daily on November 2, 1926.

Prior to April 30, 1920, the Review was published at 123 East Second Street. At the time the Ling management took over the Review, the newspaper was housed in a small building at 330 East Second Street, with a plant which included one Linotype, two job presses and a small newspaper press. In 1921, three men were employed.

On April 28, 1924, the plant was moved into its own new building at the present location, 220 East Orange Grove. The building is one story, with 50-foot frontage and a depth of 100 feet. On December 16, 1926, the Review went from a standard seven-column to a standard eight-column newspaper.

By 1930, the composing room equipment was increased by three additional Linotypes, a web newspaper press, Ludlow type-casting machine and other modern printing machinery. The number of employes had been increased to 52, including 29 carriers, and the annual payroll approached $50,000.

In June, 1930, the subscription list of the Burbank Daily Tribune was taken over by the Review and became part of the newspaper's subscribers.

The Burbank Review weathered the storm of competition through the years and effected consolidations with many local publications. Among these were the Burbank Independent, the Burbank Pathfinder, edited by Lynn Monroe, who later became one of the city's first historians; the Burbank Tribune, the San Fernando Valley Tribune, and more recently the Magnolia Park News and the Sun Valley News. The latest major consolidation was with the weekly Burbank News, which was issued as a standard-size newspaper for 10 years, from 1942 to 1952. The Burbank News was bought by Southern California Associated Newspapers in January, 1952, from James O. Linter and Associates, and was merged with the Review, which had been purchased on May 1, 1950, from Harvey Ling and the Greer estate.

On September 1, 1950, four months after the Review was purchased by SCAN, Hugh Baumberger was made publisher. Baumberger, a native of Kansas, was educated in Idaho and at the University of Southern California. He joined The Copley Press in 1928, when he became advertising manager of the Culver City Star-News. He was manager of the advertising sales production for SCAN from 1944 to 1950, when he assumed his present

THESE MEN DIRECT OPERATION OF BURBANK DAILY REVIEW

Hugh Baumberger, editor and publisher, is seated at left. Also at desk is Charles C. Christian, advertising manager. Standing, left to right, Thomas J. Hageman, managing editor; Warren L. Taylor, auditor and credit manager; Ed Dunn, classified advertising manager, and W. D. Hopkins, circulation manager.

position as editor and publisher of the Review. At one time he was connected with the Los Angeles Times.

Department heads of the Review are Thomas J. Hageman, managing editor; Charles C. Christian, advertising manager; Ed Dunn, classified manager; Warren L. Taylor, auditor and credit manager, and W. D. Hopkins, circulation manager.

In the composing room, the type-casting equipment consists of five machines in the news department and two mixers and one Ludlow type-caster in the ad alley. One news machine is equipped with a teletypesetter for tape operation. In addition are one strip-casting machine, a mitering machine and two saws.

In the stereotype department is one set of tubular plate-casting equipment, including a casting box, finishing machine, router and vacuum mat-drying machine. The flat-casting department consists of a casting box, two routers, a ruffer and a saw. The mats are made on a Goss 32-inch mat roller. All plates are cast out of a 2000-pound gas-fired metal pot. The press is a 16-page Duplex tubular high speed two-deck, rotary type, capable of producing 30,000 16-page papers an hour. The Review is published five weekdays, omitting Saturday.

In major accomplishments, which have resulted in many important industries locating in Burbank, the Chamber of Commerce and other civic organizations have had the hearty co-operation of the Burbank Review. It was through the efforts of a special committee of Chamber of Commerce leaders, including the Review publisher of that day, that Lockheed Aircraft Corp., first known as Loughead, came to Burbank from Hollywood, where it had been located temporarily after moving from Santa Barbara. In 1932, a group of businessmen purchased a struggling airplane manufacturing plant located near the Burbank Airport and the present-day Lockheed Aircraft Corp., destined to become the city's largest single industry, was started.

Later the Review, in co-operation with civic leaders and the Chamber of Commerce, launched a campaign for an air terminal in Burbank and, as a result, Lockheed Airport was established here. It was the principal airport for the Los Angeles area until the City of Los Angeles developed International Airport near Inglewood, on the western side of the city. Lockheed Airport has continued to grow in importance and, because of its freedom from excessive fog and unfavorable atmospheric conditions, is used frequently by air liners when the other major airports are fogbound.

Since 1938, Burbank has been bursting at its seams keeping up with the astonishing growth which gave it the title of "Fastest growing city in America." Defense production shot the moderate-sized Lockheed Corp. into a gigantic arsenal of freedom which at its peak during World War II employed nearly 100,000 persons. People by the thousands flocked to Burbank and homes were built as fast as carpenters could do the job.

Today the once vast grazing lands for cattle and sheep and the sprawling green vineyards, which were among the first to produce sparkling California wines, are entirely replaced by homes, factories and business establishments. Not an acre in Burbank today is under commercial cultivation.

Burbank never has stood still. As each generation thought the city had surely reached its peak of growth, the next generation calmly forged ahead.

CULVER CITY

Evening Star-News

"For a Greater La Ballona Valley"

VENICE

Evening Vanguard

"For a Greater Beach Area"

CULVER CITY, POPULATION 30,000, KEEPS GROWING

ROBERT L. CURRY
Editor and Publisher, Evening Star-News and Evening Vanguard
Vice President, Southern California Associated Newspapers

274

Evening Star-News

4043 Irving Place   Culver City, Calif.

Evening Vanguard

1916 Lincoln Boulevard   Venice, Calif.

THE CULVER CITY STAR-NEWS and the Venice Evening Vanguard were built on dreams—dreams of great development of the communities in which they were launched. In most respects, the dreams have come true. The growth and progress of Culver City and Venice have been remarkable. Of course, disappointments have occurred and difficult years were encountered, especially in the pioneering days of the newspapers and later during the depression. But through hard work and devotion to the public interest, the two newspapers, which are operated jointly, have grown and prospered with the communities they serve.

Both are printed at the Star-News plant, at 4043 Irving Place, Culver City, but they are separate newspapers. The Evening Vanguard is the older publication, having been established June 22, 1907, while the Star-News came into being on October 20, 1927, through a merger of the Culver City Star and the Culver City News. The Star was established in 1923. The News was started by F. W. Kellogg in 1925 as an adjunct to the Venice Vanguard. The Culver City News at the outset was printed at the Vanguard plant and was circulated in Culver City, but the Vanguard mechanical operation was closed late in 1929 and the place of publication was changed to Culver City, where the Vanguard since has been printed. Offices of the Vanguard are maintained in Venice.

The Vanguard and early Culver City newspapers were started in connection with real estate promotions in two communities, which lay five miles apart, and which since have grown to such extent that they have merged actually, if not politically.

Culver City is a municipal entity, whereas Venice, in 1925, became a part of the City of Los Angeles. The Culver City-Venice district, lying west of Los Angeles proper, spreads over La Ballona Valley and extends westward to the Pacific Ocean. It includes the one-time town of Palms, which now also is a part of Los Angeles, and the thriving business and residential Mar Vista area. The tributary region also includes Playa del Rey and a portion of Ocean Park, as well as Beverly Wood, Cheviot Hills, Westside Village, Westdale and Studio Village. All this area—then open fields—was embraced by Rancho la Ballona and its neighbor to the east, Rancho Rincon de los Bueyes, which were the earliest white settlements in La Ballona Valley. The post office at Palms, established in 1875, was the first postal facility west of Los Angeles.

Culver City, with a population of approximately 30,000, continues its rapid expansion. It is renowned as the home of Metro-Goldwyn-Mayer, the world's largest motion picture studio. Also located at Culver City are the RKO and Hal Roach Studios, while nearby is 20th Century-Fox.

Following World War II, industrial plants situated in the vicinity were enlarged and new enterprises were established, contributing notably to the growth and prosperity of Culver City. Products manufactured in this area include aircraft instruments, aircraft fittings and accessories, army and navy communication equipment, house trailers, heating appliances, automobile motors and exhausts, tools and dies, musical toys, ceramics, relays and switches, bottle and can openers, plastics, ball-point pens, shoe polish, leather merchandise, bakery goods and electric motors for model railroads.

The first newspaper in La Ballona Valley, a four-page glossy sheet named the Palms News, was edited by a nurseryman, Sirell C. Perrine, and W. A. Rennie. The initial number was issued on December 22, 1906. Perrine, who also was active in civic affairs in the Palms area, continued as publisher, except for a short period late in 1907 and early in 1908, until the newspaper suspended on December 31, 1910. Rennie left the Palms News soon after its inception to found the Venice Vanguard.

Perrine and Rennie, who joined forces to exert influence "for the betterment and improvement of the conditions at The Palms," as was stated in an editorial in the first issue, later devoted their energies to the promotion of Culver City and Venice. Shortly after Harry C. Culver formed the Culver Investment Co., on July 25, 1913, Perrine started a weekly, the Culver City Call. The Culver Investment Co. proposed to subdivide a portion of the Palms area lying between Los Angeles and the beach and to build a

MUNICIPAL SWIMMING POOL IN CULVER CITY

well-balanced community, "partly business, partly residential." Culver's associates and influential friends, who comprised the directors and stockholders of the company, christened the community Culver City in honor of its enthusiastic founder. No doubt Perrine was encouraged by the prospect of considerable advertising revenue from the new venture, as Page 1 of the first issue of the Culver City Call, dated November 1, 1913, was devoted to photographs of Culver's realty officials and staff, numbering 28.

At the time the Culver Investment Co. was formed, the real estate development of Venice was well on its way. Venice, as a resort city with canals, pavilions and a pier to rival that of Atlantic City, was the dream of Abbot Kinney, who had come to California in 1883, commissioned to investigate conditions of the Mission Indians.

Kinney had acquired, about 1891, an interest in a strip of ocean frontage then considered worthless, in what was known as South Santa Monica. He and his partner, F. G. Ryan, built cottages, planned parks and sidewalks, and gradually developed what became the most popular resort on the beach for a time, the old Ocean Park district. South of this area was an unimproved and apparently useless tract of land to which Kinney took title in January, 1904, and began plans for a Venice of America, with a system of canals for streets. In the beginning, his ideas were regarded with skepticism and were referred to as "Kinney's dream," but it was not long before his project was accepted with enthusiasm. In May, 1904, a map of the Venice View tract, which consisted of 67 lots, was presented to the Board of Trustees of Ocean Park, and a year later work began in earnest.

Canals were dug and were filled with water. A hotel patterned after an Italian villa was planned. A pier, 1700 feet long and 30 feet wide, was designed and contracts were let, at a cost of $300,000, for buildings and other projects. Plans were developed for an auditorium which was to be the finest structure of its kind on the West Coast, and a $100,000 breakwater was constructed to protect the pier from damage by heavy seas.

Among those having a profound belief in the future of Venice as a cultural and recreational center was Rennie, who had been co-founder of the Palms News. With little cash but much perseverance and initiative, he established the Venice Vanguard. The first issue was a four-page, four-column newspaper, 9 by 12 inches.

The canals of Venice have been filled with earth, the once magnificent pier has disappeared, and the elaborate buildings have been razed, but the Vanguard has survived.

The Vanguard first was printed in an unpretentious building on Windward Avenue. There was one chase for type and a second-hand job press, operated by footpower. The press was large enough to print only a page at a time, so every newspaper of four small pages passed through the press four times. Often the editor wrote the news, edited it, set the type, ran the press and sold or distributed the newspapers.

Within a year, a small addition, 20 by 30 feet, was built, a pony press was installed and the size of the newspaper increased to five-column folio.

Rennie's two sons, Walter W. and Robert, joined him in publishing the Vanguard and, in 1910, they became members of the firm. Offices and equipment were moved to larger quarters at the old roller-skating rink of the Abbot Kinney Co., at Trolleway and Lorelei Avenues. Later, a modern printing plant was installed at the corner of Avenue 18 and Mildred Avenue.

The founder of the newspaper, W. A. Rennie, died in 1919, and his

STAR-NEWS USES LOCAL GENEROUSLY ON FRONT PAGE

two sons continued publishing the Vanguard until May, 1920, when they sold it to George W. Tompkins. Walter left the newspaper to devote his time to the practice of law in Venice and later became a police judge. Robert remained with the Vanguard and now is a member of the Star-News staff.

Tompkins was publisher of the Vanguard for two years. In June, 1922, he sold the newspaper to F. W. Kellogg and E. A. Dickson, at which time it became part of the group of Kellogg newspapers.

When Kellogg became owner of the newspaper, he also assumed control of most of the editorial policies. Many are the stories of his eccentricities and the resoluteness of his beliefs. For example, he had an unbreakable rule against smoking in the office. Robert L. Curry, editor and publisher of the Star-News and Vanguard, relates that Kellogg walked into the office one day just before deadline and observed a man he thought was a member of the staff, smoking a cigar of an obnoxious aroma. Without a word, Kellogg stomped to the man's side, jerked the cigar from his mouth and threw it on the floor. The supposed staff member was the newspaper's best advertiser. Fortunately, the victim of Kellogg's wrath had a sense of humor.

Kellogg had been sold on the future of Culver City by its founder, Harry Culver. He could visualize the eventual merging of the boundaries of Culver City and Venice. As a result, Kellogg started the Culver City News. Kellogg later selected as editor of the newspaper a young man who

ADMINISTRATION BUILDING OF M-G-M STUDIOS

HOME OF EVENING STAR-NEWS AT 4043 IRVING PLACE

was city editor of the Santa Monica Evening Outlook. He was William Shea, who now is associate publisher and general manager of The San Diego Union and Evening Tribune.

Shea, a veteran of World War I, had been a reporter on New York State newspapers prior to locating in California. He joined the Santa Monica Outlook staff as a reporter in 1923 and later became city editor. He was appointed editor of the Star-News in December, 1927.

By 1923, seven newspapers were published for Culver City residents. Among them was the Star, published by William Smith in a small structure on Cardiff Avenue. This was the only newspaper, aside from the Vanguard, that survived competition. While others died along the way, the Star flourished.

Kellogg decided that only one newspaper was necessary to serve Culver City and Venice, so, in 1927, he bought the Star from Smith and combined it with the News. The name of the newspaper was chosen following a contest among readers, and the combined newspaper henceforth was known as

PLENTY OF PICTURES DRESS UP EVENING VANGUARD

the Culver City Star-News. Kellogg then built a small newspaper plant at 4023 Irving Place, adjoining the present site of the Star-News Building.

On January 1, 1928, Col. Ira C. Copley purchased the Star-News and the Vanguard, along with other Kellogg newspapers. He reorganized operations and made Shea publisher of the Star-News in 1929 and of the Vanguard at a later date.

Col. Copley, from the time of his first visit to Culver City, had been aware of the possibilities of great growth of the area. He once visited Culver City with J. F. Sartori, well-known banker. They were close friends. It was their prediction that Culver City eventually would be a large city. The population at that time was less than 1000.

When the picturesque canals of Venice were filled as part of a mosquito-control program, and the development of oil-producing wells in the vicinity resulted in pollution of the beaches, the area lost its appeal to summer visitors and many Venice businessmen were forced to close their stores. The Vanguard's advertising patronage dwindled and its circulation declined. Mechanical operations finally were discontinued in Venice, as an economy measure, in November, 1929, and the Vanguard was produced at the Star-News plant. It was only because Col. Copley had faith in the future of Venice that the Vanguard was not suspended.

In the spring of 1949, offices were established for the Vanguard on Lincoln Boulevard in Venice and an intensive circulation campaign put the beach paper on its feet.

The Star-News also faced many critical days during the long uphill struggle of Culver City's development into a modern community. One of the chief problems during Shea's tenure as editor and publisher was fighting off repeated attempts by Los Angeles politicians to force annexation of Culver City. Methods which had been successful in effecting annexation of Venice to Los Angeles were tried, but, due to Shea's foresight, annexation was defeated.

Another campaign was aimed at weeding out corruption in city government. Recall elections against city officials were allowed only every six months and a new recall movement was launched almost as soon as the law permitted. One of Culver City's judges, for example, gained nationwide notoriety by ordering the arrest of motorists who committed even the slightest infractions of the law and, as a result, drivers for years purposely bypassed the community. It ultimately was revealed that the judge was involved in illegal practices in levying fines on the unfortunate offenders. After this disclosure, the judge was dismissed and punished by the courts.

During the depression, the Star-News expanded its shopping editions and eventually shopper distribution extended into Beverly Hills and the

RKO RADIO PICTURES AND PATHE STUDIO, CULVER CITY

Wilshire-Western district. The newspaper also led a series of campaigns to encourage home-building and, following World War II, was instrumental in bringing a number of industrial plants to the community.

When Shea was appointed publisher of the San Pedro News-Pilot, on February 1, 1946, Robert L. Curry, who had been advertising manager, was made editor and publisher of the Culver City Star-News and Venice Vanguard.

Curry was born in Dayton, O., but most of his life has been spent in California. He started newspaper work as a carrier boy on the Fresno Bee, and later became a district circulation manager in Fresno. He attended Fresno State College. Curry joined The Copley Press on May 30, 1928, as district circulation manager on the Glendale News-Press. Late in 1929, he went to the Monrovia News-Post as circulation manager and, in 1930, was transferred to the Hollywood News, then a Copley newspaper. He became circulation manager of the Star-News and Vanguard the following year and, in 1937, was appointed advertising manager of the two newspapers. He thus was well grounded in newspaper work and was thoroughly acquainted with the Culver City-Venice field when he was named publisher.

In April, 1949, the Star-News moved into its present modern one-story building, which contains more than 10,000 square feet of floor space. The

AT STAR-NEWS AND VANGUARD CONFERENCE TABLE

Left to right, David J. Duncan, business manager; Earl V. Leavitt, composing room foreman; Arthur Carlson, classified advertising manager; Robert L. Curry, editor and publisher; Herbert Gulick, display advertising manager; Donald R. Vaughan, managing editor; Denny C. Hough, circulation manager; Lester Robinson, Evening Vanguard manager.

newspaper is printed on a four-deck, 32-page Goss rotary press, with color equipment. The press was acquired from the Illinois State Journal and Register.

Curry, an enthusiastic and energetic editor, is an outstanding foe of communism. In a location which from time to time has been beset by various shades of pink endeavors, he publishes a newspaper which reflects his vigorous opposition to all tinges of red and pink.

Department heads are Donald R. Vaughan, managing editor; Herbert Gulick, display advertising manager; Arthur Carlson, classified advertising manager; David J. Duncan, business manager; Denny C. Hough, circulation manager, and Earl V. Leavitt, composing room foreman. Lester Robinson is manager of the Evening Vanguard.

Some of these men are old-timers with the organization. Leavitt joined the Vanguard as foreman in 1919. Duncan started as a carrier. Carlson's service dates from 1926. Robert Rennie, son of W. A. Rennie, founder of the Vanguard, has been on the staff for nearly 25 years, as has Harry Roe.

Among distinguished newspapermen who once worked on the Star-News are Hal Forrest, who started his famous comic strip, "Tailspin Tommy," during his employment on the newspaper; Russell Brines, once on the staff of the Vanguard and now a top Associated Press foreign correspondent; Rembert James, one-time head of The Associated Press Moscow bureau, and now with The San Diego Union, and Tom Bernard, who won acclaim with the Stars and Stripes and American Magazine.

James S. Copley, upon graduation from Yale in 1939, gained his first practical newspaper experience on the Star-News, doing stints in advertising, circulation, editorial work and management.

The Star-News is the only daily newspaper serving Culver City and surrounding area. Its growth has kept pace with the rapid expansion of the community. It has contributed immeasurably to the development of a city that is well-balanced by industry and homes.

Glendale News-Press

"A Good Paper to Come Home To"

GLENDALE, WITH VERDUGO HILLS IN BACKGROUND

CARROLL W. PARCHER
Editor and Publisher, Glendale News-Press
Vice President, Southern California Associated Newspapers

288

Glendale News-Press

111 North Isabel Street   Glendale, Calif.

THE GLENDALE NEWS-PRESS, only daily newspaper published in Glendale, Calif., a city of 104,000 (1953), acquired its name through the merger, on February 15, 1928, of the Glendale Evening News and the Glendale Daily Press, both published daily except Sunday.

The predecessor of the Glendale Evening News was the Glendale News, the pioneer publication in the Glendale field. It was a weekly, first issued on May 1, 1905. It was published continuously from that date until August 23, 1913, when it began its career as a daily with the change of name to the Glendale Evening News.

The Glendale Daily Press was the outgrowth of the Glendale Press, a weekly, which began publication in May, 1910, and was issued regularly from that date until March 1, 1921, when it was converted into a daily.

The community which was the nucleus of today's City of Glendale just was beginning to realize its own potentialities in the rapidly expanding empire of Southern California when the Glendale News was established. Development of the Glendale Valley had its start in the 1880's and has continued steadily since then, despite occasional setbacks.

By 1905, business districts had become established on Glendale Avenue and on Brand Boulevard, in the general vicinity of what now is Broadway and then was Fourth Street. Railway connections with Los Angeles, together with tract promotions, were bringing new residents to Glendale in numbers which assured permanence of the community. A union high school and some elementary schools helped to make Glendale attractive to families with children. Two banks were about to open, a public library soon was to start under guidance of a group of civic-minded women, and it would be only a few months before Glendale would become an incorporated town.

Conditions were ripe for the services of a community newspaper. An unnamed printer from Los Angeles opened a small shop in Glendale in the winter of 1904-05 and thereby helped whet the interest of the Glendale public in the idea of a local newspaper by getting out an occasional news sheet and distributing it free. His place of business was on Glendale Avenue between Broadway and Wilson, then Fourth and Third Streets.

Then E. M. McClure, an experienced newspaperman, came to Glendale, recognized the opportunity, and joined forces with J. F. Boughton to publish a weekly newspaper, which they named the Glendale News. The paper came out each Friday. McClure and Boughton began publication of the News in quarters on the north side of Broadway, two doors west of Glendale Avenue.

In less than six months after establishment of the News, Boughton sold his interest to his partner and by mid-fall of 1905 the weekly was being published by McClure as sole owner. In 1906, he moved to another room, around the corner on Glendale Avenue, in order that Glendale's first Board of Trustees could take over his Broadway location as a board room.

McClure was aggressive and believed a newspaper should take an active part in civic affairs. He was credited with a major role in the success of the campaign for incorporation of Glendale, which was effected in 1906. Wilmot Parcher, father of Carroll W. Parcher, present editor and publisher of the News-Press, became the first mayor. While McClure knew the newspaper business and gained a fair return for his money and effort as publisher, he apparently failed to foresee the greatness of the opportunity confronting him and sold the News, on January

THE

GLENDALE NEWS.

Devoted to the best interests of Glendale, Tropico, Eagle Rock and Verdugo.

VOL. I.   GLENDALE, LOS ANGELES COUNTY, CAL., FRIDAY, JUNE 30, 1905.   NO. 10

EARLY ISSUE OF NEWS, 1905
Forerunner of News-Press

1, 1907, to E. B. Riggs and J. C. Sherer, the latter an early settler in Glendale.

The firm of Riggs & Sherer retained the Glendale Avenue location. In July, 1908, Riggs sold his interest to Sherer. Strangely enough, Sherer was forced to buy out Riggs a second time, his erstwhile partner having started an opposition paper, the Valley Independent, on Brand Boulevard. The two deals with Riggs were made not far apart.

In March, 1913, Sherer sold the News to A. T. Cowan, a newspaper-man from Illinois, who moved the plant from Glendale Avenue to what was known as the Wilson Block on Broadway, just east of Louise Street and

J. C. SHERER
Pioneer Glendale Editor in His Office, 1912

opposite the present site of the Glendale post office. The building became known in more recent years as Townsend Hall, for it was used as a club-house by local Townsend pension plan groups.

Cowan conducted the News as a weekly for only a few months. He converted it into a daily August 23, 1913. The new Glendale Evening News thus had the distinction of being the city's first daily.

The plant that Cowan bought from Sherer consisted of an old cylinder press, two job presses, two or three cases of type and the other usual accessories of a small printing establishment. The employes numbered five.

From the time the News became a daily it grew consistently in circulation and influence and a decade later was housed in a spacious modern three-story building at 139 South Brand. Modern equipment was installed. The Evening News was issued as a paper of anywhere from 10 to 16 pages, employed 75 persons and had a weekly payroll of $2000.

As a sidelight on the progress of the News, mention may be made of a Tropico publication, the Sentinel, which was launched in February, 1911, under leadership of H. W. Melrose, a printer residing in Tropico. N. C. Burch became editor. Burch was connected with the Verdugo Canyon Water Co.

Melrose sold to Burch in June, 1911. Two years later, Burch sold to Harry L. Edwards and soon afterward Mrs. Ella W. Richardson became sole owner, appointing A. J. Van Wie editor and manager. In 1916, the Sentinel passed into the hands of E. C. Gibbs, who named Miss Gertrude Gibbs as editor. In December, 1917, the Sentinel merged with the weekly edition of the Glendale Evening News.

The Glendale News had been growing for five years as a force in community affairs when, in May, 1910, Frank S. Chase, a printer, came to the city from Los Angeles and started the Glendale Press, a four-page weekly, in a small shop on Brand Boulevard. For several months the actual printing of the paper was done in Los Angeles. The editor and proprietor conducted a job printing business, which was the principal source of income at first. However, it was not long before the volume of advertising carried by the Press provided an increasing net return.

As general conditions in Glendale improved, the Press became fairly prosperous. A good plant was accumulated gradually and after a decade of effort Chase had become the owner of a valuable property. The amount of advertising usually was large enough to justify a 16-page paper.

On December 1, 1919, or about six years after the Glendale Evening News started its career as a daily, Chase sold the Press to J. H. Folz, also a printer. Folz operated the Press for approximately six months and then disposed of a part interest to J. W. Usilton, who was well known in Glendale through his connection with the Los Angeles Express and because of his activity in civic affairs.

The paper continued as a weekly for another year, when Folz, Usilton and a number of other Glendale citizens incorporated a publishing company and started the Press on its way as a daily. The first issue of the daily appeared on March 1, 1921. Shortly afterward, Folz sold his interest to Thomas D. Watson, who took over the general management. At the time, Usilton was editor and W. L. Taylor was business manager.

The Daily Press speedily became a profitable venture. In May, 1921, a Duplex double web press, with a capacity of 3600 papers an hour, was installed. The new press solved the problem of production, which had been a difficult one.

In September, 1921, F. W. Kellogg, publisher of the Los Angeles Ex-

NEWS BECOMES DAILY
Vol. 1, No. 1, August 23, 1913

DAILY PRESS LAUNCHED
Dated March 1, 1921

SAMUEL G. McCLURE   JACOB D. FUNK
Bought Evening News in 1926   *General Manager of News-Press, 1928-32*

press and other newspapers, obtained control of the Glendale Daily Press. Watson continued as general manager.

Soon after Kellogg's purchase of the Press, talk was heard regarding a prospective merger of the two dailies, the News and the Press, records of the time disclose. Glendale, growing rapidly, had an estimated population of 25,000 and was known as "the fastest growing city" in the United States, but there was a feeling that the field was somewhat restricted for two local dailies, especially in view of the competition from Los Angeles newspapers, which were reaching into the metropolitan environs for more circulation. The merger talk, whatever its source, did not achieve anything at the time beyond providing a topic of conversation.

In 1926, Samuel G. McClure, a retired Ohio newspaper publisher, and his son-in-law, Jacob D. Funk, an Illinois bank executive, purchased the Evening News from Cowan, and continued publication in the paper's own building at 139 South Brand Boulevard.

Two years later, merger of the Evening News and Daily Press actually took place. The transaction, which was one in a series of transactions, was made public in the Evening News of February 15, 1928. The story, in part, as told in the News article, was:

"The Glendale Evening News Co. has purchased the Glendale Press, including all its accounts and bills receivable, its subscription lists and circulation, plant, equipment and good will and the building and real estate at 333 North Brand now occupied by the Press.

"The Press has been merged with the Glendale Evening News. After today, the consolidated newspaper will be issued as the Glendale News-Press. By the agreement consummated, F. W. Kellogg and W. S. Kellogg have sold the entire list of Kellogg newspapers to Col. Ira C. Copley, of Aurora, Ill. The Glendale Press and the Hollywood News are transferred at once. The other Kellogg newspapers will be taken over September 1.

"Through the purchase of the Glendale Press and its sale to the Glendale News, Col. Copley becomes a large stockholder in the Glendale News-Press. The management of the News-Press will remain in the hands of Samuel G. McClure and Jacob D. Funk.

"When all the Kellogg newspapers pass under control of Col. Copley, they will be known as the Southern California Newspapers, Associated. Samuel G. McClure will be president and general manager. Jacob D. Funk will become president and general manager of the News-Press.

"F. W. Kellogg has disposed of all his interests in the Glendale Press. When the transfer to Col. Copley is completed, he will become vice president of The Copley Press, which owns Col. Copley's newspapers in Elgin, Aurora and Joliet, Ill., and which will become the holding company for the stock of The San Diego Union and Tribune, the Illinois State Journal and probably other properties."

Distinction of being the first editor of the combined Glendale Evening News and Glendale Daily Press—or Glendale News-Press—belonged to Winfield Scott Ingram, who was editor of the News prior to the merger.

A native Californian, Ingram was editor of the Oakland Tribune in 1906, when San Francisco was ravaged by earthquake and fire and, during the emergency which followed, he became editor of the combined San Francisco Call, Chronicle and Examiner, published in the Tribune Building. From Oakland he went to the Fresno Herald as editor-in-chief, from there to the Pasadena Star-News as editor and then to the Long Beach Press as editor. Then came 10 years as owner and publisher of the San Bernardino News. In 1918, Ingram became editor of the Glendale Evening News and, in 1928, of the News-Press. He died on August 23, 1938, of a heart attack, immediately following return from a vacation trip.

WINFIELD SCOTT INGRAM
First Editor of News-Press

W. S. KELLOGG
News-Press Publisher, 1932-40

When, on April 1, 1932, McClure and Funk disposed of their interests in the News-Press, to take over the Santa Monica Outlook, W. S. Kellogg became publisher of the News-Press. Kellogg also held the title of president and general manager.

Bill Kellogg, as he was known around the newspaper plant, had been with the Pasadena Post since the early 1920's. In 1926, he was taken into partnership with his father, the late F. W. Kellogg, and engaged in managing the Kellogg newspapers, including the Glendale Press. When those papers were sold by the Kelloggs in 1928, Bill remained as publisher of the Post until he came to Glendale as News-Press publisher.

He was active in the civic and social life of the city, served as president of Glendale Rotary, was prominent in the Chamber of Commerce and Community Chest, was a member of Glendale Post, American Legion, of the Elks, and other organizations.

In 1939, he was elected president of the California Newspaper Publishers Association. He was an ardent advocate of "streamlining" newspapers to make them more easily readable and during his later years as publisher the streamlined News-Press gained nation-wide attention among members of the newspaper fraternity for its format. In the years since he left the paper, some of his innovations have been dropped, others retained. He resigned, effective October 1, 1940, following the death of his father, in order to manage the estate.

Taking over as editor on Ingram's death, in 1938, was J. C. (Cliff) Safley, who, in practical effect, had been filling the position for a year or more. Due to demands on his time as an advisory assistant to Publisher Kellogg, and also because of failing health, Ingram had turned over a large share of his editorial responsibilities to Safley on top of the latter's duties as city editor. So the transition to the post of editor was not difficult for Safley.

A native of Iowa, Safley had entered the newspaper field immediately on graduation from high school, becoming a reporter on the Davenport (Ia.) Democrat. He later was on the staff of the Idaho Statesman, in Boise, and then became telegraph editor of the Moline (Ill.) Daily Dispatch. He subsequently was editor and publisher of the Idaho County Free Press at Grangeville, Ida., for seven years, selling that publication to come to California.

After several years with the Santa Ana Register as news editor, he joined the staff of the Glendale Evening News. In 1928, he was made city editor of the Hollywood News, then one of the properties owned by Col. Copley, but returned to Glendale in 1931 as city editor of the News-Press.

Safley was editor of the News-Press for approximately two years, before being promoted to the position of managing editor of the Copley newspapers in San Diego. He now is editor of The San Diego Union.

On October 1, 1940, H. C. Burkheimer, who had been publisher of the Alhambra Post-Advocate since 1934, became publisher of the News-Press. Burkheimer had been advertising salesman and later advertising manager of the Post-Advocate. He went to Alhambra from the Hollywood Citizen's advertising department. His previous experience had been in merchandising and advertising agency work and he developed a number of merchandising ideas for the News-Press. One of his promotion plans was the establishment of an "exhibitorium," an auditorium in which merchants were invited to display exhibits in booths. The center of the room was used as a meeting place for civic organizations and during the war a portion of the exhibitorium was developed as a recruiting center for various branches of the armed services. Breakfasts for groups of draftees leaving for service were held regularly and the room was in daily use for meetings and exhibits.

Shortly after Burkheimer came to Glendale, Alden C. Waite, now president of SCAN, became editor of the News-Press. Waite succeeded Safley on November 30, 1940. He long had been familiar with policies and problems of the newspapers comprising SCAN in his capacity as chief editorial writer for the group. It was not long until he was wholly familiar with all the duties of the new position and, because of his long experience in every department of newspaper operation, both on his father's paper, the San Pedro Pilot, and as co-publisher of the Westwood Hills Press, he was called upon to give advice and assistance to other departments of the paper.

Waite remained with the News-Press as editor until January 1, 1944, when he was transferred to Alhambra as publisher and general manager of the Post-Advocate. A little more than two years later, on April 19, 1946, he was promoted to the office of assistant to the general manager of SCAN, with headquarters in Los Angeles. He was made president of SCAN on February 1, 1948. He is a Glendale resident.

Succeeding Waite as editor of the News-Press was Carroll W. Parcher, a lifetime newspaperman and native son of Glendale. His extensive experience in newspaper work and wide knowledge of Glendale people and conditions made the office a natural for him.

Parcher had been writing a special column, first entitled "On the Level" and later "In My Opinion," for the News-Press, starting in 1939. He was made associate editor, while Waite was editor, in 1942, and became editor when Waite took charge of the Alhambra Post-Advocate.

Early in life, Parcher displayed an inclination and natural aptitude for newspaper editorial and publishing responsibilities. He was editor of the Stylus, annual publication of Glendale High School students, and was on the staff of the Explosion, Glendale High newspaper. This experience was followed, starting in 1921, by groundwork as a printer's devil in the composing room of the old Glendale Press, where he learned the printing trade and he also served an apprenticeship in the pressroom and stereotype department.

He was connected with the editorial departments of Los Angeles newspapers at various times. These intimate contacts with the newspaper publishing business caused him to try his own hand at being a newspaper owner and publisher. He established the weekly Ledger in Montrose, a pioneering experiment that was helpful both to him and the budding community where he was temporarily established.

After a time, the Ledger was consolidated with the Record, which had been started the year before in Tujunga by Wallace M. Morgan, to form the Record-Ledger. It was as co-publisher and later publisher of that paper that his initial experience in newspaper work proved valuable. He served in the varying capacities of printer, pressman, advertising manager, editor, office boy and bookkeeper.

Desiring to broaden his background of knowledge concerning matters political, which he noted had important relationship to the newspaper field, he served for a while as field secretary to the chairman of the Board of Supervisors of Los Angeles County and then took a similar position with the City Council of Los Angeles.

His first newspaper column was "Humble Views," which appeared regularly in the Record-Ledger. He finally altered the title to "In My Opinion," on suggestion of a columnist friend. He used the latter title when, in later years, he wrote for the News-Press after having sold, in 1937, the weekly paper and commercial printing plant which had developed into a highly successful publishing operation.

Parcher is a member of the American Society of Newspaper Editors, the American Newspaper Publishers Association, the National and Los Angeles Press Clubs, and is past president of the Los Angeles professional chapter of Sigma Delta Chi, national journalism fraternity. He is past lieutenant governor of the California-Nevada District of Kiwanis International and a member of the board of directors of the All-Year Club of Southern California.

When Burkheimer resigned as publisher of the News-Press, on November 21, 1947, he was succeeded by Parcher, who also continued as editor. For the first time in the history of the publication the combined title of editor and publisher was created.

At the same time, Charles C. Hushaw, who had been managing editor, was made executive editor, marking the creation of another title new to the paper. Hushaw had been added to the staff by Safley, in 1936, as his chief assistant on the city desk. When Safley was succeeded by Waite as editor, the new head of the editorial department selected Hushaw as city editor.

Hushaw is another lifetime newspaperman. He received his initiation

299

CHARLES C. HUSHAW
Executive Editor

WALTER F. COOK
Business Manager

into the fraternity when he was 11 years old as printer's apprentice on the Gibson City (Ill.) Courier. Later he worked in the circulation department of the Decatur (Ill.) Review, while attending school. When the family moved to St. Paul, Minn., Hushaw turned to newspaper writing, meantime continuing in school. His next stop was at Watertown, S. D. There he became editor of his high school paper and, when a student at South Dakota State College, he edited the Collegian, that institution's publication.

Coming to California, he became editor of the Bell Post and subsequently was on the city desk of the Huntington Park Signal until he came to the News-Press.

Hushaw is master of Glendale Lodge, No. 544, F. & A. M.; a member of Unity Chapter, No. 116, Royal Arch Masons; Glendale Commandery, No. 63, Knights Templar; the Los Angeles and San Francisco Press Clubs and the Los Angeles Chapter of Sigma Delta Chi.

Operation of so large a commercial enterprise as the News-Press necessarily involves a vast amount of business and financial detail. Whether it is a matter of billing, collection, payroll, purchasing, bookkeeping or any of a multitude of transactions required, all are inherently important to the smooth running of the newspaper machine.

In charge of this division of the News-Press is Walter F. Cook as business manager. He has held the position since January, 1946. He came to Glendale with a wealth of experience. A native of Philadelphia, Pa., Cook settled in California in 1912. He went to work for the San Francisco Call as display bookkeeper on November 1, 1915, when the paper was managed by F. W. Kellogg. Later Cook became cashier. He left in March, 1918, to join the Army. He served in the Army until July, 1919, as hospital sergeant with Base Hospital 47, in France. He returned to the Call, as statistician, immediately after leaving service and continued in that position until March, 1920, when he became auditor of the Pasadena Post. He left the Post in July, 1921, to take the position of auditor of the San Pedro News. He was with the News until March, 1922, when he went to the Santa Monica Outlook as business manager.

CHARLES H. RUHMLAND
Composing Room Chief, 1934-45

Cook remained with the Outlook until December, 1924. Changing his base of operations, he entered government service and was assigned to duty in Hawaii in January, 1925, where he stayed until February, 1926. At that time he returned to the Pasadena Post in his old position as auditor and remained there until February, 1932. He became outside auditor for Southern California Associated Newspapers general office after severing connections with the Post and continued in that capacity until July, 1933, when he was named business manager of the Alhambra Post-Advocate. Cook left the Alhambra paper in January, 1946, to become business manager of the Glendale News-Press.

He is a member of the Institute of Newspaper Controllers and Finance Officers, through the medium of which he is able to keep in contact with business practices of other modern newspapers.

Charles H. Ruhmland came to the News-Press as composing room superintendent in 1934 and continued in that position until illness forced his retirement in 1945, to be followed, February 23, 1946, by his death. While with the News-Press, he served as president of the Southern California Mechanical Conference.

Born in Des Moines, Ia., Ruhmland began working in a print shop in that city when he was 13 years old and remained until he was a full-fledged printer, getting his journeyman's card when he was 18. He worked on newspapers in a number of states, was composing room foreman for the Honolulu Star-Bulletin three years, and was an employe of the Pasadena Post 13 years, acting as circulation manager from 1923 to 1932. He later was circulation manager of the Los Angeles Record and a circulation district man for the Los Angeles Examiner.

Col. Copley, who foresaw the need for expansion of the News-Press plant and equipment in anticipation of the further growth of Glendale and adjacent areas served by the paper, was directing the planning of a new home for the News-Press at the time of his death in 1947. It was not many months after Parcher became editor and publisher that work actually started on a new and modern newspaper plant on the site of Glendale's first big hotel, which had been built in the boom days of the 1880's. This site extends from Isabel Street to Jackson Street, between Broadway and Wilson, and is across the street from the City Hall grounds. Work began March 6, 1948.

The building was completed in the fall. The week of October 17, 1948, became "moving week" for the News-Press and by Saturday the editorial and composing rooms had been transferred from 333 North Brand Boulevard to the new home at 111 North Isabel Street. It was not long before all News-Press departments were established at the new location.

In order that the public might become acquainted with the new building and its location, two "at home" nights were held, December 6 and 7. Throngs took advantage of the opportunity to tour the building.

Prior to the public opening, a special edition of the News-Press, called "The Glendale Story," was issued. It not only gave a detailed picture of the plant, but made the edition memorable for its unprecedented coverage of all major phases of Glendale life, including the history of the city, the churches, public and parochial schools, business and industrial enterprises, civic and fraternal organizations and numerous other aspects of community living.

ENTRANCE TO NEWS-PRESS BUILDING AT 111 NORTH ISABEL STREET

Some excerpts from "The Glendale Story," as they relate to the development and progress of the News-Press, are offered:

"This special edition is a product of the newly-erected $350,000 plant of the Glendale News-Press at 111 North Isabel. Visitors have been impressed by the spaciousness of grounds and building, by the unusual convenience for patron and employe alike provided by the arrangement of the floor space. They have noted that in style of construction and type of equipment and facilities the plant is modern to the maximum degree.

"The building contains 35,000 square feet, and has been planned to handle the publication of a daily newspaper of 50,000 or more circulation. Publisher Carroll W. Parcher and members of the staff are convinced that no more efficient plant for newspapers of comparable size is to be found in the country.

"Brilliant fluorescent lighting is featured throughout and all departments and offices are fully air conditioned. Asphaltic tile flooring is used in all offices, while all woodwork is of attractively grained birch.

"Prefabricated steel and concrete construction, known as Latis-steel, was utilized in building. The structure is 230 feet long and 120 feet in width.

WHERE NEWS-PRESS WAS PUBLISHED FROM 1928 TO 1948

OFFICES OF GLENDALE EVENING NEWS, 139 SOUTH BRAND

"The site comprises 14 lots, seven facing on Isabel, the main entrance to the building, and seven on Jackson. A parking lot for employes' automobiles surrounds the building on two sides.

"Providing space for staff meetings and for sessions by business and other groups, a large conference room has been included. Adjoining the conference room is a fully-equipped kitchen, available for special occasions and also used daily by the staff for morning coffee.

"The layout of the building has been designed for speedy and continuous flow of copy from the front counter, where offices of the display and classified advertising departments are situated, and from the editorial department, through the composing room, stereotype room and pressroom to the circulation department at the rear of the building.

"The publisher's office is located between the display and editorial departments and opens also on the main conference room. Adjacent is the secretary's office and waiting room which is connected with the office of the executive editor.

"The four-position copy desk is connected to the composing room by a pneumatic tube, as are the sports desk and social desk.

"Opening off the editorial department is a sound-proofed teletype room containing receivers for The Associated Press and United Press wires, race wire covering California tracks, and The Copley Press Washington Bureau leased wire.

"The circulation department, at the rear of the building, adjoins a long outside dock from which newspaper distribution to trucks is made. An overhead conveyor from the pressroom carries freshly printed newspapers to the circulation mail room.

"Notable in the new equipment is a four-unit Goss High Speed semicylindrical straight-line press, capable of printing 64 standard pages.

"Stereotype equipment includes a Pony Autocaster, Premier shaver, Goss 55-F curved router, Sta-Hi vacuum dry mat former, Wesel flat router, and two Kemp pots of 7000 and 2000 pounds capacity with dual carburetors.

"Thirteen Linotypes form the battery in the composing room and space has been provided for additional machines.

"The modern photography department, leading from the editorial department, has four darkrooms and a work room as well as a large studio. Stainless steel sinks and other modern equipment have been installed in the darkrooms. A new Automega enlarger has been added to the equipment. The paper's Associated Press wirephoto receiver is located in one of the darkrooms. Five rooms have been provided for the photoengraving department.

"A basement with space for storage of 60 days' supply of newsprint is under a portion of the building. A track on which to move paper rolls to the reels underneath the press runs the length of the storage space. A truck ramp for paper delivery ends at a hydraulic hoist which will lower the rolls to the basement level."

In the time intervening between the date of "The Glendale Story," on November 26, 1948, and the present writing, various additions and replacements of equipment have been made in the natural line of improvement of facilities.

Teletype equipment has been installed in the composing room with tape perforators, a transmitter and two Linotype operating units, while in the teletype room a teletype wire service machine and tape reperforator connected with The Associated Press are in use.

In the stereotype room, a Premier rotary shaver shaves flat castings to the precise thickness required on the composing room makeup table. An automatic alarm system is connected with the larger metal pot to direct atten-

FRONT PAGE OF NEWS-PRESS FOR FEBRUARY 2, 1953

tion to temperatures which rise above a safe maximum or drop below a safe minimum.

In the photographic division, a wirephoto transmitter is in service, supplementing the wirephoto receiver. In the photoengraving department, a new Robertson camera has replaced the older camera and a new Challenge proof press has been installed. The business office equipment has been increased with a National Cash Register bookkeeping machine and new Friden calculator.

As an added service both to merchants and shoppers, the News-Press Shopper was inaugurated in April, 1948, appearing each Thursday, with a combined circulation of more than 50,000 and reaching every corner of the Glendale trading area. Distribution in the city zone was put in the hands of the carrier organization under direction of W. E. Buhrle, circulation manager.

In May, 1950, the Burbank Review was purchased by SCAN and was operated as an adjunct of the Glendale News-Press until September, 1950. Publisher Parcher and department heads of the News-Press supervised the necessary steps to set up the Review as a separate unit of the SCAN system.

At the time the Burbank paper was acquired, the News-Press added the services of United Press to its news sources.

In line with its policy of providing the most complete news coverage possible, the News-Press and other newspapers in SCAN maintain a Los Angeles news bureau.

Because of the importance of the teletypesetter service and the fact that it was pioneered by the News-Press, which acted as a sending station for a SCAN teletypesetter circuit, excerpts from a news story appearing in the News-Press on January 9, 1952, are given here:

"A new method of getting the news to the reader has been pioneered by the Glendale News-Press in the Los Angeles area during the past year. It has proved successful and is now being applied on a general scale throughout Southern California by The Associated Press and the United Press.

"The new system is 'teletypesetting' and it actually enables an operator in a central station to set type in the composing rooms of a virtually unlimited number of newspapers simultaneously.

"Actually invented in 1932, teletypesetting has only in the past year come into wide practical use in the newspaper field. Since installation of a transmitter in the Glendale News-Press offices, daily news reports have been

HEADS OF FOUR NEWS-PRESS DEPARTMENTS

Standing, William D. Weigand, left, composing room foreman, and Roy B. Johnson, classified advertising manager; seated, Hoyt Cater, left, display advertising manager, and W. E. Buhrle, circulation manager.

transmitted to the offices of other members of Southern California Associated Newspapers.

"The news report is automatically set into type on Linotype or Intertype machines in the receiving office. With one operator actuating half a dozen machines at a time, real economies in newspaper production have been achieved.

"Many new techniques have had to be developed in the News-Press editorial and composing rooms to make the teletypesetter circuit effective. Members of the Glendale local of the International Typographical Union have co-operated fully in perfecting the mechanical operation of the circuit and members of the union operate the transmitting machines.

"Editors in Glendale select and edit the news and write headlines for it, so the report is ready for use by the time it is received in the offices of other newspapers on the circuit.

"The United Press and Associated Press have profited by the experience on the Glendale 'pilot' circuit from both editorial and mechanical points. Advice of Glendale editors has been sought regarding other teletypesetter circuits."

Carroll W. Parcher, editor and publisher of the News-Press, spoke, on special invitation, before the annual convention of the Arizona Newspapers Association in Phoenix on the operation of teletypesetter circuits as perfected in Glendale. William D. Weigand, foreman of the composing room, spoke at the A.N.P.A. Mechanical Conference in June, 1952, on the teletypesetter operation in Glendale.

Constructive work in civic lines is a continuous achievement in the history of the News-Press, so any attempt to list such projects would be endless, but, as an example, the role of the paper in creating a USO center in Glendale after Pearl Harbor can be cited. The Community Chest agreed to finance day-by-day operation and a hotel owner offered to supply a room, but no way of getting furnishings and equipment was in sight.

Realizing the need, Editor Alden C. Waite told the citizens' USO committee the News-Press would guarantee at least $1000 for capital outlay. With this in view, the paper inaugurated a circulation campaign which raised $1800 and provided all equipment and furnishings required. All who subscribed in the campaign were invited to a special open house of USO to see what had been done with their money. The biggest surprise came, however, when, two years later, the News-Press circulation list was checked and it was discovered that 60 percent—a phenomenally high proportion—of the USO drive subscribers still were taking the paper.

News-Press department heads are Walter F. Cook, business manager; Charles C. Hushaw, executive editor; Hoyt Cater, display advertising man-

GLENDALE'S CITY HALL IS AN IMPOSING STRUCTURE

ager; Roy B. Johnson, classified advertising manager; William D. Weigand, composing room foreman; W. E. Buhrle, circulation manager; William W. Crawford, press foreman, and Lawrence Morris, stereotype foreman.

"Once an employe, always an employe" is not true of every private enterprise, owing to persons with ambition being subject to itching feet, but it more truly applies, perhaps, to the News-Press than to most lines of business because of the excellent working conditions at the plant, the "humanness" of the executive division from the top on down and the desirability of Glendale as a city in which to live and work.

News-Press employes, who like to refer to themselves as members of the News-Press "family," are noted for their loyalty to the paper, as attested by the long records of service which many of them have.

Special pins are given employes after they have been with the paper for a year, and a diamond is added for each five years' employment thereafter. Salvador Felix, chief photographer and holder of a journeyman pressman's card, now has a service pin with seven diamonds, for 35 years' employment.

Other employes with service records of 20 years or more include Ray Wolcott, ad foreman, since 1921; Carl Hammer, Linotype operator, 1921; William D. Weigand, composing room foreman, 1923; Henry Hoefner, Linotype operator, 1923; Harper Mouthrop, printer, 1924; Logan Barr, printer, recently retired, 1925; George Goshorn, reporter and feature writer, 1925; Ruby Gates, secretary to the publisher, 1927; W. E. Buhrle, circulation manager, 1927; Sterling Parker, Linotype operator, 1930; L. A. Verna, printer, 1929; Edwin Grattan, Linotype operator, 1930; W. W. Crawford, press foreman, 1930; G. A. Boyd, Linotype operator, 1931; Lawrence Morris, stereotype foreman, 1931; Carl Fellows, Linotype operator, 1931; O. C. O'Kell, display advertising, 1931; Lloyd Glotfelty, assistant composing room foreman, 1932, and Charles Emmal, Linotype operator, 1932.

Walter Jones, Linotype operator, who died in 1951, came to the News-Press in 1918. J. W. Bailey, Linotype operator, who died in 1952, started work in 1924, and Ralph Lynd, reporter, whose death occurred in 1949, became associated with the paper in 1920.

With a roster that averages 125 employes, the News-Press can fairly justify its claim to being one of the important economic factors in the life of Glendale. Average paid circulation for February, 1953, was 20,430.

MONROVIA

DAILY NEWS-POST

"Covers the Northern San Gabriel Valley"

MONROVIA EXTENDS TO FOOTHILLS OF SAN GABRIEL RANGE

CHARLES F. DAVIS
Editor and Publisher, Daily News-Post
Vice President, Southern California Associated Newspapers

314

Daily News-Post

119 West Palm Avenue   Monrovia, Calif.

THE FABULOUS CALIFORNIA MILLIONAIRE and original real estate subdivider, E. J. (Lucky) Baldwin, was in a way responsible for the City of Monrovia. Baldwin was the first to admit he sold the morning breeze, the clouds and sunshine. When a customer complained about paying $350 an acre for rich Santa Anita Rancho land that Baldwin had bought only two years previously for $25 an acre, Baldwin answered: "I'm not selling you the land. I'm charging you a fair price for the wonderful Southern California climate, and throwing in the land."

Baldwin had bought the 6000 rolling acres of Santa Anita, originally a part of the San Gabriel Mission holdings, when he had arrived from San Francisco, with $5,000,000 in cash, received from the sale of the fabulous Ophir mine, burning a hole in his pocket. Later Baldwin was to make many other real estate purchases in Southern California, but Rancho Santa Anita always was closest to his heart.

Baldwin had begun extensive development of the property when a young Texas railroad contractor, also with money in his pocket—in fact, $100,000 from a Southern Pacific construction job—arrived at Santa Anita on a holiday buggy ride, listened to what Baldwin said, and believed him. The young railroad builder was William Newton Monroe. He bought considerable acreage, subdivided it into town lots and, with a half dozen associates, founded a city that was named Monrovia in his honor.

Monroe and Baldwin were among the first California real estate subdividers to put money value on climate. Their successors have been doing it ever since.

315

The original townsite chosen by Monroe and his associates lay in the foothills of the San Gabriel range, at the base of the mile-high mountains. More than 100 years before, in the summer of 1769, these mountains were first described by Fr. Juan Crespi, historian of a group which set out from San Diego on July 14, under command of Don Gaspar de Portola. Fr. Crespi and Fr. Francisco Gomez were sent by the command of Fr. Junipero Serra, famed head of the Franciscan order in Mexico. The Franciscans were looking for a site to build a mission.

The little party made its way slowly up through the interior. On July 27, the group crossed the Santa Ana River and two evenings later was camped on the banks of the San Gabriel. Here is what Fr. Crespi, the keen-eyed old monk, wrote about the northern San Gabriel Valley, which today is the home of the Daily News-Post of Monrovia:

"We then descended to a broad and spacious plain, of fine black earth, with much grass, though we found it burned. After traveling for an hour through the valley, we came to an arroyo of water which flows among many green marshes, their banks covered with willows and grapes, blackberries and innumerable Castilian rosebushes loaded with roses. In the midst of the verdure runs a good channel of water which, when measured, was found to have a volume of three-quarters of a square yard. It runs along the foot of the mountains, and can easily be used to irrigate the large area of good land the valley has. The valley has a length from north to south of about three leagues, and is surrounded by ranges of hills. The ones to the north are very high and dark and have many corrugations, and seem to run farther to the west. The others are not so high and run from east to west. The plain must be about six leagues long."

Fr. Crespi was looking at Monrovia Peak, and at Mt. Wilson, today bristling with television stations, and at other mountains to the north, when he described the range "high and dark" with "many corrugations." And he noted the "fine black earth" and the roses, which were not Castilian, but California wild roses.

Baldwin and Monroe probably never read Fr. Crespi's description of the foothills of the San Gabriel range, but Baldwin was the first to sub-divide this part of the ranch into parcels, and Monroe, with his friends, was the first to buy, divide his holdings and ready the lots for sale to individual homeowners.

The first lots in the new city went on sale May 17, 1886, a date that

ARTIST'S DRAWING OF MONROVIA AND VICINITY ABOUT 1874

since then has come to be celebrated as Monrovia Day. And now that the first order of business was out of the way, the founders took up the second— to get themselves a newspaper.

At this point, E. L. Buck appeared on the scene. Despite the fact that almost a complete file of his newspaper exists, little is known of Buck. Evidently he had learned that the firm of Monroe & Co. was looking for a newspaperman. Buck called on the promoters, met their not very strict requirements, and was offered a free building site, "right down town," if he would erect a building. He did. It was a two-story false-front structure, with the newspaper and job printing shop on the first floor, a residence for the proprietor on the second. A photograph of the building has been preserved by the historical department of the Security-First National Bank. It was a plain, narrow, little frame building with an outside stairway leading to the editor's parlor. Standing on the uncovered front porch was a group of figures in old-fashioned garb. At the left drowsed a burro.

But if Buck was modest in his office and home, he was not modest when he named his paper the Monrovia Mountain Planet. Said the Orange Tribune, quoted in an early issue of the new Monrovia paper:

"The Mountain Planet, a nice, clean-looking six-column local paper,

317

published in the new and growing town of Monrovia, comes to us in exchange. E. L. Buck, founder of the San Jacinto Register, is editor and proprietor. We greet the Planet and hope it will revolve for many moons."

Buck printed the first issue of the Planet Saturday, November 20, 1886. Monrovia then was 6 months and 3 days old.

Buck was enthusiastic about Monrovia. In fact, he wrote such glowing accounts of the new community that he sold himself on the idea of making his fortune in Monrovia real estate. In less than two months after he launched his Planet, he disposed of it to another newcomer, a man from Canada. J. W. Harvey had his name on the masthead with the issue of December 18. Editor Buck became Realtor Buck, though the word "realtor" had not yet been coined. The two men, one through his newspaper and the other by selling town lots, must have stirred up interest outside their own city limits, for within a short time a third newspaperman, Frank Kasson, was on the scene, full of enthusiasm and energy. He started a second newspaper. Not to be outdone in names, he called it the Leader.

The young community, however, proved unable or unwilling to support two papers, so Kasson and Harvey joined forces. They suspended the Planet and the Leader and launched the Monrovia Messenger. Kasson was editor, Harvey business manager.

Additional changes were to come. In February of the following year, 1888, Harvey retired from the Messenger and moved with his family to San Pedro, where he took editorial charge of the San Pedro Pilot. But the seashore didn't agree with him and by June he was back in Monrovia. He bought out Kasson and resumed publication of the Messenger.

THE MONROVIA PLANET WAS THE TOWN'S FIRST NEWSPAPER

Monrovia Messenger.

VOLUME 11.   MONROVIA, CALIFORNIA, THURSDAY, NOVEMBER 8, 1888.   NUMBER 51.

Monrovia + Messenger.

ISSUED EVERY THURSDAY MORNING.

KASSON & HARVEY, Proprietors.

SUBSCRIPTION RATES.
ONE YEAR, in advance..................$2.00
SIX MONTHS, " 1.00

ADVERTISING RATES ON APPLICATION.

Entered at the postoffice at Monrovia, Cal., as second
class matter.

MONROVIA NOV. 8 1888

AMERICA WINS.

Harrison and Morton Elected
by a Good Majority.

FREE TRADE DID IT, YOU KNOW.

The Republicans Elect the Entire
County Ticket.

Just how it happened is what worries

CONGRESS.
Vandever..................100
Terry..................63
Miller..................18
Scattering..................1

STATE SENATOR.
McComas..................159
Montgomery..................65
Abbot..................31

ASSEMBLY—68TH DISTRICT.
Brierly..................159
Waldron..................65
Walton..................31

CHIEF JUSTICE.
Beatty..................159
Searles..................16
Thompson..................70
Kendrick..................20

ASSOCIATE JUSTICE.
Works..................178

LATEST REPORTS.

Cleveland Gracefully Accepts His
Defeat.

The press reports received this morning make the Republican victory certain
beyond a doubt. President Cleveland
acknowledges his defeat and shows no
sign of disappointment. New York and
Indiana are both Republican, California
is safe by a majority of at least 5,000.
Now is the glory and prosperity of
America vindicated. "It is a famous
victory."

MESSENGER LAUNCHED WHEN PLANET AND LEADER SUSPENDED

The Monrovia Messenger continued alone and prospering in the field until a restless jeweler, who had come to California from Ohio, settled in Monrovia. He set up a jewelry store, he operated the flashy La Vista Grande Hotel, he played solo cornet in Monrovia's silver cornet band, and, as a member of the young city's first park commission, he and two others created Library Park. But for the purpose of this narrative, A. E. Cronenwett's most important contribution was the Monrovia News, which he started shortly after the turn of the century. The year was 1903. W. J. Rouse was business manager and Mrs. Harriet Barry, who recently had come to Monrovia from Ventura with her husband, George A. Barry, was made assistant editor, with special attention given to society news.

The News was published from a combined print shop and newspaper office on East Olive Avenue, and met with a cordial reception. The paper continued under Cronenwett's ownership until 1906, when it was bought by

MONROVIA NEWS

THE OFFICIAL PAPER OF THE CITY.

VOL. 5 NO 45   MONROVIA, CALIFORNIA, SATURDAY, NOVEMBER 28, 1908. $1.50 PER YEAR

NOT FOR US   BIG BEGINNING   THE RACE TRACK

MONROVIA FAILS TO LAND   SIX MONTHS WORK SHOWS   MONROVIA SENDS HUNDREDS
AUTOMOBILE FACTORY   PROGRESS BY THE Y. M. C. A.   OF VISITORS THE FIRST DAY

A NEW TERMINAL

MONROVIA NEWS, ESTABLISHED BY JEWELER IN 1903

a new corporation, Monrovia Publishing Co. The president was A. P. Seymour, the vice president, Paran F. Rice, a Los Angeles attorney; secretary, Hugh Sutherland, and treasurer, George A. Barry, who also was made editor and manager of the News.

The paper did well as a weekly and five years later became Monrovia's first daily, the Monrovia Daily News. Shortly afterward, the Olive Avenue premises were abandoned and the News moved into a new two-story brick building at 115 East Lime Avenue. Editor and Mrs. Barry had a comfortable and commodious apartment upstairs; below were the editorial and business offices in front, with ample space for the mechanical departments in the rear.

The Daily News at that time was a simple and economical newspaper operation. The sole occupant of the front office was Barry, editor and publisher, when he was in residence. Often he was away, for he was fond of travel. In those days

OFFICE OF PLANET
Pioneer Monrovia Newspaper

railroads were generous with passes and the editor took many a jaunt to distant points. Next in line to the manager was the general reporter, the workhorse, who was promoted to city editor when he asked for an increase in pay and couldn't be put off. His successor always started again as reporter. Then there was a girl who wrote social notes, took subscriptions and classified ads, and another girl who kept the books, made out the bills, took charge of the carrier boys and counted out the papers.

As the paper went to press, all hands, front and back, helped fold the papers as they came off the Optimus press. Bone folders were used and the job was done rather quickly. The circulation was about 600.

Rates were simple and easily understood. The subscription price was 25 cents a month, want ads were "three lines three times for a quarter."

The display rate was 25 cents an inch. In those early days, advertisements ran week after week without change. Merchants didn't advertise bargains or specials; they didn't advertise anything in particular. They "supported" the newspaper and in many cases took pride in doing so. There were no trained advertising men; customers brought in their ads scrawled on a piece of wrapping paper which the editor handed to the printer. When Barber Hinton was persuaded to advertise he wrote: "O. H. Hinton Tonsorial Parlor, shaving, haircutting, shampooing and everything in head toilet neatly executed in highest tonsorial art. Ladies' bangs trimmed."

Through some powerful connection with one of the Los Angeles officers, the little daily enjoyed an excellent run of job printing from a big oil well supply company, and often the Daily News commercial printing accounts exceeded in revenue the newspaper income.

It was in that period, the pre-World War I era, that a young man from Iowa presented himself to take the place of the current city editor, who suddenly gave up what he considered an unattractive as well as an ill-paid job. The newcomer gave his name as Charles F. Davis. Barry found him without any newspaper experience, hired him anyway, gave him a week's sketchy coaching, and left for a long visit with his son, a successful short-story writer in New York City. The paper managed to survive, Davis later said, thanks largely to the good sense of the girl who handled the books.

The young man from Iowa learned to like newspapers. He still was there when World War I came. He was granted a leave of absence by Barry and spent several months in England and France, but was back at his desk early in 1919. There he remained until shortly before the News was sold, in 1922, to C. C. Howard, who came to California from Kirksville, Mo., where he had been a successful newspaper publisher.

Howard enlarged and improved the newspaper, and moved it again, this time from its comfortable home on East Lime Avenue to its present building, the attractive Spanish-style two-story concrete structure at 119 West Palm Avenue, fronting on Library Park.

Here the Daily News continued unopposed until July 1, 1924, when F. W. Kellogg, well-known Pacific Coast publisher, owner of a group of newspapers in Los Angeles County, moved into Monrovia and launched the Monrovia Post. Kellogg bought a business lot at 416 South Myrtle Avenue and installed a newspaper plant, even to sinking a pit for the press.

However, the press never was erected. The Post was printed in Pasadena as a part of the Pasadena Post, and was distributed with the Pasadena Post and the Los Angeles Express. Editorial and business offices were in Monrovia.

The Monrovia Post bought the Messenger's mailing list and good will when the old weekly, after a long and honorable career of public service, finally gave up the ghost.

When the Post was started, J. J. Martyn, of Long Beach, was made general manager; Charles F. Davis, formerly with the Daily News, was named editor, and Miss Ellavera Nelson, assistant editor. Later Martyn resigned. Davis was promoted to editor and general manager and held the position until 1928, when the Post, as one of the Kellogg group of newspapers, was bought by Col. Ira C. Copley.

The Daily News was purchased March 1, 1929, by Col. Copley, and merged with the Monrovia Post to form the present Daily News-Post, a unit of the Southern California Newspapers, Associated. Harry W. Fredericks was business and advertising manager of the News under the Howard ownership, while Davis had edited and managed the Post for Kellogg.

Samuel G. McClure, the first head of SCNA, called the two former rival managers into his Los Angeles office, told them the battle was over, to shake hands and from then on to work together. Both promised and both tried, but they had been on opposite sides of the fence too long. Soon Davis and his assistant editor resigned. Miss Nelson went to Europe and Davis wrote a book on Monrovia.

Fredericks continued for some months as manager of the News-Post, then was succeeded by Roy Ratliff, former advertising manager. Ratliff's place later was taken by Phil M. Knox, of Long Beach.

Knox was an able newspaperman, a circulation specialist and was well liked in Monrovia. He found he was handicapped by not knowing the town, and sought the return to the News-Post of a man who had worked for one or the other of the two papers for many years. He offered the editorship to Davis, who in the depth of the depression had gone into the job-printing business, and had married Miss Nelson. The deal was made after Clark F. Waite, now chairman of the board of Southern California Associated Newspapers, had approved Davis' request that the Daily News-Post buy his job plant.

On March 1, 1934, Davis returned to the News-Post. In the fall of the following year, Knox went to the Oakland Tribune as circulation man-

'THE BEST PAPER POSSIBLE,' AIM OF NEWS-POST

ager, and Davis was promoted to publisher and manager, a position he since has held.

"When Col. Copley bought the Monrovia News from Howard and consolidated it with the Post," commented Clark F. Waite, "it would have

323

been a much better deal if the services of Charles F. Davis, editor of the Post, had been retained. But Davis, being a very modest man, did not go after the job as publisher as he might have done. He went into the job printing business on his own.

"It was Phil M. Knox, now business manager of the San Francisco Examiner, who, during his residence in Monrovia until late in 1935, discovered what a mistake had been made in letting Charlie Davis get away when the papers were consolidated. He came to know Davis well and learn how highly he was regarded by Monrovia residents. When Knox resigned as manager of the News-Post to become circulation manager of the Oakland Tribune, before joining the Hearst organization, he recommended Davis as his successor.

"So SCNA bought the job printing business of Davis in order to get him again as publisher of the News-Post. Thus the valuable good will asset that had been lost when the News and Post were consolidated was restored by the purchase of Davis' job printing business."

Elwood Irwin, managing editor, started carrying papers for the Daily News as a grammar school pupil, wrote sports in high school, then served as sports editor, general reporter and city editor before heading the editorial department.

Like newspapermen everywhere, the men who edited and published Monrovia's early-day newspapers worked in the public interest, and helped to mold their community. There were notable editors among these pioneers. Among them were Homer Fort, who left a star reporter's post on one of the great New York papers to brilliantly and wittily edit the Messenger; Charles O. Broxon, another Messenger editor, who once in Boise, Ida., edited his paper from the county jail to which he and two associates had been sentenced for contempt of court; Cronenwett, who was responsible for much of the early progress in parks and playgrounds, and Barry, whose editorials had state-wide circulation. They set examples for the late comers to follow.

Prized possessions of the Daily News-Post are the yellowing pages of these pioneering newspapers, including a practically complete file of the Planet, and a number of volumes of the Messenger. These crumbling sheets tell the week-to-week and later the day-to-day story of the town's growth, recording the minute as well as the most important happenings that, taken all together, slowly pile up like coral on the reef, to record

DAILY NEWS-POST BUILDING FACES LIBRARY PARK

time's passage and the slow but sure results of the laborers in the field of community effort. And in Monrovia, as elsewhere the country over, newspapermen have found that the community helps to build the newspaper as the newspaper helps to build the community.

Monrovia was founded on a boom, which was brought about by a sudden and fantastic inflation in real estate values, plus a railroad rate war that saw travelers buying in Chicago tickets to Los Angeles for $1. Within two years, the Southern California boom collapsed. Many an infant municipality was wiped out. Monrovia suffered less than did most communities. There was a good deal of hard cash in the little town. Besides, folk liked the climate and the high hills around about. It was almost a mountain town; if you stood at any street intersection and looked north, south, east or west, you saw mountains at the end of every street.

The 1880's ended in a great crash. Then the 1890's crept in, but instead of the "gay 90's" of song and story, they were grim 90's in Monrovia, for they brought many long years of drought that almost, but not quite, ruined the valley. The drought didn't really end until the turn of the century. But saving the orchards came first, and when the rains failed and the mountain streams dropped to a trickle, the townsfolk hauled water in barrels from the river to the parching trees. It was a tough time, but the little town fought back valiantly, and even went ahead.

By 1900, Monrovia had a population of 1500. In another decade it was up to 3756. By 1920, the population had nearly doubled again, to 5480. Another double was recorded in 1930 to 10,980, then a leveling off to 12,784 by 1940, and then to 20,015 by 1950. Today the population is in excess of 23,000.

First founded on an agricultural and horticultural economy, Monrovia, during the dry years, gradually gave up orange and lemon production. For a time it looked as though the city might become a health resort. Many had come from the East because of the dry, warm climate. But, quite early in the present century, the town took what now appears to be a permanent turn toward industry. Less than 20 miles east of Los Angeles and half that distance from Pasadena, Monrovia is ideally located as a residential city. The municipal council made wise zoning laws, and the manufacturing district is attractively landscaped and well designed. By 1948, sales of goods manufactured in Monrovia totaled $21,000,000, and in 1951 jumped to $26,875,000. The total for 1952 came close to $30,000,000, with more than 75 industrial plants well established. Industry and business, with Monrovia in the heart of the rich San Gabriel Valley, have joined hands. Retail sales in 1948 were $18,000,000, in 1952, $20,000,000.

The Daily News-Post has kept pace with the handsome, well-groomed suburban city that Monrovia has become. The present newspaper plant, built in 1922 on the north side of downtown Library Park, a square block of beautiful trees and lawns, with a Carnegie Library in the center, still is adequate for its 50 or more employes and 75 carriers. A. W. Shipton, president of The Copley Press, said Monrovia reminded him strongly of Illinois towns built around a public square.

Mechanical equipment includes a Goss 16-page straightline press, stereotyping department with a Sta-Hi former, curved and flat routers, casting boxes, mat rollers, etc., six Linotypes, one Ludlow, in an excellently-arranged 39-by-70-foot workroom. Editorial department equipment includes a Fairchild photo-electric engraver, cameras, and a well-furnished darkroom, as well as teletype printers.

The Daily News-Post has been exclusive in its field for some years. The publisher and his department heads believe the only way to deserve

DEPARTMENT HEADS OF DAILY NEWS-POST

Left to right, John A. Flood, classified manager; David G. Holmes, circulation manager; Elwood Irwin, managing editor; A. F. Grimes, advertising manager; Terrence T. Donnelly, auditor; Charles H. Ellsworth, mechanical superintendent.

the continued support of the whole community is to give it, day by day, the best paper possible. Included in the operational executives are Charles F. Davis, editor, publisher and general manager; Elwood Irwin, managing editor; A. F. Grimes, advertising manager; John A. Flood, classified manager; Terrence T. Donnelly, auditor; David G. Holmes, circulation manager, and Charles H. Ellsworth, mechanical superintendent. Each has taken an active part in the civic, business and fraternal life of the community.

SOUTH BAY

Daily Breeze

Redondo Beach—Hermosa Beach—Manhattan Beach—Palos Verdes Estates

REDONDO BEACH NESTLES ON SHORES OF PACIFIC

329

F. S. HAYNES
Editor and Publisher, South Bay Daily Breeze
Vice President, Southern California Associated Newspapers

Daily Breeze

131 South Pacific Avenue   Redondo Beach, Calif.

THE SOUTH BAY DAILY BREEZE, at Redondo Beach, Calif., was started in 1894 on an impulse by a one-time druggist, S. D. Barkley. Doc, as he was popularly known, was a round-faced, good-humored man, who held public office in the town for many years. He also had a penchant for prospecting, with the usual pattern cut by the mining fever. He often left the Breeze to its own resources while he picked fruitlessly at the rocks of Nevada.

Barkley is said to have remarked to friends one evening: "I'm going to start a newspaper in this town tomorrow and call it the Breeze, because the breeze always blows here." And the Breeze has been blowing about the attractions of Redondo Beach and nearby communities ever since.

Barkley no doubt started the Breeze for political purposes. The town was divided into two factions—the wets and the drys. The wets, represented by the four saloonkeepers in town, had strong political support. The drys, represented by the ministers and a goodly sprinkling of women, were out to close the saloons. Doc Barkley never failed to uphold John Barleycorn.

The Breeze was launched in a tiny office at 116 North Pacific Avenue. The building was a ramshackle wooden affair, half of which was occupied by Nick's Bootery.

The early history of the Breeze is vague. Files in the office of the Breeze are incomplete. They date back only to 1917, with wide gaps in between. The Redondo Beach Public Library has a complete set of files, but they date only from 1909. Efforts to obtain earlier copies have been almost fruitless. Only a portion of a 1905 issue, a section of a 1908 copy and a single sheet from a 1902 paper give glimpses of the Breeze prior to 1909.

331

Thus most of the early history of the Breeze has been gathered in the most vexatious manner, from the dim, dusty and often controversial memories of old-timers. Often they are distorted, sometimes exaggerated and usually a 2-to-1 mixture of imagination with fact.

However, by piecing together here and there, it is possible to develop a thin, though badly worn and often broken thread of early Breeze history.

City Hall records take no notice of the Breeze until August 6, 1894, when the Board of Trustees ordered Ordinance 35, prohibiting obstruction of streets and sidewalks, to appear officially in the Redondo Breeze.

An earlier weekly, the Redondo Compass, mentioned in municipal records of 1892, apparently had fallen by the wayside. Nobody in Redondo today recollects the Compass. However, a few months after the birth of the Breeze, John Steward, a former New York newspaperman, started the Redondo Reflex. For many years, the Breeze and the Reflex battled it out, with no holds barred.

When the Breeze was started, Redondo Beach numbered less than 500 inhabitants. The town consisted of a handful of wooden store buildings with typical false fronts, a sprinkling of houses, a tent city, three commercial piers, and the then magnificent Hotel Redondo, built in 1888 and boasting 225 rooms. The Los Angeles & Redondo Railway was completed in 1890, and from its inception groaned beneath the weight of tourists and freight, for Redondo was a veritable mecca for visitors and its commercial piers accommodated astonishing numbers of passengers and heavy cargoes of freight.

The census count for Redondo in 1900 was 855, and the flux of tourists and week-enders numbered in the thousands.

During the early 1900's, Barkley served as city clerk in addition to getting out the Breeze and was an active and energetic member of the Chamber of Commerce. In 1913, shortly before he sold the Breeze, he became postmaster.

In that day, the Breeze appeared every Saturday. It inevitably was a four-page tabloid. Two slogans on its front page marked its optimism and local patriotism. One read: "20,000—The Population of Redondo Beach in 1915." The other: "For Redondo's Interests, First, Last, and All the Time." The fact that the population prognostication appeared after the official 1910 census of 2935, clearly showed that Barkley was a born optimist.

However, in the light of what was happening, his optimism can be readily excused. Redondo Beach was undergoing a real estate boom comparable to the speculative booms sometimes experienced in gold camps. Real estate, though not being measurably improved, was turning over again and again in the hands of speculators, who actually lived in tents just outside the city and hawked real estate during their waking hours.

The year 1910 saw the $1,500,-000 Edison Co. steam plant in operation and also marked the opening of "the world's largest indoor plunge."

That year, the Breeze moved to the Garland Building, just north of its present location. That the Breeze moved with no fanfare, nor even an announcement, must remain a $64 question. The Breeze was quartered in the basement, where it remained until removal to the basement of its present location.

S. D. BARKLEY
Founder of Breeze

The Breeze, in 1910, won a double-header for the wets over the drys. The feeling sweeping the country, and which eventually led to national prohibition, was markedly high in the Redondo Beach of that time. Wets were wets and dry were drys, with no middle ground to stand upon.

The April election saw the drys put up their own ticket to defeat the "rule of the saloonkeepers." The Breeze promptly aligned with the wets. After a spirited election, the Breeze could jubilantly support its claims of local influence. The drys were put down hard. Not daunted, however, the drys immediately circulated a petition calling for a special election to do away with the sale of spirituous liquors in the city.

The Breeze went into action again, exhorting the people to keep their saloons open. When the smoke cleared away, the Breeze again could trumpet its triumph. "Redondo Beach Votes Wet by Big Majority," the

Breeze of May 21 gleefully chortled in headlines. The "big majority," though only 90, was tabulated at 347 wet votes, 257 dry.

The celebration of this achievement took place in the form of a torch-light parade, in which the rotund form of Barkley figured more than extensively. The toasts drunk to success that night are said to have put to shame the celebration of the opening of the Redondo Hotel, 22 years before.

In accomplishing his victory, however, Barkley's Breeze lost prestige with much of the feminine, the church-going and the sober-minded business population of Redondo Beach. Revenue of the Breeze was said to have fallen off, and of this the Redondo Reflex took advantage. But Doc squeaked through, nevertheless, and, as time healeth all things, the year 1911 saw the Breeze over its financial troubles, at least as far over them as it ever had been.

The Pacific Electric Railway, on April 1, 1911, took over the Vale, Los Angeles & Redondo Railway and the Los Angeles Pacific Railway, thus putting the Pacific Electric in command of transportation so far as Redondo Beach was concerned, although the Santa Fe still terminated in the city. Evidence of the magnitude of the throngs visiting the Redondo Beach area during those days is the report that a Catholic picnic at Redondo one Sunday was attended by 20,000 persons, practically all, if not all of whom were transported by rail at 40 cents for the round trip for adults and 20 cents for children.

The amount of shipping in those days was amazing. For example, the Breeze of August 7, 1909, gives the report of the deputy collector of the port for July as follows: Imports, 2,891,996 feet of lumber, 4,050,000 shingles, 100 bundles of lath, 300 tons of pig iron, 291 tons of merchandise, 104 barrels of oil. Two schooners and 49 steamers arrived during the month with net tonnage of 50,746, while 232 passengers arrived and 1736 departed.

No wonder, then, that Barkley and the Breeze eyed San Pedro's shipping interests with a jaundiced eye. They never lost a chance to fire a broadside at the city over the hill. C. T. Gulliver, editor of the Breeze, noted, probably during one of Barkley's prospecting trips, on the front page of the June 11, 1910, issue: "That Redondo Beach is in favor among shippers of the Orient is noted from the fact that the United States customs office at this place does a larger business and turns in more dollars to Uncle Sam's treasury than does any other port of entry south of San Francisco."

And continuing more pointedly: "While San Pedro will always do a

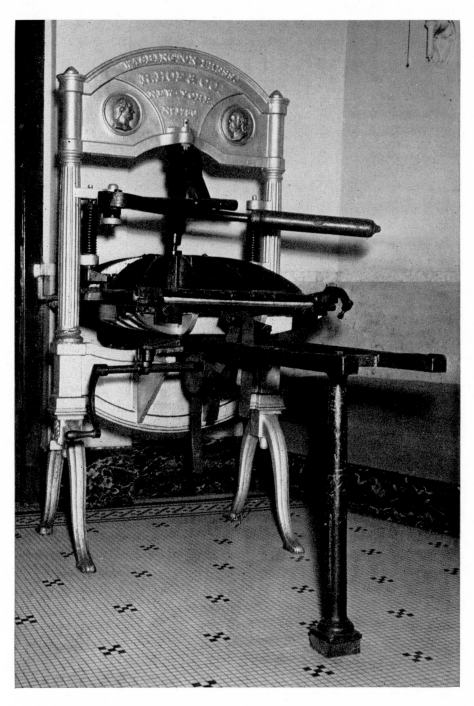

OLD WASHINGTON HAND PRESS RELIC OF LONG AGO
Displayed in Lobby of South Bay Daily Breeze

large business, its trade will be carried on in small vessels plying along the coast and in undersized foreign ships. Redondo Beach has a water depth of about 45 feet at the docks, which would admit the largest vessel afloat."

Alas for the dreams of Redondoans! Again and again were they to try to interest the federal government in a harbor and time and time again they were to fail completely, even to this very day. Redondo shipping dwindled in the same ratio that San Pedro shipping increased.

In 1912, Redondo Beach made its first try for governmental assistance in developing a harbor. A political aspirant, Harry Brolaski, new to the city, put the bee in Redondo's bonnet. He would go to Washington and induce Congress to appropriate $5,000,000 for a harbor. The Breeze was as enthralled as was everybody else. The newspaper recorded each of Brolaski's golden words of wisdom. Brolaski went to Washington and returned in a blaze of glory. Mass meetings were held at which he always was the hero-in-chief.

Finally government engineers appeared on the scene. After looking over the situation, they turned thumbs down on the project. The Breeze was glum and then truculent. After swallowing hard to choke back the tears, the newspaper fired a series of vituperative editorials at San Pedro. Something had to be done to ease the pain.

About that time, the Breeze began to report news of Hermosa Beach and Manhattan Beach. Hermosa Beach numbered 865 inhabitants and Manhattan Beach had "about 75 persons." It was not until years later, however, that the Breeze considered all three cities within its zone of influence and adopted a policy of news coverage of them in about the same ratio.

During this period, Barkley sold the Breeze to George Murphy, a chamber of commerce secretary. Murphy was born in San Diego in 1888. He was a baseball player and was hired to coach the Redondo Beach baseball team in 1910. He was a good coach, apparently, and was well liked, for he was employed also as secretary-manager of the chamber, which was a lively organization, with 150 members.

It also is quite reliably reported that Murphy was hand in glove socially, politically and spiritually with the politician, Brolaski, who had all the aspirations, desires and tendencies toward Redondo Beach that the late Huey Long had in Louisiana. Years later, Brolaski, serving a term in San Quentin Prison for overexerting himself on one of his schemes, was released from that institution, to die of cancer a few months afterward in San Francisco.

Moreover, old-timers say that Brolaski really put up the money for the Breeze and that Murphy was just an office fixture. However that may be, the Breeze vigorously reasserted itself in the politics of the town, made few friends and apparently many enemies.

Frank L. Perry, whose father, a railroad executive on the Los Angeles Railway, and who built the fourth residence in Redondo Beach, bought the paper from Murphy, "some time in the latter part of 1915."

Murphy was made postmaster, replacing, of all persons, S. D. Barkley. Thus one former Breeze publisher succeeded another in a local political appointment.

Perry owned the Breeze just nine months. Various sources claim Perry's purchase was for strictly political purposes. Perry himself, however, is rather hazy on precise dates and facts surrounding his ownership. "I bought the Breeze for $6500," he said. "I think I bought it late in 1915 and sold it in 1916 to George Orgibet, a newspaperman from Chicago. I was no newspaperman and was rather glad to get it off my hands."

When asked how much he received from Orgibet for the newspaper, Perry replied, "Exactly what I paid for it, $6500."

Corroboration came in a vague way from Mrs. George Orgibet, before her death in November, 1952, as she could recall little of her husband's newspaper work. "George bought the Breeze the year before the United States entered the First World War," she said.

Early in 1918, circulation of the Breeze was "631 paid copies." It cost the subscriber $1.50 a year and the advertising rate was 25 cents a column inch. The Breeze of 1918, besides the typical war stories, admonitions and urges peculiar to that year, was full of breakwater excitement again. In 1917, the people of Redondo Beach voted $300,000 in bonds for the construction of a breakwater. Then things hung fire. Early in 1918, however, Harry Brolaski, now a member of the Board of Trustees of the city, "had connections with a shipbuilding company," which was interested in building ships at Redondo Beach. Interest was white hot. The breakwater was to be constructed immediately. Contracts were drawn up and just about the time they were to be signed the shipbuilding corporation reneged and the hopes for a government subsidy and a breakwater at Redondo Beach were exploded again. For the second time, Redondo Beach was to face disappointment in securing a breakwater.

Rivalry between the Reflex and the Breeze was near its zenith when the war ended. Indeed, copies of both papers are full of tub thumpings of disparagement, each for the other. C. H. Turner, editor and publisher of the Reflex, never lost a chance to take a good-sized crack at the Breeze, and

BREEZE CIRCULATION GAINS RAPIDLY, EXCEEDS 13,000

George Orgibet was no slouch in retaliating. Editorial artillery on both sides was not only hot and painful, but was distinctly personal.

In a two-column, page-length editorial, for example, in the November 22, 1918, issue of the Breeze, Orgibet, under the heading, "In the Name of Decency," accused his warring competitor, Turner, of insulting a woman. One can read the editorial to the end without discovering exactly what particular specimen of womanhood was singled out for Turner's insults, but the author of this remarkable diatribe added in a *postscriptum* that he was not referring to Mrs. ————, "who can take care of herself. Our reference to woman covers all women, for when one will attack one woman one will attack all women." That piece of logic seemed to satisfy everybody, except perhaps Turner. At any rate, there is no record of a duel and subsequent issues of both papers find Orgibet and Turner still going it, hammer and tongs.

Turner tells his version of sale of the Breeze to F. W. Kellogg in the late fall of 1922. Said Turner, now retired and living in Redondo Beach: "We weekly newspaper publishers, including Orgibet and myself, were at a convention at Lake Arrowhead. Somebody, I don't remember who it was, remarked that F. W. Kellogg was looking at Redondo Beach with a view to starting a daily newspaper in connection with the Los Angeles Express. Well, you know what? Orgibet packed up and left right then, he did. Just disappeared. And you know what? When we got back to Redondo, Orgibet had sold the Breeze to Kellogg. Pretty fast work, wasn't it?"

Kellogg's acquisition of the Breeze brought about three immediate changes. The Breeze moved to the basement of the Bank of America Building at 105 Wall Street. The building fronts on Pacific Avenue and is the newspaper's present home. The Breeze almost immediately became a daily newspaper, delivered in conjunction with the Los Angeles Express. And the new staff included Hugh Pomeroy, general manager; George North, editor; "Cap" Salinas, advertising manager; Blanche Friend Austin, social editor, and Samuel G. Austin, reporter. (Austin served as Redondo Beach police judge until January 1, 1953, when he retired.) The first issue of the Breeze as a daily was dated Monday, December 18, 1922.

At the time Kellogg acquired the Breeze, circulation was estimated at 1865. Population of Redondo Beach was 4913, according to the 1920 census, Hermosa Beach was 2327, and Manhattan Beach, 1600.

The Breeze virtually limited its local news to Redondo Beach, unless

339

something of great importance occurred in the adjacent cities. The policy of S. D. Barkley to make the Breeze a newspaper representing all three cities had faded into the distant past, and was not resumed, with any degree of force, until after Col. Ira C. Copley bought the newspaper.

Redondo Beach was enjoying some prosperity. The oil lands lying directly to the east were humming with activity. The year 1922, however, brought one big disheartening setback to Redondo. The Redondo Hotel, financially waning through the years, hit the skids completely. Owners, despairing of refinancing or selling, finally had the hotel torn down. For salvage of a few thousand dollars, the pride and glory of old Redondo Beach was obliterated.

A new general manager came to the Breeze in 1923. He was Charles S. Robertson, a tall, thin and genial man, who, it was said, "sold most of the advertising for the paper." Robertson, personally popular, climbed the chairs in the local Elks Lodge and was a pillar in that organization until his death during World War II. Robertson is reported to have worked for F. W. Kellogg in Kansas City before coming to Southern California.

Until mid-1924, the Breeze, even though it was delivered in conjunction with the Los Angeles Express, confined itself largely to wire news. Local stories, despite the fact that the Breeze issued a Hermosa edition, dealt almost entirely with Redondo. The newspaper during the period usually comprised six pages, increasing up to 12 pages on rare occasions when a "special promotion" was the order of the day. Then, quite suddenly, the Breeze changed tactics and played up the local side almost exclusively, running an Associated Press story when it had national significance. Local stories, however, were overwhelmingly confined to Redondo and Hermosa, with Manhattan receiving slight coverage.

Under Kellogg's ownership, the Breeze discontinued the policy of taking a strong stand on local issues. Often it took no stand at all. Rather, it rode the fence, ceased potshotting at its rival, the Reflex, and confined its editorials to things far enough away so as not to incur local criticism. The statement of ownership, published December 6, 1927, gave the Breeze circulation as 2951.

Although Col. Ira C. Copley purchased, in January, 1928, the Los Angeles County newspapers now comprising the Southern California Associated Newspapers, transfer of the Breeze was not made officially until September 1. On that date, the Breeze printed a two-column announcement, which read:

"With yesterday's issue of the Redondo Daily Breeze, the ownership of F. W. Kellogg terminated and this newspaper appears today under new ownership, in accordance with purchase arrangements concluded several months ago and announced at that time.

"No changes in the operation of the publication are considered . . . no changes in personnel are contemplated, except that George S. Thurtle (who replaced Charles Robertson, March 11, 1928, as general manager) has been elected president of the Redondo Breeze Publishing Co."

The announcement concluded: "Redondo Beach and the South Bay communities have benefited greatly through Mr. Kellogg's interest and vision and will continue to gain further advantages accordingly as we come into full realization of that splendid growth and advancement which he had so much made possible."

On January 27, 1929, Thurtle, offered the position as business manager of the Long Beach Sun, another Copley newspaper, left the Breeze. Gail R. Fuller, who succeeded Thurtle, had been managing editor of the Breeze for about a year. Fuller, one reporter and Mrs. Fuller, who was the society editor, comprised the full force of the Breeze editorial department. Fuller was general manager for a year and was succeeded on January 29, 1930, by George F. Orgibet, a former owner of the Breeze.

Since selling the paper to Kellogg in 1922, Orgibet had engaged in the real estate business, first in Redondo Beach and then in Glendale. Prior to returning to the Breeze, he operated a job printing shop in Glendale.

In 1930, the newspaper occupied that portion of the building which now forms the composing room; that is to say, all departments, including a flatbed press, were housed there. The general manager's office was almost adjacent to the press, and as the paper ground out its daily run, conversation must have been difficult. But that wasn't all. The paper at that time did considerable job printing, and the job department also was housed in these more close quarters.

In December, 1930, daily paid circulation was 2358 and revenues from job printing and advertising were about equal. The paper sold at 10 cents a week, 50 cents a month and $4.50 a year.

At that time, news coverage in Manhattan Beach and Hermosa Beach was considerably stepped up, as the management saw possibilities of increased revenue from these closely-woven cities that comprise the South Bay district. Suddenly, in apparent line with this thinking, the name was changed from Redondo Daily Breeze to South Bay Daily Breeze.

On June 12, 1933, John J. Berry replaced George Orgibet as publisher. Berry, who for years had owned a daily newspaper in Paducah, Ky., also had been postmaster in that city before coming to California. He worked for F. W. Kellogg in Long Beach and Pasadena and later on the News in San Pedro, where he was an advertising solicitor. Berry remained with the San Pedro News-Pilot after the News and the Pilot were consolidated.

JOHN J. BERRY
Breeze Publisher, 1933-45

A quiet, soft-spoken man in his late 60's, he always was immaculately attired. Berry made friends quickly in Redondo Beach. He and Mrs. Berry soon were in the city's social picture and their courtesy and quiet way of living brought them the respect of the townspeople.

Conditions in the basement of the Bank of America Building, where the newspaper was housed, finally became unbearably crowded. When the Bank of America moved into its new building, one block south, the Breeze, with the exception of the composing room and the press, moved upstairs. The change was completed by Monday, February 18, 1935, and staffers found the banklike quarters admirably suited to their needs, although to this day an occasional stranger will wander in and inquire for the bank cashier or ask where he can deposit money.

In celebration of the move, a special edition of the Breeze, the largest in its history, was published. The 32-page newspaper was printed the hard way in four eight-page sections, each a separate press run, as the capacity of the flatbed press was eight pages at a time.

Expansion of the Breeze at that time clearly indicated the confidence

Col. Copley held for the future of Redondo Beach. The move was made during the depth of the depression. Indeed, revenue from circulation and advertising had fallen off that year from the year before.

The depression years brought small-time gambling to Redondo Beach's El Paseo, the waterfront street. As the 1930's began to wane, professional gamblers descended on the city. They built sumptuous "bingo" and "tango" establishments. The games "paid off" in negotiable cartons of cigarets. All such places paid the city a "license" fee of $25 a month for each chair, although gambling, of course, was not licensed. With their fronts of tango, many establishments permitted gambling behind closed doors. In the late summer of 1940, Les Bruneman, gangster-gambler, was shot as he walked along El Paseo. Recovering, he was released from a Los Angeles hospital a month later and was shot and killed in a Los Angeles night club. News stories hinted at an internecine gamblers' war at Redondo Beach. Local citizens began looking with anxious eyes toward their rococo bingo zone.

As the year closed, Redondo Beach was possessed of another gambling gimmick. The gambling ship *Rex*, property of the notorious Tony Carnero, was anchored off the coastline and passengers were transported from Redondo's Monstad Pier.

In the spring of 1940, members of the Junior Chamber of Commerce solicited the aid of the Breeze and civic organizations in an effort to drive all gambling from Redondo Beach. They sent informal ballots to all registered voters and the returns showed the citizens to be overwhelmingly opposed to gambling. Gamblers, unaccustomed to this sort of procedure, retaliated with threats and nuisances. Grant Cooper, Los Angeles attorney and former assistant to Buron Fitts, district attorney, was solicited by the Junior Chamber to aid in exposure of gambling in Redondo. This he did with a technique that would do credit to a film director. At a mass meeting, sponsored by the Junior Chamber, Cooper named names and gave an enlightening history of most of the men running El Paseo, including a direct tie-up by two of the concerns with the gangster, Bugsy Siegel. That did it. Gamblers in Redondo Beach silently folded their tents and stole away.

In 1938, the Breeze played a strong part in a $300,000 bond issue to match federal funds for construction of a breakwater. The bond issue passed and work on the breakwater started in January, 1939. With completion of the breakwater in 1939, Redondo Beach received the first of many assaults of the shoreline by the sea, in a four-block area just south of the

HOME OF SOUTH BAY DAILY BREEZE

breakwater. Early in 1940, an assault swept away an entire half block of residences and apartment buildings along the waterfront.

Throughout the war, Redondo Beach suffered almost yearly damage from the sea along the four-block waterfront as high tides smashed at buildings on the Strand. Although efforts were made to obtain government aid to extend the breakwater as a potential harbor, they were in vain.

The Breeze entered the war years with the same trepidations that beset all newspapers. The problems of limited newsprint, curtailed manpower and the necessity of operating under drastic restrictions contributed toward keeping everyone on his toes. Circulation of the Breeze for 1941 stood at 3145 and the newspaper hit a new high of 115,553 in total advertising inches.

On September 4, 1945, John J. Berry dropped dead while working in his garden. On recommendation of Clark F. Waite, F. S. Haynes, just coming out of service, was appointed his successor by Col. Copley.

Haynes, advertising manager of the Breeze from April 13, 1936, to September 30, 1943, had come to the paper from the San Pedro News-Pilot, where he was classified and display advertising solicitor. He joined the News-Pilot May 13, 1931.

During 1945, the Breeze ran 151,235 inches of paid advertising and its circulation stood at 5205.

The war years wrought changes to the South Bay area. Although virtually without industries, the beach cities filled with an overflow of war-plant workers and their families from industrial towns. The old tourist and seasonal days became history.

The next five years saw tremendous growth of the South Bay region as a residential district. There came a steady influx of new businesses which contributed to the growth of the newspaper. The 1940 census, for example, gave Redondo Beach a population of 13,363. The 1950 census showed 25,176. Most of the growth, however, came after the war years. The same pattern held true for Hermosa Beach (7197 population in 1940, and 12,432 in 1950), and Manhattan Beach (5320 population in 1940, and 16,367 in 1950).

A special census, taken in 1953, gave Redondo Beach a population of 35,706. Manhattan Beach, where the Breeze has shown most of its circulation increase on a percentage basis, recorded a population of 26,315. Estimates are that Hermosa Beach will show a 30 percent gain over 1950.

Breeze circulation increased admirably through the years from 5646 in 1946, to 9215 in 1950, to 10,000 in September, 1951, and had climbed to 13,221 on June 1, 1953. Advertising has kept pace in the same manner, the Breeze striking a new high in 1952 of 403,165 inches of total paid advertising.

The press is a Goss 28-page, 3-decker, serial No. 603, with the lower deck three plates wide and the upper decks two plates wide. The capacity is 19,000 newspapers an hour. The typesetting equipment consists of five Linotype machines, one Intertype mixer and a Ludlow. There also is an Elrod material maker. One of the Linotypes is equipped for teletypesetter operation.

The Breeze of 1953 is manned by a corps of 55 regular and part-time employes. In addition to printing the daily newspaper, it produces two shoppers, each with a press run of 11,000 and distributed in two zones.

The Breeze owns the building that houses it and an adjacent store facility now occupied by Firestone Stores. Upstairs are office rooms. Across

BREEZE PUBLISHER AND HEADS OF DEPARTMENTS

Around the table from left, S. C. Stewart, managing editor; Mrs. Leo Tremblay, classi-
fied advertising manager; F. S. Haynes, publisher; Robert A. Macklin, circulation manager;
Lloyd Nicholson, advertising manager; Jess Moore, auditor; Frederic Kaessinger, mechanical
superintendent.

the hall is an immense ballroom. The Breeze probably is the only newspaper in the United States that can boast its own ballroom.

S. C. Stewart is managing editor. He formerly was managing editor
of the Standard-Examiner in Ogden, Utah. Jess Moore, is auditor. Moore
came to the Breeze from the Alhambra Post-Advocate. Lloyd Nicholson is
advertising manager. He was promoted to that position from classified
advertising manager. Mrs. Leo Tremblay is classified manager. Robert
Macklin is circulation manager. He came to the Breeze three years ago from
the Evening Tribune in San Diego. Frederic Kaessinger, former owner of a
job shop in Hawthorne, is mechanical superintendent.

SAN PEDRO NEWS-PILOT

"Where Ship and Rail Meet"

SAN PEDRO ONE OF WORLD'S GREAT SEAPORTS

BYNNER MARTIN
Editor and Publisher, San Pedro News-Pilot
Vice President, San Pedro Printing & Publishing Co.

San Pedro News-Pilot

356 Seventh Street   San Pedro, Calif.

WHEN CLARKE F. WAITE came to San Pedro in the spring of 1909, the little California seaport was split and arguing over whether it should consolidate with the City of Los Angeles.

The San Pedro Daily News was opposed to the idea. So were most of the San Pedro city officials and employes. The News, supporting the San Pedro city administration, almost daily ridiculed or assailed the consolidation plan. The move to merge the harbor communities of San Pedro and Wilmington with Los Angeles stemmed from the long and bitter "Free Harbor" fight. This was a battle extending over a generation and in which San Pedro, backed by Los Angeles, finally won over Santa Monica for improvement as a harbor by the federal government.

Work on the breakwater, a major step in harbor development, already was under way when Waite arrived. But much more needed to be done to build a harbor to serve the expanding trade of Los Angeles. Many San Pedro residents believed an adequate harbor could be achieved only by enlisting the strength and power of Los Angeles.

Clark Waite, a veteran newspaperman, saw two opportunities in San Pedro: first, to help win the consolidation fight; and secondly, to take root and grow with the harbor, the gateway between the Seven Seas and the Southwest.

Waite talked with John T. Gaffey, E. D. Seward, Frank Burns and other San Pedro leaders in favor of consolidation, and with Los Angeles leaders backing the move.

When Waite told them he planned to start a newspaper which would support the consolidation program, they greeted him with open arms and pledged full support.

In April, 1909, Clark Waite began publishing the San Pedro Pilot as a weekly, thus giving the consolidation faction its first local newspaper voice to combat the Daily News.

Waite came to the job well prepared. While only 31 years old, he already had been in the newspaper business for 15 years. He practically grew up in a newspaper office, working with his father, W. J. Waite, who published the weekly Exeter (Neb.) Enterprise. When Clark Waite was 16, he attended the World's Columbian Exposition in Chicago. Upon his return, he went into full-time work with his father. Later they bought the Geneva (Neb.) Gazette in the Fillmore County seat, and Clark ran that paper for several years.

In those early years, Clark Waite learned all phases of the newspaper business, from setting type by hand and operating a Washington hand press to trading a subscription for such farm produce as potatoes, eggs, bacon and ham. In Exeter, he met the daily train and thus kept tab on who was going and coming and why. He did not bother to write these personals. Instead, he went back to the shop and set them in type directly from his notes.

Early in 1906, Waite sold out in Nebraska and came to Southern California, living first in Pomona and then in Santa Ana, where he was business manager of the Santa Ana Register. Afterward, while working as manager of a Huntington Beach weekly, he read the San Pedro Daily News, received among the exchanges, and became interested in the San Pedro situation.

Later, Waite published the Scout at La Mesa, near San Diego, for a year, but he kept thinking of the harbor controversy. Finally he wrote to John T. Gaffey, who with others invited him to come to San Pedro.

Clark Waite started his paper in the plant of the defunct San Pedro Times, which a few months before had sold its subscription list to the Daily News. The equipment, formerly owned by E. B. Scott, included a flatbed press, a supply of hand-set type and other items, but no Linotype. In order to speed composition, he mailed his copy to a Los Angeles commercial shop, where it was set. Each week he rode the Pacific Electric Railway to Los Angeles to fetch home the galleys of type.

San Pedro in 1909 had a population of less than 6000. The business buildings clustered close to the main channel, along Front Street (now

Harbor Boulevard) and Beacon Street, between Fourth and Seventh Streets.

The residential areas fanned out to the north, west and south. But in those days few houses were west of Pacific Avenue. Small as it was, San Pedro was a cosmopolitan town, made up of many nationalities and factions.

Politically it was controlled by the liquor interests. There were 14 saloons as well as several "blind pigs" in Happy Valley, the "night town" section of the city. The most profitable business in town was the one wholesale liquor house, owned by the political leaders of San Pedro. There were more saloons than any other type of business and they ran wide open, practically night and day.

Church folk and others in the community protested in vain. At election times, they campaigned vigorously, but never were able to break the liquor element's control.

Waite soon saw that attacks on the saloon situation offered a fruitful avenue to rally support for consolidation. Once the two cities were merged, San Pedro would be ruled by Los Angeles city and its police department. Throughout the election campaign, he hammered at the San Pedro city administration and the liquor element and pointed out the advantages of consolidation.

Stung by the barbs, the Daily News struck back with ridicule or scathing editorials. The fact that the News took note of the little weekly San Pedro Pilot worked to Waite's advantage. Residents who otherwise might not have bothered to read the Pilot bought it because of the News' jibes and jeers.

At that time, John C. Wray was editor and W. C. Miller publisher of the News. The News contended that, even if the consolidation went through, nothing would be done about the excessive terminal rates then existing in San Pedro, and that the increased taxes would be out of proportion to the benefits received. The News also scoffed at the possibility of Los Angeles carrying out any of the pledges it might make.

All Los Angeles newspapers backed consolidation, but Waite's hard-hitting campaign was a major factor in the victory. At the election, on August 12, 1909, San Pedro voted, 726 to 227, to consolidate with Los Angeles.

Wray took the defeat in good grace. In his first issue after the election, the banner headline read: "Merger Landslide Greatest in History of San Pedro." And the several secondary heads said: "In the Face of the Will of the People as Expressed Yesterday at the Polls, It Is the Duty of Every Man to Get Busy, Put His Shoulder to the Wheel and See to It that San Pedro Receives Every Possible Advantage from the Victory. The News Made the Best Fight Possible, and Lost, and that Tells the Whole Story."

It did for a time. In subsequent issues, Wray needled Los Angeles officialdom and business associations, claiming certain deals had been made which, if known, might have changed the result of the election. One of these deals, Clark Waite learned later, was that the San Pedro saloon operators had been promised secretly in Los Angeles that their licenses would be protected.

As the years passed, both the News and the Pilot criticized Los Angeles for slowness in fulfilling consolidation pledges for improvements.

In 1909, the first notable change came after consolidation in the closing of the saloons on Sundays. In a report on the innovation, the Pilot said that the newly-assigned Los Angeles officers had nothing to do the first Sunday until late in the afternoon when a woman, "apparently unaware that San Pedro and Los Angeles had been merged, created a disturbance in Happy Valley and had to be locked up."

The saloon operators said they lost $1200 in business, but the Pilot remarked that much of the business came from out of town and conditions aboard the electric cars now would be much better on Sundays for passengers who did not patronize the saloons.

Wilmington eight days earlier also had voted, 107 to 61, to consolidate with Los Angeles. The San Pedro victory thus brought the harbor under the jurisdiction of the great city.

Los Angeles had prepared for this avenue to the sea by annexing, on May 26, 1906, a "shoestring strip" of land from its southern border to Wilmington's boundary.

San Pedro's branch City Hall is 25 miles from the Los Angeles City Hall, and is 54 miles from Los Angeles city's northernmost boundary.

The consolidation of the cities marked the beginning of a new era for San Pedro, an era in which Clark Waite played a major role through his newspaper in developing harbor facilities and commerce to the point that Los Angeles a generation ago became and still is the leading port on the Pacific Coast.

With 28 miles of water frontage and 2780 acres of land area, the har-

SERVING SAN PEDRO'S CIVIC, CULTURAL AND BUSINESS INTERESTS

bor today spreads over San Pedro, Wilmington and Terminal Island, and represents an investment of more than $125,000,000.

In a boat trip around the harbor today, cargo and passenger vessels may be observed from most of the maritime nations of the world. One sees

353

the breakwaters, the channels, the piers, transit sheds, the ship- and boat-yards, lumber, fish canneries, oil terminals, copra plants, yachts, tugs, ferries, fishing boats, a great naval base and naval shipyard and warships anchored in the roadstead.

Advanced as the harbor is, the job of building is far from done. The harbor department completed in 1953 an $8,250,000 terminal for the Matson Line in the East Basin, and has plans for additional construction. Los Angeles Harbor, lying on the western shore of San Pedro Bay, is man-made, a tribute to American genius and perseverance.

Yet this was San Pedro's destiny. Historically, the harbor dates back to 1542, when Juan Rodríguez Cabrillo, a Portuguese navigator sailing under the Spanish flag, made reference to Point Fermin and the slough that was to be developed into a harbor. Later, the early Spaniards and padres from the Old World and Mexico used San Pedro Bay for trade in hides and foodstuffs.

As the Spaniards moved north in the late 1700's, they established presidios, missions and pueblos. Los Angeles was founded in September, 1781. Then came the grants of the ranchos. San Pedro today stands on parts of two famous ranchos, Rancho San Pedro and Rancho los Palos Verdes.

American shipmasters began trading at San Pedro in 1805. The American sailing ship *Lelia Byrd*, Capt. William Shaler, anchored in Avalon Bay, at nearby Santa Catalina Island, where its officers and crew could safely defy the Spanish law forbidding commerce between Californians and foreign vessels. From Catalina, the Americans sent small boats carrying silks, shawls and shoes to San Pedro to barter for hides, tallow and provisions.

This was the beginning of a trade which in a few years made San Pedro the greatest hide shipping port on the coast. Commerce grew and became more varied following the Gold Rush of 1849 and California's admission into the Union in 1850.

But it was not until the 1850's that San Pedro began to develop as a town. And it was not until 1882 that San Pedro's townsite was laid out on a 400-acre tract set aside for the purpose in the partitioning of Rancho los Palos Verdes. San Pedro was incorporated March 1, 1888.

Little can be found in the files about early San Pedro newspapers. But apparently more than a score of weekly newspapers were started and later suspended prior to 1900.

Some of the earliest newspapers in the state were published in San

NEWS-PILOT PUBLISHED IN THREE-STORY BRICK BUILDING

Pedro. They included the San Pedro Clipper, the Harbor Advocate, the Sun, the San Pedro Record, an early San Pedro Pilot, and the San Pedro Times.

Ever since the News and the Pilot were consolidated in 1928, the News-Pilot has carried in its masthead a statement that the San Pedro Daily News was established in 1901. But research for this history disclosed that the date actually was 1903.

No one currently associated with the News-Pilot can recall the source of the 1901 date. The files of the News from its inception until January, 1906, have been lost. Apparently, at the time of the merger of the News and the Pilot, some one asserted that the News was established in 1901, and it was so stated in the masthead.

But the record in the office of Secretary of State Frank M. Jordan, at Sacramento, shows that the San Pedro Morning News Co. was incorporated November 11, 1903. The incorporators were S. A. Conner, of San Pedro, and J. Mills Davies, Daniel Neuhart, Frank G. Finlayson and M. T. Collins, all of Los Angeles.

The corporation was capitalized at $5000, with shares at $10 each. Conner and Davies were the major investors, each subscribing for $1500 worth of stock. Neuhart put in $110, Finalyson $50, and Collins $10.

Two years later, on December 14, 1905, the San Pedro Morning News Co. forfeited its charter for failure to pay its state taxes. But this was the result of a change in ownership and the formation of a new company to publish the paper.

In a special edition, issued March 24, 1906, the News reported on its heritage in these words:

"The San Pedro Daily News was established a little over two years ago as a morning newspaper. It was founded by Messrs. Davies and Conner, who formed the San Pedro Morning News Co., a corporation.

"The Daily News seemed to fill a long-felt want from the very start, and was not long in securing a large circulation and a generous advertising patronage. The original founders of the paper, however, sold it after a few months and sought other fields.

"More than a year ago, the present owners, Messrs. Miller and Hogaboom, secured control of it. The paper had in the meantime been changed from a morning to an evening paper.

"The present owners organized a new corporation, the San Pedro Publishing Co., which has purchased the stock of the old corporation and all the material and good will of the company, and since the first of the year has been doing business under the new organization. The company is capitalized for $25,000. A majority of the stock is owned by Messrs. Miller and Hogaboom. W. C. Miller is president and general manager of the company and W. H. Hyatt is secretary. Winfield Hogaboom is editor of the Daily News and treasurer of the San Pedro Publishing Co."

Hyatt was an attorney and secretary of the San Pedro Chamber of Commerce, and was not active in the operation of the paper.

In 1906, the News plant was located at 220 Sixth Street, but on March 8, 1906, without fanfare in its columns, was moved to 519 Beacon Street, where it remained until 1915.

ARTHUR L. WAITE
Joined Pilot in 1909

JULIUS A. (DUDE) WAITE
Started with Pilot in 1910

Under the impetus of the consolidation fight, Clark Waite's Pilot soon became a strong competitor against the News. Within a year, the Pilot became a semi-weekly with editions on Wednesdays and Saturdays. Arthur L. Waite joined his brother in the fall of 1909, and Julius A. (Dude) Waite, the third brother, joined the Pilot in January, 1910. Harry Johnson was the first printer outside the family to work for the Pilot. Johnson still is with the company.

In 1914, the Waites' father, W. J. Waite, sold his business in Nebraska and came to San Pedro. Warned by a doctor that he probably had only six months to live because of a heart condition, W. J. Waite soon settled into a job of editorial writer and real estate editor and lived until 1931.

In 1912, the Pilot became a daily paper and from then until it was merged with the News in 1928, it was published by the Waite brothers. The Pilot's first carriers were John Gaudino and Marco DeNicolai. Both now are prominent San Pedro business men. Gaudino is manager of the Bank of America's Tenth Street and Pacific Avenue branch, and DeNicolai is manager of the E. K. Wood Lumber & Supply Co. office.

Gaudino and DeNicolai recall that Sixth Street was the dividing line for their territories. Gaudino carried the four-page papers on the north side

357

of the town and DeNicolai on the south side. For their services as carriers and other work around the plant, each received $1.50 a month.

In those early days, DeNicolai recalls, Dude and Art Waite slept on cots in the rear of the print shop. Clark Waite, a married man with a family, had a house.

The Pilot's first plant was in a frame building on Beacon Street, between Sixth and Seventh Streets. Within six months, Waite moved the Pilot into quarters in the new and modern Ferl Building, of brick construction, on the northwest corner of Seventh and Beacon Streets. This was the Pilot's home until Memorial Day, 1918, when the plant was moved to 246 Sixth Street, next door to the News.

The News had moved in January, 1915, to 254 Sixth Street. In maintaining publication while making the transfer from 519 Beacon Street, the News encountered some

W. J. WAITE
Wrote Editorials

difficulties and frustrations which it reported to its readers.

For example, in the issue of January 7, 1915, the News complained that an electric power break had delayed the printing of the paper, and added: "This inconvenience, coming after the chaotic condition which invariably prevails during moving time, is more than exasperating to the News and its staff of employes."

But six days later, the News, in a large display advertisement, announced that the moving was done, and boasted: "We now have one of the best lighted, ventilated and convenient offices of its size on the coast; with individual motors on all machinery, controlled by the latest electrical devices, and are in a position to serve you with the newest in type, ink and paper. We wish to thank our friends and customers for their indulgences during the stress of moving. With this issue everything is installed and in complete operation. No more delays or late editions are expected."

The News, like others, had no complete guard against human frailty. In its issue for January 22, 1915, one of its pages was blank except for this message in large type: "This page of today's issue was accidentally pied at the last moment. Give the devil his due. He did it!"

When the Pilot moved next door to the News, competition between the papers became more intense. At World Series time, the papers tried to outdo each other in size of scoreboard and speed in reporting the progress of the baseball games. The News was a member of The Associated Press and the Pilot subscribed to United Press.

The papers also tried to excel each other in covering the news, getting advertising and circulation, and business for their job shops. Even as they competed avidly for leadership, both played strong roles in the development of the community.

John C. Wray, the editor with whom Clark Waite dueled with words during the consolidation fight, left the News late in March, 1916. His departure was as unheralded as had been his appointment as editor more than eight years before. Winfield Hogaboom was editor of the News until August 13, 1907, when he announced he had sold his interest in the paper to George M. Braxton, of Julesburg, Colo. Braxton became editor, but little more than two months later, on October 25, 1907, Braxton's name was replaced in the masthead by that of Wray.

Wray was a crusading editor. He frequently wrote long and forceful articles about conditions in the community or about some phase of city administration. Most San Pedro old-timers, when asked in 1953 about the early days of the News, remembered only Johnny Wray.

Wray's name was removed from the masthead without explanation. A week later, on April 1, 1916, General Manager W. C. Miller announced he had sold an interest in and turned over the management of the News to Edward M. Boyd, a 52-year-old newspaperman, who had worked in Pittsburgh, Washington and Honolulu.

Boyd ran the News for 18 months, when unexpected death ended his career. He was fatally injured, October 16, 1917, in an automobile accident in Mill Creek Canyon, as he was returning from a duck-shooting trip to Big Bear Lake. His widow, Mary D. Boyd, became editor of the paper and W. J. Williams became business manager.

This arrangement lasted less than six months. Williams left the News on March 27, 1918, and two weeks afterward, on April 10, 1918, the News was sold to F. W. Tenney and C. H. Fawcett. Tenney and Fawcett bought the publication, the plant, and the stock of the San Pedro Publishing Co. The stock was owned by W. C. Miller, Mrs. Mary D. Boyd and Mrs. H. M. Gibbs, Miller's sister.

Announcement of the sale said that Tenney formerly had a half interest in the Baker (Ore.) Herald and had been at Baker for six and a half years. Prior to that time he had worked on the Boston Journal and the New York Evening Journal. At the News, he became the manager of the editorial and advertising departments.

Fawcett had worked for three and a half years at the Baker Herald as circulation manager, the announcement said, and later with the Examiner (presumably the Los Angeles Examiner). Fawcett became circulation manager of the News.

World War I brought a surge of growth to San Pedro. Shipyards sprang up and vessels were built to carry supplies to Europe; harbor commerce boomed; Fort MacArthur teemed with men preparing for service, and the Navy established a submarine base in the Outer Harbor.

San Pedro was unprepared for the influx. Hundreds of persons literally camped in the town, living in tents on vacant lots. The Pilot in May, 1918, estimated the population at 16,000, an increase of 37 percent within a year.

But in 1921 the war boom had ended. The shipyards had shut down and the servicemen had gone home. That San Pedro business dropped off may have been the major factor in Tenney's and Fawcett's decision to sell the News to F. W. Kellogg. The sale was announced October 17, 1921. Kellogg bought the News as a link in a chain of a dozen Los Angeles area community papers which he forged by purchase or by starting new papers.

Kellogg appointed Joseph Frishman as business manager of the News; Edward Reese, circulation manager; Thomas R. (Speed) Evans, city editor; Wayne B. Cave, telegraph editor, and Walter F. Cook, auditor. Frishman left the Pilot to become manager of the News. He first worked for the Pilot as a printer, later as an advertising salesman.

Kellogg had an arrangement with the Los Angeles Express, an afternoon daily, by which he offered News subscribers both the Express and the News at a club rate of 65 cents a month. At the time, the News subscription rate was 50 cents and that of the Express 65 cents. The Express was so eager to gain circulation, however, that the paper was delivered to News subscribers regardless of whether they agreed to pay the additional 15 cents under the club rate.

Kellogg immediately added more shop equipment and improved the News in content and makeup. The News carried more syndicated features, but the files show that the Pilot put more emphasis on local news and names.

Clark Waite was quick to point out to advertisers a basic weakness in the News and Express circulation arrangement. He emphasized that, when the Express and the News were delivered to a home, 85 percent of the advertising was for Los Angeles stores, only 15 percent for San Pedro stores. The Pilot, Waite declared, did not accept competitive Los Angeles or Long Beach advertising. The Pilot's policy was to build business in San Pedro, not in Los Angeles.

Kellogg was determined to make the experiment work. Three years after he bought the News, he built a new plant for the paper at 356 Seventh Street, the building which today (1953) is occupied by the News-Pilot.

Shortly after Kellogg's purchase of the News, business picked up in San Pedro when a real estate boom developed. New subdivisions were opened and home building proceeded at a fast pace. By 1925, the population was estimated at 36,000.

The News and the Pilot competed strongly for business, each periodically claiming leadership in circulation, and each ever alert to point out the shortcomings of the other.

By 1927, the real estate boom had subsided and San Pedro settled down to a slower pace. Late in 1927, Kellogg began negotiations which resulted in the sale of his newspapers to Col. Ira C. Copley. The sale of the News to Col. Copley was announced on February 15, 1928.

At the time these negotiations had been going on, Col. Copley was dickering with the Waite brothers for an interest in the Pilot and its merger with the News. Three weeks after Col. Copley bought the News, the consolidation of the two papers was announced. Clark Waite was named general manager and president of the San Pedro Printing & Publishing Co. The announcement was made on March 5, 1928, and the first issue of the combined papers was published the next day.

The announcement stated that the merged papers had a circulation in excess of 10,000 and would be better able to serve advertisers and residents of San Pedro. In checking the subscription lists, it was found that only 674 homes had been subscribing to both the News and the Pilot.

In its first issue, the News-Pilot carried a dozen congratulatory messages from prominent San Pedro residents. Typical of the comments were the statements by John T. Gaffey and Mrs. Rudecinda F. S. de Dodson, the latter a member of the pioneer Sepulveda family.

Gaffey said: "I congratulate you. The consolidation is good for you and means a lot to San Pedro."

Mrs. Dodson said: "One paper, I think, is a very good idea, because it will give better service to the community."

Apparently there was no criticism of the merger. In fact, Clark Waite complained in his column a week after the consolidation that no one had approached him to argue about it and he therefore had not had the chance to point out in person all the advantages of the new arrangement.

In the same column, Waite reaffirmed the promise to provide San Pedro and the harbor area with a better newspaper, fair to all. He said that, under the stress of competition, neither the Pilot nor News had been making a fair profit, but, with the savings effected by the consolidation, the management could now operate profitably and at the same time give advertisers and subscribers more for their money.

The following year, the News-Pilot remodeled its building to make better use of space on the top floor which for several years had been occupied by the San Pedro branch of the municipal court. The second floor of the three-story forward part of the 45-by-125-foot brick building was cut back halfway, making it into a mezzanine. Decorative iron grillwork was installed, new desks and chairs were purchased, and the entire plant was redecorated. To celebrate the transformation, the News-Pilot, on November 29, 1929, issued a 24-page special edition and held open house.

Within a year after the consolidation, Clark Waite was asked to assist in the management of the Hollywood News, one of the Kellogg papers acquired by the Southern California Newspapers, Associated. But he kept in touch with the News-Pilot and retained the titles of president and general manager.

When he went to Hollywood, his brother, J. A. Waite, became acting manager of the News-Pilot. This arrangement continued until February 11, 1931, when J. A. Waite was appointed general manager.

W. H. (Bill) Bastedo was managing editor at the time. Bastedo, in November, 1929, had succeeded Lowell Jessen as managing editor. Jessen, who had been editor of the News, now is editor and publisher of the Beverly Hills (Calif.) Citizen. Shortly after J. A. Waite's formal elevation to general manager, the name of the third brother, Arthur L. Waite, was inserted in the masthead with the title of advertising manager. Arthur Waite later became business manager, a job he held until his death, August 8, 1945.

J. A. Waite guided the News-Pilot through the tough years of the depression. It was during that decade, in late 1937, that the News-Pilot was picketed, so far for the only time, in protest to an editorial.

The editorial criticized the national leadership of the Workers Alliance, an organization formed by some of the persons employed on Works Progress Administration projects.

A delegation of a dozen called upon J. A. Waite, demanding that he "retract" the statements made in the editorial. Waite's reply was that he would not retract the statements, but would print their rebuttal. The delegation scorned this and began picketing. Twenty-five pickets appeared the first day and fewer the second and third days, after which the picketing ended.

J. A. Waite continued at the helm of the News-Pilot through World War II. His biggest problems were getting enough help to produce the paper and enough newsprint to accommodate the growing circulation.

At the end of 1941, the News-Pilot's paid circulation was 11,416. At war's end, in December, 1945, the circulation was 13,288. The News-Pilot's peak in circulation—13,734—was reached in March, 1946.

World War II brought another boom to San Pedro similar but on a grander scale than the one the town experienced during World War I. Five shipyards mushroomed to build cargo and naval vessels, and a half dozen boatyards were busy with smaller craft.

The Navy built a new base on Terminal Island and brought in thousands of personnel. The Army expanded at Fort MacArthur, established anti-aircraft stations along the coast, and raised barrage balloons in San Pedro. The government built four housing projects in San Pedro, two in Wilmington and one in Harbor City to accommodate the influx of war workers.

San Pedro's population jumped from the census figure of 43,005 in 1940 to an estimated 61,000 in 1945.

Sixty percent of the stock of the San Pedro Printing & Publishing Co., owner of the News-Pilot, is held by Southern California Associated News-

RUTH MASSEY WAITE
Early Stockholder

LILA WAITE
Inherited Husband's Interest

papers, while 40 percent is the property of the Waite family. The minority interest originally was held by Clark F. Waite; his wife, Ruth Massey Waite; J. A. Waite and Arthur L. Waite. Following the death of Mrs. Ruth Massey Waite, her interest passed to her son, Alden C. Waite, and her daughter, Mrs. Marjorie Wanglin. When Mrs. Wanglin died in 1949, her holdings went to her husband, Byron Chase Wanglin II. Mrs. Lila Waite inherited the shares of her husband, Arthur L. Waite, when he died in 1945.

J. A. Waite remained as publisher of the News-Pilot until February, 1946. By then he had completed 35 years of active newspaper work. He stepped out of the job of publisher, but continues as president of the San Pedro Printing & Publishing Co., and as an adviser.

William (Bill) Shea succeeded Waite as publisher of the News-Pilot. Shea came to San Pedro from Culver City, where for 19 years he had been publisher of the Star-News, another SCAN paper.

Shea arrived as San Pedro was beginning to readjust from the peak activity of the war years to a peacetime pace. The shipyards shut down and the military service personnel headed home. San Pedro lost population as war workers returned east or moved to other localities where they could find employment.

The News-Pilot readjusted, too, expanding its local news and picture coverage and encouraging work on a host of community projects which had been stymied because of the war.

Shea managed the News-Pilot a little more than two years. In May, 1948, he became general manager of the Union-Tribune Publishing Co., in San Diego, and later was appointed associate publisher.

Bynner Martin was appointed to succeed Shea as publisher. Martin had joined the News-Pilot staff in September, 1929, as suburban news editor. He later served as sports editor, then telegraph editor and in August, 1937, was named managing editor, succeeding W. H. Bastedo, who went to the Los Angeles Times.

Martin's family first came to San Pedro from Kansas in the summer of 1910, when he was 7 years old. The family remained a year, then moved to Tropico, now part of Glendale, but returned in the spring of 1918, at the height of the World War I boom. Martin was graduated from San Pedro High School and Pomona College. He worked a year as a sports

BYRON CHASE WANGLIN II
Acquired Wife's Holdings

MARJORIE WANGLIN
Daughter of Clark F. Waite

SAN PEDRO NEWS-PILOT DEPARTMENT HEADS

Seated, left to right, Carl A. Johnson, composing room foreman; Lewis H. Puryear, managing editor; Helen J. Anderson, auditor; Robert U. Davies, press foreman. Back row, left to right, Arnold F. Ecklund, display advertising manager; George A. Coverdale, classified advertising manager; William R. Watson, circulation manager, and Alex Karbownik, stereotype foreman.

writer on the Los Angeles Record, prior to joining the News-Pilot staff.

When Martin succeeded Shea as publisher, he named Lewis H. Puryear, an employe of the News-Pilot since August, 1937, as managing editor. Other department heads then and now (1953) are Arnold F. Ecklund, display advertising; George A. Coverdale, classified advertising; Helen J. Anderson, business office; William R. Watson, circulation; Carl A. Johnson, composing room, and Alex Karbownik, stereotyping department. Bertram G. (Gerry) Burke, press foreman at the time, went to The San Diego Union and Tribune-Sun in November, 1948, and Robert U. Davies was appointed press foreman.

The News-Pilot staff today comprises 55 full-time employes. The shop equipment includes two Intertype mixers and four Linotype machines. One of the Linotypes is equipped with a teletypesetter for the setting of Associated Press copy and SCAN features. The paper is printed on a Goss double-width quad decker type press with a color deck. Built in 1910, the press has a capacity of 32 pages and a top speed of 32,500 copies an hour. It was purchased from the Salt Lake Tribune and installed at the News-Pilot in 1938.

Since the war, San Pedro's development has been slow, compared with other Los Angeles area communities. The population dropped from 61,341 as estimated in a special U. S. census check in January, 1946, to 54,378, the 1950 census figure.

Few new business buildings have been erected since the war, but, beginning in 1949, home construction has gradually increased. In the last three years, four subdivisions, with a total of 350 houses, have been completed. Besides these, about 500 houses have been built throughout the town. They compensate in part for loss of residents in public housing. One temporary housing project of 998 units has been vacated, and another of 2000 units is half empty.

San Pedro, situated on the eastern slopes of the Palos Verdes Hills, is not so well suited for mass building as communities located on flat land. However, the slopes of the Palos Verdes gradually are becoming dotted with fine homes and it is inevitable that some day all of these hillsides will be covered by dwellings.

A notable event in 1952, in which the News-Pilot played a prominent role, was the successful campaign for community financing of an $800,000 resort-type hotel to be built on a Palos Verdes knoll.

As these hundreds of acres of land are developed, San Pedro will become more and more a city of homes. San Pedro has little land for light industry, no land for heavy industry. The main pillars of San Pedro's economy for years have been nearby oil refining, the commercial fishing industry, and shipping and its related activities. A growing source of income will be the money spent by people who choose San Pedro as a place to live, but who work elsewhere.

The News-Pilot will endeavor to serve these people and seek to weld them into the civic, cultural and business life of San Pedro.

Washington Bureau

"A Capital Listening-post for Copley Press City Desks"

THE NATIONAL CAPITOL

369

ROBERT W. RICHARDS
Chief of Washington Bureau
The Copley Press, Inc.

370

Washington Bureau

Suite 1200   Washington, D. C.
National Press Building

T HE WASHINGTON BUREAU of The Copley Press was born amid
war. It was weaned on the curdled milk of a doubtful peace, while the
nation was torn within as it had been threatened from without. Its layette
was scant—a ream of onion tissue and three battered rental typewriters. The
manger for the infant was a tiny room in which the staff literally tucked
heads 'neath one another's arms.

The address read: Suite 314, National Press Building, but that was a
misnomer. The office comprised only 150 square feet. Its one window
looked west, admitting the broiling sun of Washington's midsummer and
the raucous clatter of traffic from the capital's busiest corner, Fourteenth
and F Streets, Northwest. To be sure, cool vistas of the White House
grounds lay only a couple of blocks away. But they were obscured behind
the aging weather-stained Willard Hotel and the U. S. Treasury. So it was
that the Washington Bureau first saw the light of day.

Space for its initial striving to thrive and grow shriveled under a dimin-
ishing return of scanty newsprint. Nurtured by plenty of printer's ink, it
could in time prove its right to survive—move on to maturity. For a period
it got that nourishing diet of type irregularly.

Editors of those Copley newspapers who fed it vitamins of regular play
and featured position were rewarded, they were good enough to acknowledge, with quickening reader interest.

Why a Washington Bureau? Some Copley executives pondered that
question at the bureau's nativity. Quite naturally some were dubious. Copley

371

newspapers had been successful without such trappings. And where would room be found for the bureau's maiden effort? The famine of wood pulp already had pared local news to the bone and required the pitching of reams of wire-service copy into the wastebasket. Even advertising, which paid the way, was rationed.

Margins had been reduced, headlines compressed, features eliminated. Scrimping was necessary on other time-tried content. Already most of the Copley papers were carrying one or more Washington columns, written by nationally-known writers. If not always authoritative, they often were provocative, and in any event well read. And they cost only a few dollars a week—far less than a cub reporter's wage. Syndicate salesmen were hounding publishers to brighten editorial pages with other big names.

Here was a new bureau, elbowing for a spot in already tight columns. Could its copy compare with the Washington coverage already flowing into Copley city rooms from the seasoned staffs of The Associated Press, United Press and International News Service?

Whoever heard of Robert W. Richards, or Frank Macomber, or Frank Kuest, or Richard Pourade (a member of the original bureau staff, now associate editor and managing editor of The San Diego Union), or any of the several girls, from Mary Hoke to Juanita Williams, who have toiled in the federal garden for The Copley Press? Would their by-lines mean anything? And would readers differentiate between Copley reporters, reflecting their own impression of the national scene, and those writers laboring for the wire services? Or did they care how news came to them, so long as it was fresh and readable?

Was there, then, sound reason for all of America's great papers, scores of lesser ones and others in lands across the seas, to maintain expensive establishments in Washington? The late Col. Ira C. Copley, founder of The Copley Press, believed there was.

Today more than 500 daily papers are represented in the capital by nearly 1400 newsmen and women, with another 500-plus working for magazines, radio and television. Many of the bureaus are being expanded because editors believe critical times in which the republic finds itself require greater enlightenment on how their government functions.

Col. Copley was convinced, when he envisioned and launched the Washington Bureau in 1944, that the already strong community flavor of his newspapers would be substantially enhanced by interpretations from his

FRANK MACOMBER
Correspondent

FRANK KUEST
Correspondent

own on-the-spot observers of what makes Washington tick. For what Washington does touches every home and reaches into every pocket.

He desired understanding home-town eyes through which the readers might peer into Washington's crystal ball, clarifying what they saw therein as to its probable bearing on their own pursuit of life, liberty and happiness —those inalienable rights willed them by the Founding Fathers, for those rights have seemed on the verge of washing down the drain.

His son, James S. Copley, now board chairman of The Copley Press, agreed. The young man who now controls the 15 Copley newspapers had been stationed in Washington as a naval officer during World War II. His is a first-hand understanding of "what gives" in the seat of the federal government.

By way of explaining what he was about, Col. Copley cited a circumstance to Bob Richards, whom he had asked to head his new venture as chief of bureau.

It was a sultry May evening in 1944, the war's end still more than a year away. Richards had been an operations officer for Gen. William J. (Wild Bill) Donovan's intelligence agency, the Office of Strategic Services, living in the questionable glamor of a city, sardine-packed with a million and a quarter war and government workers, thrice the number it could comfortably house and feed.

The teeming town was a far cry from the Washington of two decades before, then a quiet and beautiful community, easygoing in its semi-southern setting on the Potomac Flats, with restaurants noted for fine cuisine, excellent hotels and attractive residences.

JUANITA WILLIAMS
Secretary

It seemed in urgent need of a psychiatrist. The press of war's demands beat against a lust for power by forces swirling out of the previous global maelstrom and its aftermath of economic depression. Richards' yearnings at that time were for the quieter eddies of life. He was a country boy at heart, looking for the vine-covered cottage and a hammock slung between spreading elms. But there was a job to be done. Col. Copley outlined it in detail, and with the following example:

Franklin Roosevelt, in 1944, was the seeming eternal occupant of 1600 Pennsylvania Avenue, which had become the No. 1 address on this troubled planet. His legendary power to sway the Congress, though earlier challenged, had reasserted itself, since none could say him nay during the nation's hour of peril.

In a pique at Capitol Hill's rejection of his demand for stiffer levies, he just had vetoed a tax bill, with so acrimonious a tongue-lashing of the lawmakers that in the most deliberative body on earth—the U. S. Senate—up rose the president's senior spokesman, Majority Leader "Dear Alben" Barkley, later to become vice president.

Unable longer to take more of the abuse he had endured so patiently for so long, his face red with anger and his voice shaking with emotion, Barkley hurled defiance at his White House master and resigned forthwith.

PRESIDENT EISENHOWER STRESSES POINT TO RICHARDS

It was a high moment in the era Roosevelt, marking a definite return to legislative independence.

"We should," Col. Copley remarked, "have been in on that and should have reported what our senators and congressmen thought about it."

The telegraphic services had covered the Barkley revolt, as Col. Copley knew. It was his thought, however, that his papers needed more than generalized accounts of this big story.

The A.P., U.P. and I.N.S., necessarily beamed for the many, are limited by time and space to little more than a lick and a promise of events in Washington having specific interest to the Copley-served communities. The bureau was to apply an inquisitive finger to the capital's pulse with special regard for the well-being of the folk in those cities, most of whom are readers of Copley newspapers. This was to be its principal assignment—a Washington listening-post for the papers' city desks, just as they watch local municipal buildings, courthouses, police and fire stations, which are standby sources of information.

375

In this strong emphasis on local and regional news, The Copley Press Washington Bureau differs sharply from most other news bureaus in Washington, which focus attention almost exclusively on the center ring. The metropolitan dailies keep busy staffs of from half a dozen to as many as 36, the number of reporters and sub-editors the New York Times regards as necessary to its journalistic pre-eminence, and second only to the 75 men retained by both the A.P. and U.P. on the firing line, and backed by another 100 in the office for rewrite, liaison, and other duties.

The large bureaus deploy their staffers to the White House, various executive departments such as State, Treasury, Defense, Senate and House wings of the capitol, congressional committees, Supreme Court and other agencies of government. Essentially they duplicate the wire services, rather than supplement them.

This duplication is expensive, but the prestige it affords, in the highly competitive big cities, has been held by publishers to be worth the cost. In their concentration on strictly national and world affairs, such bureaus often disregard that lifeblood of the daily newspaper—local news. With some exceptions, they mostly ignore Washington echoes in their home bailiwicks, a few even looking down their noses at such grist as trivia, unworthy of superior talents.

Some of the smaller bureaus confine their efforts to an interpretive sidebar on the leading Washington story of the day, with background, cause and effect, as the correspondent sees them.

The Copley Bureau attempts a more difficult job. Where one general piece might suffice for all the papers it services, its search for local news is made for widely diversified interests. So the Washington staff has divided its responsibilities. Each is a "native son," so to speak, of those areas for which he maintains a news vigil in the capital.

Richards, who came of age in Illinois, covers for the five Copley newspapers in that state. They are the Aurora Beacon-News, Elgin Courier-News, Joliet Herald-News and the Illinois State Journal and Register at Springfield, Illinois' capital city.

Frank Macomber was graduated to the bureau from the city desk of The San Diego Union, where he learned to know the burgeoning Southern California city like the palm of his hand. Not a day passes when there are not some San Diego reverberations in the nation's capital, as his long string of exclusives attests.

KUEST INTERVIEWS VICE PRESIDENT NIXON

The Pentagon gets high priority on the Macomber beat because of the prime importance to San Diego of the U. S. Navy and Marine Corps. Not infrequently editors of The San Diego Union and Evening Tribune call him by telephone asking confirmation from official sources of a story breaking in their own front yard, but which the San Diego command has tried to keep under wraps.

The whole labyrinth of government is as diligently mined for rich lodes of news as local as though they had been dug out of the San Diego Civic Center. Many of San Diego's major problems have Washington angles that Macomber is asked to investigate and screen. With San Diego the southwest gateway to Mexico and all Latin America, Macomber taps the State Department or Immigration Bureau, for example, for many a headliner.

The fate of California's desperate fight for more water for its thirsty soil and ever-increasing millions will be determined in Washington, where the Congress, the Supreme Court and the executive branch of government all have a hand in it. The water problem has been a continuing saga, flowing over the leased wires linking the capital to Copley newspapers in California.

Before the San Diego Journal discontinued publication, Macomber "wore out" six rival bureaus set up by the opposition. The Journal's management conceded that his hot pace was a contributing factor to that paper's demise.

The city desk of the Glendale News-Press provided Frank Kuest as a springboard to a coveted Washington correspondency for the Southern California Associated Newspapers, The Copley Press group in Greater Los Angeles.

Reportorial stints in Glendale and San Diego and as a staffer for the Los Angeles Bureau of The Associated Press and the Paris edition of the army newspaper, Stars and Stripes, during World War II, gave Kuest solid grounding, not only in digging out nuggets of news beamed to catch the eye and hold the interest of Southern California, but in tightly-written and thoroughly readable copy.

Macomber traded places with Pourade in the summer of 1945, a year after the Washington Bureau was established. Kuest came to the capital in 1946 and quickly established a reputation for journalistic competence against the best in the business.

Kuest's particular Washington coverage is the California congressional delegation. The two California senators and their office assistants, as well as the representatives and their aides, know and respect him and his work. He is especially fitted to bat for Macomber, because of a year on The San Diego Union, or pinch hit for the Illinois members of The Copley Press.

The latter facility may be attributed to Cupid. A bachelor when he arrived in Washington, in little more than a year he had wooed and won the secretary to the chief correspondent, the former Elizabeth Krantz, a one-time employe of The Copley Press general offices in Aurora. Thus was born a knowledge of and a feeling for Illinois, enabling Kuest to fill in whenever the Illinois reporter is absent.

The fourth member of the Copley Bureau staff is Miss Juanita Williams, who has diverse duties that only one so versatile as she could perform.

Miss Williams came to the bureau in 1951, after five years on the Washington firing line in the Department of the Interior, two of the five

ADM. WILLIAM M. FECHTELER TALKS—MACOMBER LISTENS

in the office of the secretary. With the poise and mental equipment of a Washington hostess, Miss Williams can and does:

Fashion a pert feature for the daily bureau report, turn out a thorough research job on any subject from politics to tariffs, transcribe a White House press conference, penetrate by telephone the secretarial "iron curtains" protecting high government brass, keep the financial books and records for the bureau with astonishing accuracy and pay its bills, attend the files, which she completely reorganized and keyed for ready reference, type the weekly mail columns of the correspondents, execute the duties of a secretary and charm visitors who pour into the bureau from various Copley Press communities.

These guests may be the governor of Illinois or California, mayors, industrialists, important advertisers, lobbyists on the local or state level, or simply friends of the publishers.

Some of them, awed by the great marble facade of government, need guidance and help in meeting their senators, congressmen, or officials in one or another agency of the executive establishment. The bureau arranges these interviews, though they often are unproductive of news. Others seek assistance on immigration, passport, military or naval problems.

Not a few ask hotel reservations, train or plane transportation, or just a guide to the capital's historic places. Three of the Copley newspapers in Illinois have given trips to Washington as prizes in spelling contests, with the bureau arranging entertainment for the winners. Now and then a visitor expresses a desire to dine in the crystal-hung Senate Restaurant, reserved for senators and their guests, or will request a conducted tour of the F. B. I. offices, or some other tourist mecca. For these visitors the bureau staff rolls out the red carpet, either at the National Press Club, conveniently located just one floor above the bureau's suite and a showplace in itself, or at one of the famous Washington cafes, such as Harvey's or the Occidental, celebrated the world around.

Time-consuming though this multiple activity of Washington lobby-travel agency, escort service and what not, may be, it appears from all reports to pay off in reciprocal good will for the individual newspapers from those who have benefited. Copley executives have been warm in their accolades to the bureau for maintaining a friendly oasis in Washington for Illinois and California notables a long way from home.

When a deluge of out-of-towners from Copley communities descends all at once, it taxes the capacity of the bureau to play the gracious host to all and still meet deadlines. Yet it never has failed to discharge both responsibilities.

If the regional sideshows of the capital get first call, the bureau does not ignore the main tent. Rather does it listen to the sound and fury from Washington's power-hungry stargazers through the ears of neighbor and friend. It attempts to take its audience along with it to the oval office of

COPLEY PRESS GROUP IN FRONT OF WHITE HOUSE, APRIL, 1947, DURING CONVENTION OF ASNE

Front Row—Rear Adm. Robert Henderson, USN, ret., Frank J. Macomber, Clark F. Waite, Robert W. Richards, V. Y. Dallman, James S. Copley.

Standing—Charles W. Hoefer, C. Raymond Long, Mrs., A. W. Shipton, A. W. Shipton, Miss Jean Richards, Carroll W. Parcber, J. Emil Smith, Mrs., Clark F. Waite, Edward T. Austin, Mrs., Eilif C. Hansen, Mrs., James S. Copley, Mrs., Edward T. Austin, Mrs., Robert W. Richards, Mrs. James A. Gutbrie, Mrs., Charles W. Hoefer, Mrs., Chase Wanglin, Mrs. Frank J. Macomber, John F. Lux.

the president or to the press galleries of Congress, describing, just as the fellow next door would relate it, what is seen and heard and what it all means.

The bureau received its baptism at the nominating conventions of the major parties in the summer of 1944. Then it followed their standard-bearers almost twice across the continent, endeavoring meanwhile to intro-duce those rivals for the highest gift within the American people to bestow, into the parlors, the dining rooms and the kitchens, so to speak, of Copley newspaper subscribers.

It counted the heart-beats on the ailing winner of that memorable cam-paign until they were stilled forever. It watched his successor being sworn in, recorded the high points of his honeymoon and the thorny path he since has trod. It caught the thrill of one war's ending from his lips—as com-mander-in-chief and from across his desk—and then flew 20,000 miles to be in on the kill at the Pacific show—the surrender of Japan.

The Copley Press Washington Bureau diligently kept score on the Truman administration, meantime not overlooking those Washington stories that were of purely local interest to the newspapers the bureau serves. The presidential conventions of 1948 and the campaign that followed were faith-fully recorded. Richards traveled with Gov. Thomas E. Dewey, the Republi-can nominee, on his campaign tours.

The final outcomes of the Republican and Democratic National Con-ventions of 1952 were foreseen by The Copley Press correspondents. The Eisenhower-Nixon ticket was named three days before G. O. P. delegates confirmed it and the Stevenson nomination was forecast almost as far ahead of Democratic action.

The 1952 campaign was one of the most hotly contested in the life of the republic. Richards traveled with Gen. Dwight D. Eisenhower by train, plane and motorcade, for 51,376 miles. Kuest, close friend of Sen. Richard M. Nixon, accompanied the vice presidential nominee.

These reporters, and others, supplied the Copley newspapers with play-by-play coverage of the overthrow of a long-entrenched political power which many veterans of the Washington scene were convinced never would be uprooted. It was apparent to Richards, riding the Eisenhower special train, after observing the reaction of the throngs which turned out to greet the Republican nominee, that Ike was in. This also seemed clear to Kuest, traveling with Nixon.

In the face of hostility to Gen. Eisenhower by many reporters, The Copley Press representatives assured readers of the impending tidal wave of votes for the Eisenhower-Nixon ticket. The Copley newspapers were among the few correctly to tag the Republican landslide before the record vote was polled and counted.

The telegraphic file by Richards, while on tour with Gen. Eisenhower from start to finish, ran to 500 words daily. The stories were dispatched, either directly, or via the Washington Bureau leased wire, to the news desks of the 15 Copley newspapers. Long-distance telephone was used when telegraphic facilities were swamped in handling the reports of 100 or more newspaper, magazine and radio-television correspondents accompanying the General.

Such detailed campaign reports were undertaken at the direction of James S. Copley, chairman of the corporation of The Copley Press, who found that wire-service dispatches at times were pro-Democratic. When the verdict was returned by the electorate, Gen. Eisenhower and his advisers commended The Copley Press for its integrity in reporting the campaign, for courageously calling attention to political bias in stories written by some widely-known press correspondents, and for its contribution toward restoring moderation to the conduct of government in Washington.

Annual Conferences

COFFEE HOUR AT 1953 CONFERENCE IN LA JOLLA, CALIF.

RECESS DURING 1953 SESSION AT CASA DE MANANA

Left to right, Albert L. Hopkins, head of the Chicago law firm of Hopkins, Sutter, Halls, DeWolfe & Owen; Thomas H. Beacom, vice president and head of the trust department, First National Bank of Chicago, director and member of the executive committee of The Copley Press; A. W. Shipton, president of The Copley Press, and James S. Copley, chairman of the corporation of The Copley Press.

Annual Conferences

THE ANNUAL CONFERENCES have been an important factor in the development of COPRESS and its executives. They have been held regularly, starting in 1929, except for omission of a session in 1932. Col. Copley often remarked that he had learned much while a utility operator in his attendance at national conventions and regional meetings. He, therefore, conceived the idea of annual COPRESS conferences in order to enable him to get better acquainted with his executive personnel and at the same time to give them the opportunity to know him better. His further thought was that these family affairs would make it possible for all members to become closer to one another.

No printed record was made of the proceedings of the first, second and the last six meetings. During the intervening years, excluding 1932, when no conference was held, a full report of each assembly was published. These reports have been available to the officers of the company for reference.

The first gathering of the top executives of the organization took place in 1929. Convening on Tuesday, February 12, at the Los Angeles downtown office, Fifth and Spring Streets, Robert P. Holliday, Santa Monica Outlook publisher, welcomed the Illinoisans. Edward Cortlett, then head of the Joliet Herald-News, made fitting response.

Col. Copley then made a brief talk, outlining his plans for the organization, his program for annual conferences and his hopes for the future development of COPRESS. Samuel G. McClure, who presided at the meeting, concluded with announcement of luncheon at Paramount Studios. The following two days were devoted to an automobile trip to all the

COPRESS plants in Southern California, interrupted on Thursday evening by a dinner at the Montmartre in Hollywood. The Friday of that memorable first conference completed the SCNA plant visits and in the evening the party arrived at Hotel del Coronado. Saturday morning the group visited the San Diego Union and Tribune plant and the naval installations on North Island. Following a luncheon aboard the Copley yacht, *Happy Days,* the party went to Tijuana.

The meeting held the following year, in 1930, took on the pattern for the conferences of succeeding years. It was held at Hotel del Coronado and covered four days late in February. The program included guest talks by George W. Marston, pioneer San Diego merchant, and Frank J. Belcher, Jr., a San Diego banker. At this conference, the plan of having each publisher or executive read a prepared paper on a subject of his own choosing was introduced. This gave Col. Copley opportunity to see what his associates were thinking about, to note also how they handled themselves, and finally to appraise their management qualifications. The individual papers were continued on succeeding annual programs through 1947, the year of Col. Copley's death.

At the 1930 meeting, the afternoons were left free for whatever the conferees wished to do, except on one day when a trip was made through a naval repair ship stationed in San Diego Harbor. At the conclusion of the rather lengthy but interesting tour, a reception was held at the Copley house in Coronado. A newcomer to the 1930 conference was R. Eaton Fedou, who, as publisher of the Elgin Courier-News, succeeded D. A. MacKenzie and C. B. Strohn, both then recently deceased.

The 1931 conference also was held at Hotel del Coronado, February 24 to 28, inclusive. It marked the first time Albert M. Hirsh was present. He had succeeded A. M. Snook, who died the preceding fall, as publisher of the Aurora Daily Beacon-News.

In his opening remarks, Col. Copley analyzed the reasons for the depression, then upon the country, and prophesied a return to the former high economic level by a slow climb. As to his newspapers, he said: "We are going to just draw up our belts one notch more, buckle into this thing and go through with it. I have been through four of these since I have been in business. They are not pleasant, but we are going to get through and we are all going to live."

The 1931 conference was the first to be attended by Charles D.

MRS. ELEANOR MACAULAY
Guest at Early Copley Press Conferences

389

(Chuck) Chaffee. In the early winter, he had resigned as circulation manager of the Aurora Beacon-News to direct this phase of newspapering for the SCNA group. His efficiency in this endeavor has been evidenced in the number of individual circulators from the group who have advanced to greater fields. Chaffee later became circulation director of The San Diego Union and Tribune-Sun just a few months before his death in April, 1942.

A third newcomer that year was George F. Orgibet, who succeeded Gail R. Fuller at Redondo. Social highlights were a luncheon at Agua Caliente, a reception at the Copley house in Coronado, and a luncheon aboard the *Happy Days*.

Mrs. Eleanor Macaulay, a sister of Mrs. Edith Strohn Copley, was a guest at several of the earlier conferences.

The next meeting came early in September, 1933, and was held at the Stevens Hotel, now the Conrad Hilton, in Chicago. Clark F. Waite was the presiding officer. Five newcomers joined the gathering. Four were publishers—Lester G. Bradley, San Diego; John Lux, Joliet; Phil Knox, Monrovia, and John Berry, Redondo. Arthur L. Waite, advertising director at San Pedro, substituted for his brother, J. A. (Dude) Waite, who was on a journey to South America.

Col. Copley reported the necessity for sale of three of the properties—the Long Beach Sun, the Pasadena Post and the Hollywood News. He told of the burden the depression had put upon him, but said he felt sure the bottom had been reached and that business was on the upgrade, but the going would be slow. The conference brought an introduction to W. W. Tracy, a long-time friend of Col. Copley, who then became counselor of the group.

Under way in Chicago at the time was the Century of Progress Exposition. In spite of the oppressive early September heat, many found it convenient and interesting to attend the exposition nearly every afternoon and evening. Social features were a dinner-dance at the hotel and an old-fashioned chicken-fry, served outdoors at the Copley home in Aurora. Visits to the newspaper plants in Aurora, Elgin and Joliet were made. James S. Copley was with the group at the home.

The next year, 1934, again in September, the conference convened at Hotel del Coronado. A new man at the gathering was H. C. Burkheimer, who had become publisher at Alhambra, replacing Ed Elfstrom, resigned.

Col. Copley's opening talk was directed toward constructive criticism of the Roosevelt administration. He thought it had got along fairly well for a year, but again was in a fog because it appeared to be a government ruled by college professors. He still was optimistic that bad times soon would vanish. Miss Rose Ladenburg, Col. Copley's secretary, recorded the conference, as she had done the year before in Chicago.

Features that year were a dinner at Caesar's in Tijuana, followed by attendance at the Mexican opera, a reception at the Copley house in Coronado, and a joint luncheon with the San Diego Ad Club, to hear an address by Col. Copley.

In September, 1935, the Sixth Annual Conference was held at the U. S. Grant Hotel, San Diego. No personnel changes at the executive level had been made since the preceding year.

Col. Copley made his usual appropriate opening and closing addresses. He had marked ability in developing men and he took advantage of every opportunity to inspire them to new heights of leadership. Former President Herbert Hoover was a guest and made a brief talk.

New conferees at the 1936 meeting, held once more at the U. S. Grant Hotel, San Diego, were Charles F. Davis, who succeeded Phil Knox at Monrovia, and Nelson Roberts, who followed Morris Penter as advertising director at San Diego. Knox had gone to the Oakland Tribune as circulation manager. Penter had become assistant to the publisher of the San Francisco Examiner.

Bob Holliday returned to the 1936 conference, his first time with the group since 1929. During the interim, he was publisher of the San Francisco Call-Bulletin. Some months prior to this meeting, he and Paul West had purchased the M. C. Mogensen Co. and Holliday had become head of the national representative concern.

In his opening address, Col. Copley said: "Last year we were all anticipating a great deal. These anticipations have since been put into concrete deeds. This has been the most successful year that these newspapers have had since 1930, and it has been brought about by many things, not the least of which has been the spirit of loyalty, the friendly spirit of emulation which has been engendered in great part by these meetings. I, myself, am a great believer in letting men develop themselves, and when I say to you, after watching the figures carefully, I have satisfaction from day to day and from month to month, and have seen every one of you develop himself automatically up to the standard for the best in whatever particular line he may be in."

It was at this conference that the round table—a question-and-answer period—was introduced at each session. A. W. Shipton served as chairman. So well did interest in the innovation develop and so constructive did the discussions become, that the round table, for the last six years, has comprised the entire business program.

At the September, 1937, conference, Maj. Gen. John H. Russell, retired commandant of the U. S. Marine Corps, joined the assembly. He had been retained to write a Sunday column on naval affairs for The San Diego Union. Until his death in 1946, he made many valuable contributions to the annual meetings.

Charles W. Hoefer, advertising director at Aurora, substituted for Al Hirsh that year. Hirsh had been badly injured in an automobile accident that brought death to Ben Alschuler's brother, George.

September, 1938, was the month of the desert wind. Southern California was hotter than central Illinois in August. None the less, a splendid meeting was held at Coronado. The previous year had marked a turning point in employe-management relations. Appropriate to this subject, William S. Kellogg, Glendale publisher, spoke on his "Personal Experience with the American Newspaper Guild." Lester G. Bradley talked about the "Union-Tribune Publishing Co. versus the National Labor Relations Board." It was the consensus that there might be trouble ahead, especially for the larger papers of COPRESS.

The tenth annual conference was held at Coronado in September, 1939. Col. Copley's address was devoted principally to the war in Europe. He carefully analyzed the situation and appraised the possibilities. It was the talk of a man who possessed a thorough knowledge of history and world economy.

Jim Copley, having been graduated from Yale in June, joined the 1939 conference. He was from then on to become more and more closely associated with the organization.

In 1940, Forrest Eagle, predecessor of Dick Smith, joined the conference at Coronado. He had a wide knowledge of taxation and in his talk pointed out the trends that were developing in that field. Suffice to say, many of these trends now have become facts.

Edward T. Austin, editor-in-chief of the San Diego newspapers, was introduced at the 1940 conference. He remained with the organization until 1949. He now is in charge of public relations for Rohr Aircraft Corp., at Chula Vista, Calif.

The 1941 meeting brought in two new conferees. One was Pete Ritcha, who followed Burkheimer as publisher at Alhambra. Burkheimer had replaced Bill Kellogg, who had resigned at Glendale. The other was Charles W. Hoefer, who had been appointed publisher at Aurora following the death of Al Hirsh.

It was at this conference that Jim Copley made his first speech. In it he outlined his experiences at Culver City, Alhambra and Glendale. He demonstrated the thorough care with which he observed things and learned. It was evident from his talk that he had acquired a talent for detail, later to be extremely important in directing his many interests.

J. Emil Smith and V. Y. Dallman joined the assembly at the 1942 meeting. Smith was editor of the Illinois State Journal; Dallman was editor of the Illinois State Register, and Smith also was publisher of both newspapers at Springfield. A lease of the publication rights of the State Register had been made by Col. Copley the previous April.

The attack on Pearl Harbor on December 7, 1941, had brought the United States into war with Japan and a few days later with Germany and Italy. Bob Henderson had resumed his captaincy in the Navy and Jim Copley had signed up in the same branch. Col. Copley's opening talk had to do in great part with the world conflict. He was beginning to see that it would last longer than he first thought, but he had no doubt as to the ultimate result.

The 1943 meeting convened at Coronado on September 21. Absentees were W. W. Tracy and Ben Alschuler, along with Jim Copley and Bob Henderson. Appropriate telegrams of greetings and regret were sent to each. Hugh Baillie, president of United Press, was a guest speaker, his subject: "American Troops in Sicily." He recently had visited the war front there.

The 1944 conference was held in late September at the Biltmore Hotel, Los Angeles. Newcomers were Dick Smith, who recently had become assistant to F. M. James; Alden C. Waite, publisher at Alhambra, succeeding Pete Ritcha, deceased; Les Pefferle, secretary of Radio Station WCBS, Springfield; Will McConnell, of Springfield, newly-appointed assistant to

Counselor Tracy, and Hugh Baumberger, chain store advertising director for SCAN.

The 1945 meeting, again at the Biltmore, brought Bill Haynes into the sessions for the first time. He succeeded John Berry as publisher at Redondo. The latter died shortly before the conference got under way. Haynes read the paper Berry had prepared for the program.

It was the first conference for Ray Long, successor to Eaton Fedou as publisher at Elgin. Fedou died within a week after his return home from the 1944 conference. Col. Copley's talk was confined to an expression of his pleasure at the organization's progress during the preceding year.

The 1946 conference, again at Coronado, in mid-September, brought more new faces — Robert W. Richards, chief of the newly-established COPRESS Washington Bureau; Bart Heiligers, new publisher at Alhambra, following Alden Waite, who had gone into the general office as SCAN vice president; Bob Curry, publisher at Culver City, following Bill Shea, who had become publisher at San Pedro; Walter Schneider, business manager at San Diego, and Grover Shipton, appointed, after his return from the Army, as assistant to the publisher at Springfield.

Col. Copley's opening talks had grown shorter as the years went on. In 1946, he expressed appreciation of the splendid work the executives were doing and said he was particularly happy that Jim Copley was back with the group. Jim made a talk on the newsprint situation.

Bill Copley, with the assembly for the first time and indoctrinated into the newspaper business as a reporter for the San Diego Tribune-Sun, spoke on the subject, "Covering the Water Front." He told of his trials and tribulations as a reporter.

There was a reception at the Copley Coronado place and a dinner was given by the Copleys at the hotel.

The 1947 meeting, the last Col. Copley was destined to attend, convened at Coronado on September 16. In his closing remarks, there was pathos when the chief told how difficult it was for him to say goodbye. In concluding, he said: "As long as I am living, I want these yearly meetings to be carried on. It has been more and more difficult for me to say goodbye." He died six weeks later.

The conferences in 1948, 1949 and 1950, were held at the Moraine Hotel, Highland Park, Ill. In 1951, with all coast publishers going on to New York for the ANPA convention, the meeting was held at the new office of COPRESS, at 428 Downer Place, Aurora. The 1952 session was in Coronado in February.

The 1953 conference was held February 16 to 19 at Casa de Manana, in La Jolla, with Clark F. Waite as chairman. Alden Waite was round table moderator and Bob Henderson conference manager.

Beginning in 1948, the form was changed to a round table, with each publisher first making a report on his town and business prospects. These later meetings have been very successful. It was at the 1948 conference that Nelson Roberts bought Paul West's interest in the West-Holliday Co.

Every occasion has been worth while, so much so that the organization has grown strong and continues to develop. In 1950, the Burbank Daily Review was purchased, with Hugh Baumberger selected as publisher. It is a growing paper, which some day will take more important rank in the group.

The annual conferences have added to the knowledge of the publishers and executives. Strength has come to COPRESS through these meetings. They have been a tribute to the foresight and wisdom of Col. Copley.

FIRST ANNUAL CONFERENCE, LOS ANGELES, FEBRUARY 12-17, 1929

Seated—M. C. Mogensen, Mrs. J. D. Funk, Mrs. W. S. Kellogg, Mrs. E. S. Kellogg, Mrs. Samuel G. McClure, Mrs. C. B. Strohn, Mrs. Robert P. Holliday, Mrs. A. W. Shipton.

Standing—John Callan O'Laughlin, James MacMullen, Robert Henderson, Fred O'Lovesky, Mrs. Fred O'Lovesky, Mrs. A. M. Snook, E. S. Kellogg, Mrs. James MacMullen, F. M. James, C. B. Strohn, Mrs. Eleanor Macaulay, A. W. Shipton, A. M. Snook, Robert P. Holliday, W. L. Beebe, Mrs. Clark F. Waite, J. D. Funk, Mrs. William Shea, F. Karl Lamb, Mrs. Edward Corlett, W. S. Kellogg, Edward Corlett, Col. Ira C. Copley, William Shea, Clark F. Waite, William R. Wheeler, Samuel G. McClure.

396

SECOND ANNUAL CONFERENCE, HOTEL DEL CORONADO, FEBRUARY 25-28, 1930

Seated—F. M. James, Edward Corlett, William R. Wheeler, A. M. Snook, Samuel G. McClure, Col. Ira C. Copley, John Callan O'Laughlin, James MacMullen, Clark F. Waite.

Standing—M. C. Mogensen, J. D. Funk, W. L. Beebe, R. Eaton Fedou, E. S. Kellogg, Robert Henderson, William Shea, A. W. Shipton, W. S. Kellogg, Harry W. Fredericks, Gail R. Fuller, William V. O'Farrell.

397

THIRD ANNUAL CONFERENCE, HOTEL DEL CORONADO, FEBRUARY 24-28, 1931

Seated—Clark F. Waite, William R. Wheeler, Edward Corlett, James MacMullen, Samuel G. McClure, Col. Ira C. Copley, A. M. Hirsh, Robert Henderson, F. M. James, M. C. Mogensen.
Center Row—A. W. Shipton, W. S. Kellogg, Paul West, George Orgibet, W. L. Beebe, William Shea, J. D. Funk, R. Eaton Fedou, W. G. Matthews.
Back Row—H. W. Fredericks, J. A. Waite, E. F. Elfstrom, Arthur K. Whyte, Charles D. Chaffee, H. F. Best.

FOURTH ANNUAL CONFERENCE, HOTEL STEVENS, CHICAGO, SEPTEMBER 5-8, 1933

Photograph taken September 9, 1933, at the residence of Col. and Mrs. Ira C. Copley in Aurora.

Front Row—George Doerr, Jr., M. C. Mogensen, Mrs. E. W. Hayes, Miss Rose M. Ladenburg, Mrs. Eleanor Wilbourne, Miss Eleanor Goodwin, Mrs. P. M. Knox, Mrs. E. F. Elfstrom, Mrs. John F. Lux, Robert Henderson. Second Row—Mrs. Fred C. Flanders, Mrs. B. P. Alschuler, Mrs. Lester G. Bradley, Mrs. C. R. Tichenor, Mrs. Arthur L. Waite, Mrs. Ira C. Copley, Mrs. Eleanor Macaulay, Mrs. Morris A. Penter, Mrs. M. C. Mogensen, Mrs. William Shea, Mrs. Arthur K. Whyte, Mrs. Clark F. Waite, Mrs. John J. Berry, Mrs. R. Eaton Fedou. Third Row—Fred C. Flanders, Miss Mae Barclay, Mrs. Charles D. Chaffee, Mrs. A. W. Shipton, Col. Ira C. Copley, Mrs. W. S. Kellogg, James S. Copley, Mrs. Robert Henderson, Mrs. F. M. James, Miss Fannie Hirsh, Mrs. Paul West, Mrs. C. K. Gittings, Mrs. C. O. Goodwin, Charles D. Chaffee, E. F. Elfstrom, Arthur L. Waite, P. M. Knox. Fourth Row—Lee N. Goodwin, R. Eaton Fedou, A. M. Hirsh, W. S. Kellogg, C. R. Tichenor, W. G. Matthews, F. M. James, William Shea, E. W. Hayes, Fifth Row—W. W. Tracy, John F. Lux, B. P. Alschuler, A. W. Shipton, Lester G. Bradley, C. K. Gittings, Paul West, Clark F. Waite, Arthur K. Whyte, Morris A. Penter, John J. Berry.

399

FIFTH ANNUAL CONFERENCE, HOTEL DEL CORONADO, SEPTEMBER 24-28, 1934

Front Row—Robert Henderson, F. M. James, Clark F. Waite, Col. Ira C. Copley, Miss Rose Ladenburg, Lester G. Bradley, W. W. Tracy, B. P. Alschuler.
Second Row—M. C. Mogensen, Paul West, A. W. Shipton, Arthur K. Whyte, Morris A. Penter, W. S. Kellogg, William R. Wheeler, John J. Berry.
Back Row—C. A. Johnson, A. M. Hirsh, John F. Lux, William Shea, H. C. Burkheimer, J. A. Waite, R. Eaton Fedou, Charles D. Chaffee, Phil Knox.

SIXTH ANNUAL CONFERENCE, U. S. GRANT HOTEL, SAN DIEGO, SEPTEMBER 17-20, 1935

Seated—W. W. Tracy, A. M. Hirsh, Miss Rose M. Ladenburg, Col. Ira C. Copley, B. P. Alschuler, Clark F. Waite, Lester G. Bradley, F. M. James.
Center Row—Merril Reed, Morris A. Penter, A. W. Shipton, Arthur K. Whyte, Floyd Sparks, W. S. Kellogg, Paul West, Robert Henderson.
Back Row—J. A. Waite, M. C. Mogensen, Charles D. Chaffee, H. C. Burkheimer, R. Eaton Fedou, John F. Lux, William Shea, Phil M. Knox, John J. Berry.

SEVENTH ANNUAL CONFERENCE, U. S. GRANT HOTEL, SAN DIEGO, SEPTEMBER 15-18, 1936

Seated—Robert Henderson, Arthur K. Whyte, Paul West, F. M. James, Clark F. Waite, Col. Ira C. Copley, W. W. Tracy, A. M. Hirsh, Lester G. Bradley, A. W. Shipton, Robert P. Holliday.
Standing—John J. Berry, Charles F. Davis, H. C. Burkheimer, R. Eaton Fedou, Charles A. Johnson, R. S. Nicholson, William Shea, John F. Lux, W. S. Kellogg, J. A. Waite, Nelson Roberts, Charles D. Chaffee.

EIGHTH ANNUAL CONFERENCE, HOTEL DEL CORONADO, SEPTEMBER 21-24, 1937

Seated—Robert Henderson, A. W. Shipton, Clark F. Waite, Maj. Gen. John H. Russell, Col. Ira C. Copley, B. P. Alschuler, W. W. Tracy, F. M. James, Lester G. Bradley.

Center Row—R. Eaton Fedou, John J. Berry, Charles W. Hoefer, J. A. Waite, Robert P. Holliday, W. S. Kellogg, William Shea, Charles D. Chaffee, Arthur K. Whyte.

Back Row—Paul West, John F. Lux, R. S. Nicholson, Nelson Roberts, Charles F. Davis, H. C. Burkheimer.

NINTH ANNUAL CONFERENCE, HOTEL DEL CORONADO, SEPTEMBER 27-30, 1938

Seated—Robert Henderson, F. M. James, Clark F. Waite, B. P. Alschuler, Maj. Gen. John H. Russell, Col. Ira C. Copley, W. W. Tracy, A. M. Hirsch, Lester G. Bradley, A. W. Shipton, R. Eaton Fedou.
Center Row—William Shea, John F. Lux, John J. Berry, H. C. Burkheimer, W. S. Kellogg, Paul West, Nelson Roberts, Charles D. Chaffee.
Back Row—Arthur L. Waite, Robert P. Holliday, Arthur K. Whyte, R. S. Nicholson, Charles F. Davis.

404

TENTH ANNUAL CONFERENCE, HOTEL DEL CORONADO, SEPTEMBER 26-29, 1939

Seated—Robert Henderson, W. S. Kellogg, R. Eaton Fedou, F. M. James, Maj. Gen. John H. Russell, Col. Ira C. Copley, W. W. Tracy, Clark F. Waite, Lester G. Bradley, A. W. Shipton, John F. Lux.
Center Row—James S. Copley, R. S. Nicholson, William Shea, H. C. Burkheimer, Arthur K. Whyte, Charles F. Davis, Nelson Roberts, Charles D. Chaffee.
Back Row—Robert P. Holliday, Paul West, John J. Berry, J. A. Waite, R. B. Whitcomb.

405

ELEVENTH ANNUAL CONFERENCE, HOTEL DEL CORONADO, SEPTEMBER 10-13, 1940

Seated—Robert Henderson, R. Eaton Fedou, Clark F. Waite, A. M. Hirsh, B. P. Alschuler, Col. Ira C. Copley, W. W. Tracy, Maj. Gen. John H. Russell, F. M. James, Lester G. Bradley, A. W. Shipton, John F Lux.

Center Row—James S. Copley, Robert P. Holliday, Edward T. Austin, Arthur K. Whyte, W. S. Kellogg, Charles F. Davis, Forrest L. Eagle, Charles A. Johnson, Nelson Roberts, Charles D. Chaffee.

Back Row—R. S. Nicholson, Paul West, William Shea, R. B. Whitcomb, J. A. Waite, H. C. Burkheimer, John J. Berry.

TWELFTH ANNUAL CONFERENCE, HOTEL DEL CORONADO, SEPTEMBER 9-12, 1941

Seated—Robert Henderson, A. W. Shipton, F. M. James, B. P. Alschuler, Col. Ira C. Copley, Maj. Gen. John H. Russell, Lester G. Bradley, Clark F. Waite, R. Eaton Fedou.

Center Row—James S. Copley, John F. Lux, Robert P. Holliday, Arthur K. Whyte, Charles W. Hoefer, Paul West, Edward T. Austin, Charles D. Chaffee, Nelson Roberts.

Back Row—R. S. Nicholson, Forrest L. Eagle, Arthur L. Waite, H. C. Burkheimer, P. E. Ritcha, William Shea, John J. Berry, Charles F. Davis, R. B. Whitcomb.

407

THIRTEENTH ANNUAL CONFERENCE, HOTEL DEL CORONADO, SEPTEMBER 15-18, 1942

Seated—F. M. James, A. W. Shipton, B. P. Alschuler, Col. Ira C. Copley, W. W. Tracy, Maj. Gen. John H. Russell, V. Y. Dallman, Clark F. Waite.
Center Row—Robert P. Holliday, R. S. Nicholson, John F. Lux, R. Eaton Fedou, William Shea, Arthur K. Whyte, P. E. Ritcha, Paul West, Edward T.
Austin, Lester G. Bradley.
Back Row—Forrest L. Eagle, Charles F. Davis, H. C. Burkheimer, John J. Berry, J. Emil Smith, J. A. Waite, Charles W. Hoefer, Nelson Roberts,
R. B. Whitcomb.

408

FOURTEENTH ANNUAL CONFERENCE, HOTEL DEL CORONADO, SEPTEMBER 21-24, 1943

Seated—R. Eaton Fedou, J. Emil Smith, A. W. Shipton, Col. Ira C. Copley, Clark F. Waite, Maj. Gen. John H. Russell, F. M. James, Lester G. Bradley.
Center Row—Forrest L. Eagle, H. C. Burkheimer, John F. Lux, Arthur K. Whyte, Robert P. Holliday, Edward T. Austin, Nelson Roberts, R. S. Nicholson.
Back Row—John J. Berry, Charles W. Hoefer, J. A. Waite, William Shea, V. Y. Dallman, Paul West, F. E. Ritcha, Charles F. Davis, R. B. Whitcomb.

FIFTEENTH ANNUAL CONFERENCE, BILTMORE HOTEL, LOS ANGELES, SEPTEMBER 26-29, 1944

Seated—F. M. James, W. W. Tracy, Clark F. Waite, A. W. Shipton, Col. Ira C. Copley, B. P. Alschuler, Maj. Gen. John H. Russell, Will H. McConnell, R. Eaton Fedou.

Center Row—Lester G. Bradley, John J. Berry, Charles F. Davis, H. C. Burkheimer, Charles W. Hoefer, J. A. Waite, V. Y. Dallman, J. Emil Smith, Arthur K. Whyte, Nelson Roberts, John F. Lux.

Back Row—Hugh Baumberger, Robert P. Holliday, H. E. Deckert, R. S. Nicholson, William Shea, Alden C. Waite, Paul West, L. G. Pefferle, Edward T. Austin, Richard N. Smith, R. B. Whitcomb.

410

SIXTEENTH ANNUAL CONFERENCE, BILTMORE HOTEL, LOS ANGELES, SEPTEMBER 18-21, 1945

Seated—Robert Henderson, J. Emil Smith, Lester G. Bradley, Clark F. Waite, Maj. Gen. John H. Russell, Col. Ira C. Copley, A. W. Shipton, F. M. James, John F. Lux, Charles W. Hoefer, C. Raymond Long.
Back Row—Charles F. Davis, V. V. Dallman, H. C. Burkheimer, Hugh B. Baumberger, J. A. Waite, William Shea, Alden C. Waite, R. S. Nicholson, F. S. Haynes, Edward T. Austin, R. N. Smith, Thomas G. Foley, Nelson Roberts, Will H. McConnell.

411

SEVENTEENTH ANNUAL CONFERENCE, HOTEL DEL CORONADO, SEPTEMBER 17-20, 1946

Seated—Robert Henderson, Clark F. Waite, Charles W. Hoefer, J. Emil Smith, W. W. Tracy, Col. Ira C. Copley, A. W. Shipton, Maj. Gen. John H. Russell, Lester G. Bradley, F. M. James, C. Raymond Long, John F. Lux.

Second Row—Arthur K. Whyte, Alden C. Waite, William Shea, Richard N. Smith, Edward T. Austin, L. G. Pefferle, V. Y. Dallman, Barton Heiligers, H. C. Burkheimer.

Third Row—Thomas G. Foley, Grover E. Shipton, Robert L. Curry, Paul West, H. E. Deckert, Robert W. Richards, Robert P. Holliday, F. S. Haynes.

Back Row—R. S. Nicholson, Walter J. Schneider, Will H. McConnell, Charles A. Johnson, Nelson Roberts.

412

EIGHTEENTH ANNUAL CONFERENCE, HOTEL DEL CORONADO, SEPTEMBER 16-19, 1947

Seated—Robert Henderson, Edward T. Austin, Lester G. Bradley, Mrs. C. O. Goodwin, A. W. Shipton, Col. Ira C. Copley, Clark F. Waite, Vice Adm. William S. Frye, James S. Copley, F. M. James, J. Emil Smith, John F. Lux.

Center Row—Alden C. Waite, Barton Heiligers, H. C. Burkheimer, Richard N. Smith, Robert W. Richards, C. Raymond Long, Charles F. Davis, Charles W. Hoefer, Walter J. Schneider, Paul West, Robert P. Holliday, Will H. McConnell, L. G. Pefferle.

Back Row—V. Y. Dallman, Charles A. Johnson, Thomas G. Foley, William Shea, Robert L. Curry, F. S. Haynes, H. E. Deckert, Nelson Roberts, R. S. Nicholson.

413

NINETEENTH ANNUAL CONFERENCE, MORAINE HOTEL, HIGHLAND PARK, ILL., SEPTEMBER 12-15, 1948

Seated—John F. Lux, Alden C. Waite, F. M. James, William N. Copley, Mrs. C. O. Goodwin, James S. Copley, A. W. Shipton, Clark F. Waite, Lester G. Bradley, J. Emil Smith, Charles W. Hoefer, C. Raymond Long, Robert Henderson.
Center Row—Grover E. Shipton, Edward T. Austin, Robert P. Holliday, Paul West, R. S. Nicholson, H. E. Deckert, V. Y. Dallman, Bynner Martin, Robert L. Curry, Richard N. Smith.
Back Row—Robert W. Richards, Barton Heiligers, William Shea, Nelson Roberts, Carroll W. Parcher, Will H. McConnell, L. G. Pefferle, Charles F. Davis, F. S. Haynes, Edward F. Blettner, Jr.

414

TWENTIETH ANNUAL CONFERENCE, MORAINE HOTEL, HIGHLAND PARK, ILL., SEPTEMBER 11-14, 1949

Seated—John F. Lux, J. Emil Smith, Charles W. Smith, Edward F. Blettner, Jr., F. M. James, James S. Copley, A. W. Shipton, Mrs. C. O. Goodwin, Lester G. Bradley, Alden C. Waite, William Shea, Edward T. Austin, Robert Henderson.
Center Row—Robert W. Richards, Charles F. Davis, H. L. Dewing, Jack Heintz, L. G. Pefferle, Nelson Roberts, Robert P. Holliday, Charles A. Johnson, R. S. Nicholson, H. E. Deckert, Will H. McConnell, Bynner Martin, Robert L. Curry, Grover E. Shipton.
Back Row—V. Y. Dallman, Barton Heiligers, Carroll W. Parcher, F. S. Haynes, Richard N. Smith.

TWENTY-FIRST ANNUAL CONFERENCE, MORAINE HOTEL, HIGHLAND PARK, ILL., SEPTEMBER 10-14, 1950

Seated—Robert W. Richards, J. Emil Smith, Thomas H. Beacom, Mrs. C. O. Goodwin, Clark F. Waite, A. W. Shipton, James S. Copley, Alden C. Waite, Lester G. Bradley, F. M. James, William Shea, Robert Henderson.

Center Row—Hugh B. Baumberger, V. Y. Dallman, Carroll W. Parcher, Richard N. Smith, R. S. Nicholson, Robert P. Holliday, Nelson Roberts, Charles A. Johnson, H. E. Deckert, H. L. Dewing, Jack Heintz, L. G. Pefferle.

Back Row—Barton Heiligers, Charles F. Davis, Bynner Martin, Charles W. Hoefer, Grover E. Shipton, Will H. McConnell, F. S. Haynes, Norman R. Tyre, James P. Baxter, John F. Lux, Robert L. Curry, C. Raymond Long.

TWENTY-SECOND ANNUAL CONFERENCE, HEADQUARTERS OF THE COPLEY PRESS, AURORA

MAY 1 and 2, 1951

Front Row—Robert W. Richards, Alden C. Waite, John F. Lux, Clark F. Waite, Hazel K. Burghart, Mrs. C. O. Goodwin, Ila M. Hunter, F. M. James, Charles W. Hoefer, J. Emil Smith, Robert Henderson.

Center Row—C. Raymond Long, Charles F. Davis, Barton Heiligers, Robert L. Curry, Edward F. Blettner, Jr., James S. Copley, Thomas H. Beacom, Bynner Martin.

Back Row—Hugh B. Baumberger, Lester G. Bradley, F. S. Haynes, A. W. Shipton, Carroll W. Parcher, Richard N. Smith, Norman R. Tyre, William Shea.

417

TWENTY-THIRD ANNUAL CONFERENCE, HOTEL DEL CORONADO, FEBRUARY 11-14, 1952

Seated—Robert W. Richards, Lester G. Bradley, F. M. James, Albert L. Hopkins, James S. Copley, A. W. Shipton, Clark F. Waite, Mrs. C. O. Goodwin, Thomas H. Beacom, Alden C. Waite, Robert Henderson.

Second Row—C. Raymond Long, Grover E. Shipton, V. V. Dallman, John F. Lux, Will H. McConnell, Thomas G. Foley, R. S. Nicholson, Robert P. Holliday, Nelson Roberts, H. E. Deckert.

Third Row—Donald F. Hartman, Robert L. Curry, William M. Hart, Carroll W. Parcher, William Shea, Richard N. Smith, Bynner Martin, Walter J. Schneider.

Back Row—F. S. Haynes, Alex De Bakcsy, Hugh B. Baumberger, Norman R. Tyre, Jack Heintz, James P. Baxter, Barton Heiligers, Charles F. Davis.

418

TWENTY-FOURTH ANNUAL CONFERENCE, CASA DE MANANA, LA JOLLA, CALIF., FEBRUARY 16-19, 1953

Front Row—Robert W. Richards, William Shea, Lester G. Bradley, F. M. James, Thomas H. Beacom, A. W. Shipton, James S. Copley, Clark F. Waite, Mrs. C. O. Goodwin, Albert L. Hopkins, Alden C. Waite, Norman R. Tyre, Robert Henderson.
Second Row—Richard N. Smith, Will H. McConnell, William M. Harl, J. Emil Smith, John F. Lux, C. Raymond Long, Malcolm C. Smith, H. E. Deckert, Robert P. Holliday, R. S. Nicholson, Thomas G. Foley, Nelson Roberts.
Third Row—F. S. Haynes, Charles F. Davis, Bynner Martin, Barton Heiligers, Donald F. Hartman, Robert L. Curry, V. Y. Dallman, Hugh B. Baumberger.
Fourth Row—Carroll W. Farcher, Walter J. Schneider, Alex De Bakesy, Jack Heintz, Grover E. Shipton, H. Richard Wilking.

419

Radio

TRANSMITTER TOWERS OF RADIO STATION KSDO, SAN DIEGO

JACK HEINTZ
Manager, Radio Station KSDO
San Diego

Radio

Radio Station KSDO
1029 Second Avenue

San Diego, Calif.

RADIO OF THE MID-1930's was an untried and erratic enterprise. In addition, those were depression days, which tried men's souls and gave successful businessmen pause to think twice before buying into even the best-going concerns. Radio stations, in general, seldom came under the "going" classification.

It therefore is a source of wonder that Col. Ira C. Copley was induced to invest in the then questionable medium. A. W. Shipton can be credited with influencing Col. Copley to the effect that a profitable future was possible in radio and that, along with his important newspaper ventures, radio would be another means of serving the community.

On October 7, 1937, Col. Copley decided to purchase a 50 percent interest in a struggling part-time radio station in Springfield, Ill. The station, then known as WCBS, now is WCVS. (The call letters WCBS, now used by the main Columbia Broadcasting System station in New York, were the property of the small Springfield station until 1944.) Col. Copley felt certain that, with the watchful encouragement of Shipton, this baby radio enterprise would develop into a strong, healthy addition to the great and highly respected Copley newspaper, the Illinois State Journal, in Springfield.

In those early days, WCBS broadcasting facilities consisted of a tiny studio and a still smaller office with two used desks. The studio also served as a control room, housing two turntables for records and transcriptions—and it was the records that were most often used. The location was above a jewelry store, the owner of which received rent in the form of time signals advertising his luxury wares.

The small 250-watt transmitter shack was situated in the midst of a

423

lumber yard at the edge of the city. The rent there also was a trade deal—spot announcements in exchange for the site. This system of rents was followed by many radio stations of that time.

Local independent stations, in those days, were not held in particularly high esteem by listeners. They preferred the radio fare broadcast by the "powerhouse" stations in Chicago, Cincinnati, St. Louis, and other major cities. Because something had to be done to attract listeners, Jack Heintz, manager of WCBS, turned writer-producer. He made up shows that faintly resembled some of the major station and network productions, adding purely local flavor. Everything from old fiddlers' contests broadcast from movie-house stages to participation quiz programs was used. Evidently the novelty, backed up by the enthusiasm of the station's limited sales personnel, sold the shows to local merchants. Furthermore, local listeners began to tune in the programs with regularity and talked about them on the day following the broadcast.

With the purchase of the radio station by Col. Copley, something else was added that had been needed to attract listeners—advertising promotion. The news items concerning programs and daily display advertisements carried in the Illinois State Journal and later in the Illinois State Register, subsequently acquired by Col. Copley, proved to be a great promotional force. In addition, empty store windows, plentiful in those days, were utilized for displays of the "stars" and programs. While part of this was amateurish compared with today's promotion standards, station WCBS entered into an era of respect and prosperity and became a vital force in community affairs.

Despite the newspaper ownership association, the radio station was not directed from the editorial department, or the publisher's office. It was permitted to experiment with its own destiny. This was not an idea too easily understood by newspaper-owned stations in other cities. In fact, Heintz remembers particularly an inquiry from a radio enterprise in a neighboring state to the south which wanted to know how a radio station could operate independently from the policies of the parent newspaper organization. This query was but one of a number of sources of comparison with other operations that impressed Heintz most strongly that Col. Copley wanted each of his businesses to stand on its own feet. That evidence of confidence in management to solve its own problems has been one of the proudest possessions of The Copley Press. It is a quiet sort of thing that money never could buy.

Listeners frequently asked the question: "When will WCBS get a network in addition to the shows you already have that we like?" At first not too much thought was given to this question but, since the owners and managers were making plans to enhance and enlarge the station's facilities, the network idea was added to the plans.

As the radio station entered a period of major growth in the late 1930's, plans were drawn for modern studios and offices in the Leland Building. In 1940, with its increased personnel, the station was moved into one of the finest Midwestern radio plants. In the meantime, an affiliation was made with a network to be launched coast-to-coast, to be known as the Transcontinental Broadcasting System, under the guidance of Elliott Roosevelt. This was an ill-fated affair and ended on the day it was to start. Announcement over a closed circuit was made to the effect that, due to circumstances beyond the control of the network, it would be unable to start its facility.

A later affiliation was made with the National Broadcasting System, and Springfield finally had a network service that was free from interference.

It began to look as though the future was unlimited. However, effective with the nation's entry into World War II, an extra-heavy strain was placed on manpower by the needs of Uncle Sam. Program, sales and engineering staffs were seriously affected and so finally was management, when Heintz entered the Naval Reserve. Times were lush, however, and WCBS, like all other stations, recovered quickly from the first shocks of war and rose to even greater heights than before.

In radio circles, it was the thinking during the last years of the war and immediately following that Frequency Modulation (FM) was the radio of the future. Plans were formulated by Copley Press executives to operate four FM stations on the West Coast. These stations were to be located in California cities in which The Copley Press owned newspapers. The plans for FM were influenced considerably by the new system of news broadcasts known as Facsimile. This was a startlingly new method of delivering news to the home by means of direct broadcast. Under the system, the householder would buy or lease for use in his home an instrument which would receive a complete miniature edition of the newspaper he had been receiving at his door each day. The idea was revolutionary and, according to the plans, it was hoped that it would be the newspaper of the future. Experimental installations were made in many parts of the nation, but the idea did not have popular appeal and enthusiasm for the project soon waned.

In January, 1947, negotiations were begun for the purchase, in San Diego, of an AM station, at that time in the planning stage, and which was to be operated on a frequency of 1510 kilocycles, with 5000-watt power. Some of the principals in the original application, who were not residents of San Diego, felt their interests elsewhere in California would demand all of their time and they wanted to dispose of a 50 percent interest in the projected new station. After several months of negotiations, Col. Copley decided to purchase the 50 percent interest.

C. ARNHOLT SMITH
President of KSDO

The new station had been the dream of C. Arnholt Smith, San Diego banker, businessman and ship-builder. He had selected the call letters KUSN, which were appropriate to the U. S. Navy background of San Diego and to the U. S. National Bank, of which he was president.

In June, 1947, Heintz assumed management of the proposed radio station KUSN and its auxiliary KSDO-FM station. (After leaving the naval service in December, 1945, Heintz had been connected with the general office of SCAN in Los Angeles.) Months of heartaches and unrelenting labor culminated in the christening of KUSN on October 4, 1947, with a gala broadcast featuring top Hollywood talent and the initial program in its long list of radio sports firsts for San Diego.

On March 1, 1948, the Aurora Beacon-News opened Radio Station WBNU, under the supervision of Charles W. Hoefer. The studio and tower were located on top of the 21-story Leland Hotel in Aurora and exceptionally fine reception was received. The biggest difficulty was that very few homes had FM sets, and, as a consequence, it was difficult for the station to earn sufficient revenue. The station was discontinued on August 31, 1950.

In March, 1949, the call letters of KUSN in San Diego were changed to KSDO, and the broadcast frequency was changed from 1510 to 1130. From the beginning, it had been realized that the 1510 frequency was far out of the "traffic zone" of long years of San Diego listening habits. Much discussion had gone into the final solution of the problem as it was a toss-up as to whether the wisest plan was to set aside a staggering budget to promote listening on this unknown frequency or to try to obtain a better frequency on the dial. A solution was presented in 1948, when KUSN principals were approached by the owners of a local daytime station (KYOR) on the desirable frequency of 1130, who were seeking to sell their station. Purchase of this station was favored by Smith, half-owner of KUSN, James S. Copley and Shipton, and, after many months of negotiations, a contract to purchase was agreed upon and the Federal Communications Commission granted permission for its acquisition by The Copley Press and C. Arnholt Smith.

GENERAL OFFICES OF RADIO STATION KSDO

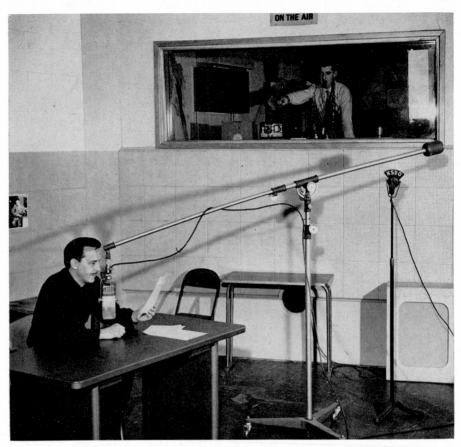

ON THE AIR

BROADCASTING AND CONTROL BOOTHS OF KSDO
Al Hunter at Microphone, Bob Austin in Control Room

In addition to the change in call letters and frequency, a new transmitter site was necessary. The KUSN location on the mesa near San Diego State College would not permit the enhanced broadcasting pattern to be used on the 1130 frequency so, with the permission of the Federal Communications Commission, a new transmitter site was located in Mission Valley.

A novel means of introducing the new broadcast facility was used. San Diego had been warned well in advance, through many advertising promotions and excellent stories in The San Diego Union and Tribune-Sun, that, at the opening of an exhibition baseball game between the San Diego Padres and the Los Angeles Angels, a ship's bell would start ringing on KSDO on 1510, and, in a matter of seconds, it would cease there and the listeners were asked to find it ringing on the new frequency of 1130. Ship's bells long have been a part of the San Diego scene and thus were an appropriate means of launching KSDO on a new and successful career as an important part of the lives of San Diegans.

On October 14, 1949, KSDO-FM began operation as an adjunct to KSDO-AM. It was operated strictly as an auxiliary to KSDO and carried a duplication of the standard station broadcasts during a six-hour daily operation. (The standard band station was an 18-hour daily facility.) After less than a year of operation, KSDO-FM was discontinued on July 19, 1950, due to extra costs and little hope for income.

KSDO celebrated its fifth anniversary on October 4, 1952. It was a time for quiet retrospect. Ownership was thanked by management for the extraordinary confidence shown during the five years of operation. Never had there been the slightest indication that that confidence had wavered. Most of the original, loyal personnel still was with the station, augmented by newer valuable employes. To them went a great "Thank you and well done" for the selfless devotion they had given.

Thoughts during the celebration were turned to the various pioneering San Diego firsts that KSDO initiated in its programming. That this alertness to the public need was appreciated by listeners was proved by the very high-rated audiences shown daily by the station and by the ever-increasing volume of business placed with the station by local, regional and national advertisers. It was pleasant to look back on the remarks made to Jack Heintz earlier by various Los Angeles radio executives, who questioned the advisability of trying to build up an unknown station "at the wrong end of the dial" in what they thought was an overcrowded radio city. It was pleasant to realize that seeming insurmountable obstacles had been hurdled. Radio, and Copley Press radio in particular, had come a long way and a greater future lay ahead.

Officers of Radio Station KSDO are C. Arnholt Smith, president and treasurer; James S. Copley, vice president; Jack Heintz, vice president, and D. R. Giddings, secretary. Directors are Smith, Copley, A. W. Shipton and Giddings. Studios are located at 1029 Second Avenue.

The Copley Press disposed of its Springfield radio interests on December 16, 1950.

"Where There's a Newspaper There's a Market"

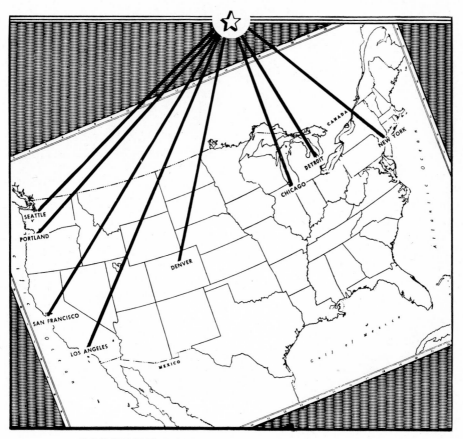

LOCATIONS OF WEST-HOLLIDAY CO. OFFICES

431

ROBERT P. HOLLIDAY
Chairman, West-Holliday Co., Inc.

West-Holliday Co., Inc.

Headquarters, San Francisco

New York—Chicago—Los Angeles—Detroit—Denver—Seattle—Portland

By ROBERT P. HOLLIDAY

Chairman, West-Holliday Co., Inc.

T HE WEST-HOLLIDAY CO. and The Copley Press first entered upon business relations long before the first formal contract was signed at the Biltmore Hotel, Los Angeles, in 1928, between M. C. Mogensen and Col. Ira C. Copley. As publisher of the Santa Monica Evening Outlook, I was sitting in the Colonel's suite when Mogensen, derby hat, spats and all the other regalia then considered regulation by the advertising fraternity, emerged from the room where he had been in conference with the Colonel, with a contract in his hand. I never had seen Mogensen before, but I was to become well acquainted with him in the ensuing years.

Prior to the purchase of the Kellogg newspapers by Col. Copley, I had been an executive on the Pasadena Evening Post and the Evening Outlook and for years had been demanding, beseeching and imploring Kellogg to do something about a representative for his Los Angeles County newspapers. Kellogg was not interested in securing general advertising for those papers which at that time were circulated in common with the Los Angeles Evening Express. The Express obtained general advertising through the courtesy of our circulation and we had the unique experience of trying to make large profits with newspapers that carried little or no general linage.

Naturally I was more than glad to see Mogensen's spats go flying down the hall, because I realized that we were entering an era where the Express no longer would dominate our business policies and we, in the natural course of events, would secure from the four corners of the United

433

NELSON ROBERTS
President, West-Holliday Co., Inc.

States linage that hitherto had been denied us. I also was happy because I had a small hand in bringing such a glaring shortcoming to the attention of the Colonel.

The first time I met Col. Copley, he had asked me what we could do to improve the newspapers he was about to acquire. Among other things, I had stressed the importance of securing more general advertising and suggested we should be allowed to have our own live and alert representative. Knowing the Colonel as many readers of this chapter did, it takes little imagination to realize how quickly he made up his mind and how quickly he acted.

For fear some readers may not clearly understand the functions of a national advertising representative, it might be fitting to describe those activities and then go into the history of the West-Holliday Co.

We do not create advertising. We are a research and sales organization, responsible to The Copley Press, the Union-Tribune Publishing Co. and the Southern California Associated Newspapers, for representing them in the markets of North America. And while representing them, it is our business to know all there is to know about the territories served by these newspapers. We furthermore are charged with the responsibility of seeing that the knowledge so derived be brought into the proper focus on the paramount problems then uppermost in the advertising world. In other and simpler verbiage, we sell advertising all over the United States and Canada for these excellent newspapers. In order to do this, it is necessary that we keep in close touch with the growth and development of each community, see that our salesmen frequently visit these territories, and glean all the information on them that is helpful. We also offer advice upon occasion.

This vast amount of information then is relayed to our various offices throughout the nation and made available through our sales corps to the wholesalers, distributors, manufacturers and advertising agencies which are eager to sell their products in those markets.

This is not a simple process by any means. After 40 years of being associated with the publishing business, I have come to the conclusion that there is no ramification of that great industry that is more complicated, that calls for more hard work and demands more of its organization than the selling of general advertising and the consequent maintenance of an adequate organization to accomplish such sales. I believe I am competent to testify in this regard, for in those 40 years I have sold retail advertising,

R. S. NICHOLSON
West Coast Supervisor

PAUL WEST, JR.
Chief in San Francisco

been an editorial writer and executive and publisher. And after 40 years of looking at the whole picture and 16 years of looking at this one phase in particular, I say, "If you don't believe me try it."

The history of the West-Holliday Co. goes back into the mists of San Francisco and is so surrounded with hearsay and legend that it is practically impossible to give concrete facts and figures. Suffice to say that, according to records in our head office, the company was approximately 25 years old when I entered the picture in 1936. This makes it one of the oldest organizations of its kind in the United States. The company operated on the Pacific Coast only, until 1928, when Col. Copley and Mogensen entered into their first and historic contract.

Approximately 10 years before that, Mogensen had been brought into the business by Fred Kimball. Before long the business was known as the Kimball-Mogensen Co., and within a comparatively short time Mogensen was in, Kimball was out, and the business started to grow and prosper.

However, it was not until Mogensen had secured the representation of the Copley newspapers that the business really began to grow. One of the provisions of the new contract was that offices were to be opened in New York, Chicago and Detroit. Thus the impetus that the Copley contract gave to the Mogensen Co. enabled the company to expand and set up a truly national organization, which in most respects met the definition of adequate service.

Mogensen surrounded himself with an outstanding corps of young, enthusiastic and tireless salesmen. Quite a number of these men still are with the company, all of them, however, in executive posts, the reward for long, faithful and intelligent service. Today these men have under their direction an up-and-coming cadre of salesmen and junior executives who are the senior executives of tomorrow.

In 1930, Col. Copley and I parted company on the most amicable terms. I thought larger and greener fields were beckoning and he thought and said I was crazy to think so, and probably he was right. Neither of us had the remotest idea of how we would join forces again, if at all. In 1936, having had my little fling in the outside world, I was ready to get back into business and started looking for opportunities. Then, as now, all the newspapers that were for sale seemed to be too high in price. But, in the course of looking around the state, I heard that Mogensen wanted to

THOMAS G. FOLEY
Heads Los Angeles Office

GENE DECKERT
At Helm in Chicago

437

retire. So one day I went into the Palace Hotel in San Francisco, engaged a room and sent for him. The result is history.

I did not know much about the newspaper representative business, but it seemed to me that there was a place in it for a man with the instincts and the experience of a publisher. However, I knew there was a man in the organization who knew the business thoroughly and I determined that he would make a good partner in the new venture. Before closing the deal, it occurred to me that I had better get in touch with the Colonel. Much to my delight, he seemed to feel that I was the proper person to accent those services in the right direction.

At first, Mogensen retained a small interest in the company and the new venture was known as the West-Holliday-Mogensen Co. Within a year, Mogensen decided to retire, and the company assumed its present name, West-Holliday Co., Inc.

Paul West, a partner in the company, immediately moved to Chicago as general sales manager and remained there during his long and successful association with the company. I remained on the Pacific Coast, where most of our newspapers are located.

In the 17 years that I have been with this company, tremendous things have been happening in the newspaper industry. In these, the West-Holliday Co. has played a major role. We were helpless to do anything for our publishers in the face of ever-rising costs of labor and materials, but we could help offset those costs by seeing to it that our organization kept abreast of the times, that new blood was injected from time to time, that a research organization was set up and, above all things, seeing to it that our papers have kept up with the march or rather the flight of the rate structure.

We have been consistent advocates of two things: First, the highest possible rate that a newspaper circulation could support; and second, we have felt for years that the reader must assume an increasingly larger share of the cost of the product.

The West-Holliday Co. functions through a series of zone offices stretching across the nation from north to south and from east to west. These offices are interconnected, not only through the closest possible supervision, but by a system of intercommunication that has been built up over a long period of years. One of our principal functions is to gather intelligence. We not only must know what is going on in each community we

JOHN W. FITTING
In Charge at Portland

MORRIS D. TOWNSEND
Zone Manager, Denver

represent, but we by all means must be aware at all times of what the manufacturer and his advertising agency are thinking.

Many years ago the problem of knowing what an agency or manufacturer was thinking was comparatively simple. There was no radio nor television to complicate matters and clutter the air. Most space buyers, as also is true now, were young and just out of college. They had learned to read by the intelligent process of following the news and sports in the daily newspaper. When they became space buyers, which they did by flocks, they knew all about newspapers. They knew how important they were in the home and how important they were to the merchant, because in most cases they could well remember the day they decided to go out and buy their first pair of long pants after having read an attractive ad in their daily newspaper. The chances were that they first had become attracted to that particular brand of merchandise by looking at an outstanding color ad in a national magazine. Naturally the newspapers and the magazines received first consideration when it came to making up space lists.

But something happened, and it was called radio, and later another thing happened, and it was called television. Today we are contacting a group of advertising executives brought up on radio, and tomorrow we will be thrown into contact with a group educated by video. These people feel, and will continue to feel, that newspapers are old-fashioned. It becomes more important every day to jar them loose from that fallacy, and it also becomes more difficult.

To accomplish that end, we use a rather simple formula, at least it looks simple on the surface, but appearances sometimes are deceiving. The formula is this: Know everything there is to know about the community you are selling. Keep visiting that community in order to get more and more information. Know more about it than anyone else possibly can know. Then correlate that information into a neat package and see to it that it gets into the hands and in front of the eyes of the man responsible. Next contact the wholesaler, the distributor and the manufacturer. Educate them to the full value of all newspapers and this newspaper in particular—and keep everlastingly at it. The formula works.

We have done this so successfully that today the average advertising agency man is fully aware that he can get the complete merchandising and sales picture of any Copley newspaper in any of our zones merely by calling us on the telephone and telling us what he wants. He knows we have it and is aware that we know how to get it to him in a hurry.

Who are the men who do this excellent job? The company is headed by Nelson Roberts, president, who for many years was an advertising executive on The San Diego Union and Evening Tribune. Roberts came to us four years ago and has added a vitality and enthusiasm which is greatly appreciated, not only by our own organization, but by the publishers we represent. He makes his headquarters in San Francisco, where one of his principal jobs is the correlation of the eastern and western operations. This is extremely important, as the major portion of linage placed on the Pacific Coast originates in that area, but its ultimate destination still is influenced in the East.

The entire Pacific Coast operation is under the supervision of R. S. Nicholson, who started in this organization 23 years ago. Nicholson has a close grasp on advertising matters pertaining to the coast. The offices he controls are Seattle, Portland, San Francisco and Los Angeles.

Thomas G. Foley has been in charge of the Los Angeles office for the last eight years and has been with the company 24 years. Foley is an acknowledged authority on food advertising in Southern California and is a great trainer of salesmen.

Paul West, Jr., has been in charge of the San Francisco office for

JAMES E. THOMSON
Directs Seattle Business

JACK SHAFER
Manager in Detroit

seven years, with the exception of the time he was away during World
War II. West is one of the best-informed men on the Pacific Coast on automotive matters.

In Seattle, James E. Thomson is in charge, at the same time keeping
a supervisorial eye on the Portland office. The Pacific Northwest has grown
as rapidly as California and it has been a man-sized job to keep abreast
of this expansion. This Thomson has ably done.

John W. Fitting, who came with our organization directly out of the
service, occupies the chair of authority in Portland. He is a young man with
a great deal of analytical ability, and a product of Foley's finishing school
in Los Angeles.

We maintain a zone office in Denver, not only to look after the accounts that come to the Pacific Coast, but to supervise the closely-knit group
of newspapers that we represent in that area. In charge of the Denver
office is one of the outstanding members of our organization, Morris D.
Townsend. Townsend has devoted his entire life to selling advertising and
has a fundamental grasp of its many problems.

Gene Deckert, in charge of our Chicago office, also has supervision
over Denver and Detroit. Deckert has built for himself a wide reputation
in general advertising circles. He has the confidence of all the Copley pub-

lishers and the agencies and has been a tower of strength in this organization for a great many years.

The Detroit office is in charge of Jack Shafer, a young man of the go-get-'em type, who has been with the organization long enough to know his way around the entire Midwest.

New York probably is our largest, if not our most important office. This is true because New York is the fountainhead of all authority in the general advertising field, even though a vast amount of influence wielded in the Midwest or on the Pacific Coast is needed to impress that authority. The problems of selling advertising, of making contacts and distributing information in New York City, are infinitely greater than in any of our other offices. These problems were met for many years by Charles A. Johnson, who, prior to his New York arrival, worked on the Pacific Coast for this company. Ably

MALCOLM C. SMITH
Assigned to New York

seconded by Harold Lessersohn, he did an outstanding job of co-operating with all the other offices and the newspapers we represent. Johnson's health failed late in 1952, and he died on February 8, 1953. The New York office now is in charge of Malcolm C. Smith, who, since leaving Ohio State University, had been with this company on the Pacific Coast and in the Midwest.

The problems in the publishing business are multiplying all the time. That also is true in our business. New competition is springing up from all sides. New approaches, new methods of purveying information and new research must be developed. An eight-hour day is an anomaly in the representative business. If you stop thinking, someone outwits you the next morning. If you stop moving, someone gets there first.

We feel that we are both thinking and moving in the right direction and have been doing so for many years. And furthermore, we intend to continue to do so.

West Tacoma Newsprint Co.

MANUFACTURING NEWSPRINT AT WEST TACOMA

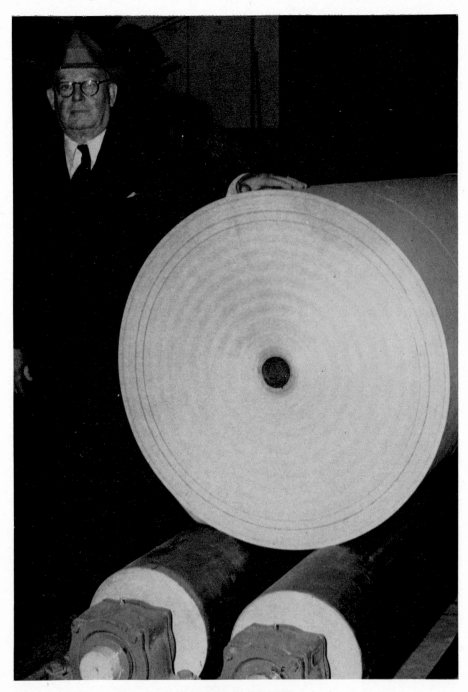

FRANK S. BAKER
First President, West Tacoma Newsprint Co.
Displays Initial Roll Produced May 9, 1947

444

West Tacoma Newsprint Co.

Steilacoom, Wash.

WHEN A COMMODITY is in short supply, the price rises. The advance in price usually tends to increase the supply, with the result that production eventually attains a point where the amount of goods reaches or exceeds the demand, and then prices decline. Thus, under economic laws, stabilization ensues. But so much cannot be said of newsprint in recent years. The demand for newsprint has been so heavy, due to greatly enlarged newspapers, and to enormous growth in circulation, that newsprint for more than a decade has been in short supply, and prices have soared.

Other factors also have entered the trying newsprint situation. Among them have been government controls in time of war; the conversion of newsprint mills to the manufacture of other types of paper, in which profit is higher for the manufacturer; shortage of labor in the logging camps, and the growing remoteness of the source of raw materials, as vast areas are logged off for the pulp and paper mills.

Scarcity of newsprint, the uncertainty of an adequate supply and possibility of transportation difficulties also have contributed to the extraordinary demand by publishers for paper and have caused them to purchase and store in warehouses reserve inventories as a protection against emergencies.

The Crown Zellerbach Co., the Powell River Mills, in British Columbia, Holmen Bruks & Fabriks, in Sweden, and the Finnish Paper Mills Association long have supplied most of the newsprint used by Pacific Coast newspapers. They did everything in their power to meet the increased demand for newsprint created by the war, and which continued after the war. How-

445

ever, they were unable to do so and newspapers were confronted by a very serious problem.

Early in 1946, it developed that the Cascade Paper Co. mill at Steilacoom, Wash., near Tacoma, could be purchased from the Everett Pulp & Paper Co. An engineering survey showed it was feasible to convert the mill from manufacture of fiberboard to newsprint, with an annual production of 15,000 tons. Prior to making fiberboard, the mill produced newsprint. While the survey showed that the cost would be more than the then going price of newsprint, the newsprint shortage was so acute that a group of publishing companies, none of which had desired or intended to enter into newsprint business on a commercial basis, incorporated the West Tacoma Newsprint Co., on May 21, 1946, bought the mill and started conversion.

The participating papers were the San Francisco Chronicle, Los Angeles Times, McClatchey Newspapers at Sacramento, Fresno and Modesto, Calif.; Oakland (Calif.) Tribune, Union-Tribune Publishing Co., at San Diego, Calif.; Tacoma (Wash.) News-Tribune, Yakima (Wash.) Herald and Republic, Eugene (Ore.) Register-Guard, Everett (Wash.) Herald, Bellingham (Wash.) Herald and Aberdeeen (Wash.) World.

The original officers were Frank S. Baker, Tacoma News-Tribune, president; George F. Russell, Tacoma News-Tribune, vice president and treasurer; L. L. Thompson, Tacoma attorney, secretary, and James E. McPherson, assistant secretary.

The original directors were C. E. Gilroy, San Francisco Chronicle; Richard G. Adams, Los Angeles Times; John J. Hamlyn, attorney, McClatchey Newspapers, Sacramento; Werner Rupp, Aberdeen World; George F. Russell and Frank S. Baker, Tacoma News-Tribune; H. L. Price, attorney, Oakland Tribune, and Lester G. Bradley, Union-Tribune Publishing Co.

Price was replaced on November 12, 1946, by Howard C. Stobel, who was succeeded by J. R. Knowland, Jr., of the Oakland Tribune, on February 26, 1947. The original officers and directors (with the exception of Price, whose place is now held by Knowland) are the present (1953) officers and directors of the West Tacoma Newsprint Co.

Production of the mill, which started operation in May, 1947, was increased from an estimate of 15,000 tons a year to 24,000 tons by plowing back depreciation and making a further investment. The increased production was reflected in a material reduction in the cost of newsprint, but the

AIR VIEW OF MILL AND LOG STORAGE POND

cost was such that the mill continued to be what is known as a "marginal" mill and could not meet the selling price of other mills.

In July, 1951, two groups of engineers presented a proposal whereby the output of the mill could be increased by 30,000 tons annually, which expansion would take the mill out of the marginal class and place it in the position of producing newsprint at a cost comparable to the larger news-print mills. In September, 1951, the expansion program was approved and the capital of the company increased.

As the needs of the original participants were not sufficient to use the added production of the mill, and since other newspapers had indicated a desire to become participants in the West Tacoma Newsprint Co., should it ever be determined to expand, applications for membership were accepted from the following:

Seattle (Wash.) Times; Santa Ana (Calif.) Register; Tucson News-papers, Inc., comprising the Arizona Daily Star and Tucson Daily Citizen; Peninsula Newspapers, Inc., comprising the Palo Alto (Calif.) Times, Red-wood City (Calif.) Tribune and the Burlingame (Calif.) Advance; Speidel Newspapers, Inc., a group extending from California to New York, with headquarters in Palo Alto; San Bernardino (Calif.) Sun; Bremerton (Wash.) Sun; Riverside (Calif.) Daily Press; Rotoprint Service Co.; Cowles Publishing Co., publisher of the Spokesman-Review and Chronicle at Spo-kane, Wash.; Vallejo (Calif.) Times-Herald; Whittier (Calif.) News; Sacramento (Calif.) Union; Colorado Springs (Colo.) Free Press; Pasadena (Calif.) Independent; Sheridan (Wyo.) Press; Provo (Utah) Herald; Santa Monica (Calif.) Outlook; Cheyenne Newspapers, Inc., publisher of the Wyoming Eagle and Wyoming State Tribune; Albany (Ore.) Democrat-Herald; Eureka Newspapers, Inc., publisher of the Humboldt Standard and Humboldt Times, in Eureka, Calif.; Fairbanks (Alaska) News-Miner; Longview (Wash.) Daily News; Medford (Ore.) Mail Tribune; Pomona (Calif.) Progress-Bulletin; Roswell (N. M.) Record; Oregon Statesman, at Salem; San Rafael (Calif.) Independent-Journal; Wenatchee (Wash.) World; Vancouver (Wash.) Columbian and Sun; Anchorage (Alaska) News; Anchorage (Alaska) Times; Imperial Valley Press, in El Centro, Calif., and Temple City (Calif.) Times.

Index

INDEX

INDEX

451

INDEX

INDEX

INDEX

INDEX

INDEX

457

INDEX

INDEX

INDEX

Union-Tribune Publishing Co., 4, 6, 10, 61, 161, 208, 211, 212, 213, 365, 392, 435, 446
United Press, 223, 308, 310, 359, 372, 375, 376, 393
Usilton, J. W., 293
U. S. S. *Constitution* (illus.), 170

Valentine, Sam, 258 (illus.)
Vallejo Times-Herald, 448
Vancouver Columbian and Sun, 448
Vanderlip, Frank A., 80, 91
Van Wie, A. J., 292
Variety, 256
Vaughn, Donald R., 285 (illus.)
Vaughn, John Early, 140
Venice *Evening Vanguard*, 4, 228, 237, 251; history, 273-286; Feb. 7, 1953, edition (illus.), 282
Venice Publishing Co., 228
Verna, L. A., 312
Viscaino, Commander Don Sebastian, 167
Vogt, Albert L., 213 (illus.), 214

Waegner, Miss Eleanor C., 5, 14 (illus.)
Waite, Alden Clark, 4, 6, 229 (illus.), 233-235, 255-256, 298, 310, 364, 393, 394, 395, 410-419 (illus.)
Waite, Arthur L., 231 357 (illus.), 358, 363-364, 390, 399 (illus.), 404 (illus.), 407 (illus.)
Waite, Clark Francis, 4, 5, 6, 9, 226 (illus.), 231, 233-235, 255, 322-324, 344, 349-350, 352, 357, 358, 361-362, 364, 381 (illus.), 390, 395, 396-414 (illus.), 416-419 (illus.)
Waite, Julius A. (Dude), 4, 9, 231, 357 (illus.), 357-358, 362-364, 390, 398 (illus.), 400-403 (illus.), 405-406 (illus.), 408-411 (illus.)
Waite, Lila (Mrs. Arthur L.), 4, 231, 364 (illus.), 399 (illus.)
Waite, Ruth Massey (Mrs. Clark F.) 231, 364 (illus.), 381 (illus.), 396 (illus.), 399 (illus.)
Waite, W. J., 350, 357, 358 (illus.)
Walter, William, 150
Wanglin, Byron Chase, II, 4, 231, 234, 364, 365 (illus.)
Wanglin, Marjorie (Mrs. Byron Chase, II), 231, 364, 365 (illus.), 381 (illus.)
Ward, Clayton I., 249, 250, 255 (illus.), 257
Washington, the National Capitol (illus.), 369
Washington Bureau, The Copley Press, 108, 223; history, 369-383
Washington Hand Press, *South Bay Daily Breeze*, (illus.), 335
Washington Star, 80
Wasson, Maxine E., 236 (illus.)
Watson, Thomas D., 293-294
Watson, William R., 366 (illus.)
Watsonville Pajaronian, 190
Weber, George R., 150
Weed, Thurlow, 78
Weigand, William D., 309 (illus.), 310, 311, 312

Weiland, C. C. (Chris), 5, 9, 14 (illus.), 15, 235
Welch, A. P., 268
Welch, J. B., 268
Wenatchee World, 448
West, Paul, 391, 395, 398-410 (illus.), 412-414 (illus.), 438
West, Mrs. Paul, 399 (illus.)
West, Paul, Jr., 436 (illus.), 440-441
Western Public Service Co., 34
Western United Gas Coal Co., 34
Western United Gas & Electric Co., 13, 15, 29, 32-35, 55, 82, 236
West-Holliday Co., Inc., 108, 232, 237, 395; history 431-442
West-Holliday Co., Inc., map showing location of offices (illus.), 431
West-Holliday-Mogensen Co., 438
West Tacoma Newsprint Co., history 443-448
West Tacoma Newsprint Co. plant (illus.), 443, 447
Westwood Hills Press, 234, 298
Wheeler, William R., 203, 208, 396-398 (illus.), 400 (illus.)
Whitcomb, R. B., 405-410 (illus.)
White, Kendall, 104, 105 (illus.)
White, W. H., 122
Whitely, Simeon, 78
Whiting, R. H., 29, 31
Whittier News, 448
Whitney, Glenn, 121 (illus.), 133 (illus.), 134
Whyte, Arthur K., 209, 210 (illus.), 232, 398-410 (illus.), 412 (illus.)
Whyte, Mrs. Arthur K., 399 (illus.)
Wilbourne, Mrs. Eleanor, 399 (illus.)
Wilbourne, William W., III, 54
Wilking, H., Richard, 6, 419 (illus.)
Williams, Eugene F., 214, 215 (illus.)
Williams, Forrest, 6
Williams, Juanita, 372, 374 (illus.), 378-380
Williams, W. J., 359
Willis, William E., 246
Willis, Mrs. William E., 246
Wilmer Ophthalmological Institute, 23, 51
Wilmer, Dr. William Holland, 23
Wilson, B. D., 241-242
Wilson, President Woodrow, 38
Witwer, C. S., 122
Wolcott. Ray, 312
Wolfskill, Mr. 241-242
Woodruff, C. E., 122
Woodruff, Dr. H. W., 122
Woods, Robert Mann, 120
Woodstock Republican, 9
Woog, Raymond, 47, 50
Wray, John C. (Johnny), 351, 359
Wright, Carleton, 228
Wright, Worth, 214 (illus.)
Wyoming Eagle, 448
Wyoming State Tribune, 448

Yakima Herald and Republic, 446

Zarley & Co., 117
Zarley, C., 117
Zarley, Reason, 117